St. Albans

History and Folklore of a Missouri River Town

For George,
Happy memories of
visits to "Fairfield"

Lucie Furstenberg Huger

11/2/01

Lucie Furstenberg Huger

First edition

Fairfield Publishing Company
1623 View Woods Dr.
Kirkwood, Missouri 63122-3522

Library of Congress Cataloging-in-Publication Data
Huger, Lucie Furstenberg
St. Albans: History and Folklore of a Missouri River Town
Includes bibliographical references and index.
1. History—Missouri—Franklin County—St. Albans
2. Lewis and Clark Expedition 3. Folklore—Missouri

Book design by Ken Gilberg Studio, Wildwood, Missouri
Printed by Independent Publishing Corporation, Manchester, Missouri

ISBN# 0-9706343-0-7

Please visit **www.stalbanshistory.com**

This book is lovingly dedicated to my family

My husband Bernard

And my children

Lucie
Bernard
Gregory
Raymond
Catherine
Mary
Cynthian

And my grandchildren

Anna
Lucie
Bernard
Anthony
Genevieve
Marianne
George
Angela
Charles
Vallee
Claire
John
Katherine
Molly
Andrew

Theodore Link overlooks St. Albans, the Missouri River and Honeybee Point about 1910.
Photo probably taken by St. Louis Artists' Guild photographer, J. W. Mack.

CONTENTS

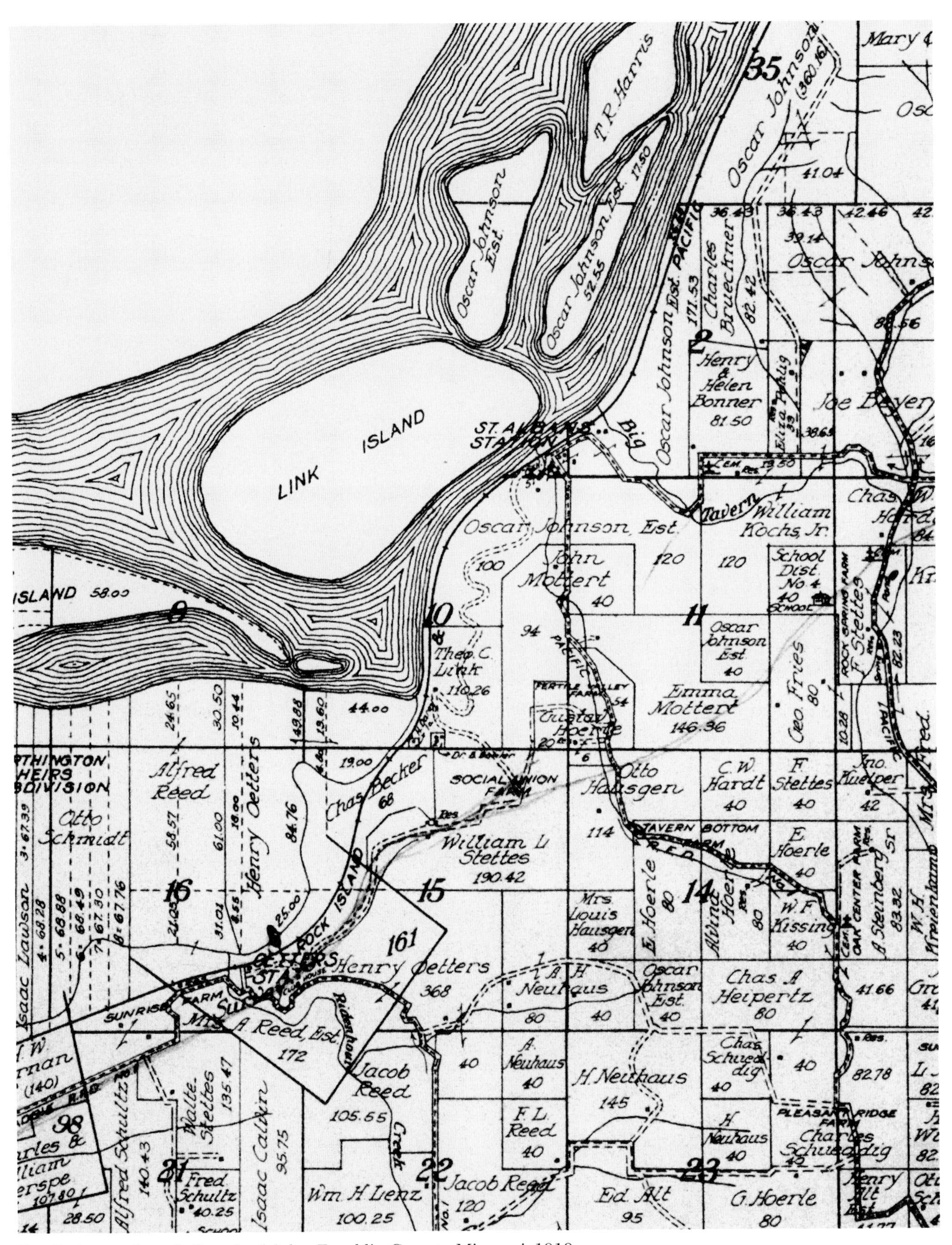

Detail of a page from the Standard Atlas, Franklin County, Missouri, 1919.

INTRODUCTION

This book has been in the making for many years. When my husband Barney and I moved to St. Albans in October 1950, our eldest daughter Lucie was seven years old; Bernard was five; Gregory, four, and Ray was two. I was pregnant with Cathy. There was no problem getting to St. Mary's Hospital when Cathy, and later Mary, were born, but with Cindy it was a different story. Dr. Reardon was no longer on the staff at St. Mary's Hospital. I will never forget driving over slippery, icy roads in an ice storm all the way to North Kingshighway Boulevard to DePaul Hospital.

We had heard, through our friend Jack Butler, that the Funstens were selling their place. He was a friend of Ada Ohmeyer who owned property across the road from the Funstens. We loved it at first sight. We bought *Fairfield* in the spring of 1950, took possession on June 22, which happens to be the feast day of St. Alban, and moved in that Fall. The Funstens had given the name *Fairfield* after a family place in Virginia, and we asked permission to retain the name.

When we bought the property it consisted of 420 acres, more or less. It was made up of four tracts of land: 80 acres from William Stettes; 200 acres from Mrs. Irene Johnson; 114 acres in the Otto Hausgen farm and 40 acres from Clemens; all located in Township 44 Range 2 East. Later we added the Dutton place, so called by us because we bought it from Elmer Dutton, but it was better known as the Neuhaus place. Then we purchased 200 acres from Oscar Johnson Jr. that rounded our property to 760 acres approximately.

Living so far out and driving the hills in all weather conditions was sometimes a problem. Barney's office was at Seventh and Chestnut Streets in downtown St. Louis, so he drove the children to school on his way. They attended City House and Barat Hall; later Villa Duchesne and St. Louis Priory School. As the children got older and had social affairs to attend, they would spend the night with friends in town and we would meet them at Mass on Sunday to bring them home. We did not allow the children to drive that distance through the hills at night.

We had horses and cattle at Fairfield. The children helped on the farm, bucking bales, picking vegetables, etc. Their friends would come out to spend the weekend, an experience many remember today. Camping out, riding the horses, and exploring were great fun. We always had a family living at the farmhouse on Little Tavern Road who did the work of the farm. We entertained our friends from St. Louis, Labadie, Union and Washington with dinner parties. Barney always took great pride in saying that everything served came from the farm. One of the first things I bought when we moved there was a pasteurizer and a butter churn. It was a wonderful life and a great way to raise a family.

Shortly after moving in, we joined the Franklin County Historical Society. I remember its meeting at Sullivan in 1956. Carl Otto of Washington was the president. Mrs. G.L. Russell of Sullivan spoke about writing the history of Sullivan for their centennial. I suggested members start writing the history of their towns while information was still available. It was then that I started interviewing neighbors, collecting news articles, pictures and stories.

Although I was busy with my family and doing what you do in the country, canning and preserving all the wonderful fresh fruits and vegetables, the history project was never forgotten. I talked with everyone I could for more information; Ulmont Kraush, Benny Pohlig, Wilbert and Gertrude Horn, John Pfeiffer, Mae Head and many others.

I am grateful to Reverend William Barnaby Faherty, S.J., of St. Louis University, a well-known historian and author of many books, who read my manuscript and made valuable suggestions. I am also especially indebted to Reverend Timothy Horner, O.S.B., of St. Louis Abbey, who is an author and taught English at St. Louis Priory School. Father edited my manuscript very thoroughly and found many corrections or changes that needed to be made. Barat and Jim Sparks both proofread the book near its completion and enhanced the text further. Ken Gilberg shared information and did the layout for the book. My daughter Mary made a special trip to St. Louis to help me in finding a printer. Each of the children read the manuscript and gave me his or her suggestions and comments.

In 1968, I was asked to write a short history of St. Albans for the Franklin County Sesquicentennial Commemorative Book. At that time, my information on St. Albans and Dr. Peter Kincaid, its founder, was based on the account given in Goodspeed's *History of Franklin County*.

> Dr. Peter Kincaid, a Scotchman, and a very prominent physician and surgeon who served under Napoleon Bonaparte, settled on the Missouri River in 1818 and in 1837 laid off St. Albans, which was washed away by the great flood of 1844.

When I read this, I determined to continue the history after 1844. Since then, I have found it contained some inaccurate data which I have attempted to correct. (See Chapter 3.)

Most of the people in the area worked for St. Albans Farms, living in Farm houses. There never was a church, bank, drug, hardware or clothing store. Head's Store had most needed items, plus a gas pump. People went to Pacific, Washington, Union or St. Louis for their shopping.

It is very interesting to see how history ties people and events together. The Johnson family was the greatest force in developing St. Albans. Mrs. Irene Walter Johnson, Sr., was a member of the Daughters of the American Revolution (DAR). Her daughter-in-law, Eleanor Clark Church Johnson, is a direct descendant of William Clark of the Lewis and Clark Expedition. It is most fitting that the DAR erected a monument honoring the visit of the Lewis and Clark Expedition to the Tavern Cave and Cliffs. The dedication of this DAR marker as part of the National Lewis and Clark Trail on October 1, 1997, marks the final date in this history.

During her senior year at Maryville College, our daughter Lucie Clara took a course in Ozark folklore. She was fascinated with the stories and remedies she heard around the pot-bellied stove at Head's Store. She would go down there when the farm men gathered at the end of the day and tape their stories and answers to her many questions. Cordie Bolin, who lived on our farm and helped at the house, came from the Bootheel in the Missouri Ozarks. She knew folk tales and many ballads which she sang for Lucie to record. Lucie also started collecting stories from our neighbors. She had hoped to put it all in a book but died in 1969 and left these notes, which are included as a part of this history.

My children are all married now. My husband died at *Fairfield* in September, 1977. It was too much for me to stay out there. At that time Mary and Cindy were still in school and living at home. We moved to St. Louis County and subdivided 276 acres of *Fairfield*, including the house, and retained the rest for the family.

This history is the story of pioneer farmers with little farms, development of larger farms and finally the amalgamation of many of these farms into one gigantic operation. Many friends have prodded me to put into book form the information I have compiled over the last forty-five years. I'm sure there is a lot that could be added, but I hope those who read this will find it interesting and appreciate the unique story of this small but historic community.

Lucie Furstenberg Huger, April, 2001

ACKNOWLEDGMENTS

I am indebted to many, many people for the stories, histories and pictures that made this book possible. It has been forty-five years since I started collecting information and photos, so I am sure I will not remember every person who helped me. I will name as many as I can recall. These names include those with whom I had personal interviews, telephone conversations and correspondence.

I wish to thank: Joan Baricevic, Everett Barnhart, Emmet Becker, Mary Berthold, Peter Bickford, Chris Blair, Hazel Meier Bower, Marvin Bowler, Bernard M. Brown, Ruth Horn Campbell, Norma Steines Cunningham, E. Dutton, Dr. Barbara F. Fulton, Jean and Harry Gibbs, Edna Gilsinn, Lelia Godair, David Godair, Anna Lee Grone, Susan Guignard, Tosca Hallock, Mary Christie Hawes, Mae Head, Joan Heisel, Gertrude and Wilburt Horn, Darold Jackson, Eleanor Church Johnson, Oscar Johnson, Jr., Rita Jones, Viginia Pendleton Jones, Dorris Keeven, Josephine Kilpatrick, Ulmont Krausch, Brian Lail, Ted C. Link, Jr., John Maher, Rita Mae Morrison, Mrs. Herman Neuhaus, Dr. Lawrence W. O'Neal, Christy O'Shaughnessy, Barbara Ossenfort, Alta Pate, John Pfeiffer, Benjamin Pohlig, Marie Pohlig, Lawrence R. Rainey, Dorcas Robinson, Sylvia Ross, Erna Schlake, Lucille Graves Schoelich, Ruth Schultz, Jeanne Seipp, Floyd C. Shoemaker, Dr. William D. Small, Eugene Stettes, Louise Stettes, Verna Stovall, Minnie Stricker, Richard Williams and Peter Young.

I wish to thank John Karel for the reproduction of his original Frank Nuderscher painting for the cover of this book.

I appreciate the cooperation I have received from the St. Albans Development Company and in particular, Joe Pottebaum.

Thanks to Chris Thompson, of *Saddle & Bridle Magazine*, who contributed the articles on Fleet Mount Farm.

Special thanks to Jim and Barat Sparks for proofreading the manuscript, making positive suggestions and taking on the huge task of indexing the entire book.

Ken Gilberg not only did the layout but shared his collection of St. Albans memorabilia, including Oscar Johnson, Jr.'s original photographs; copies of the original photographs from Theodore Link's "Hotel Register" and scrap book which was lent by Mr. Link's great-grandson, Ted C. Link, Jr. Ken also graciously allowed me to use his beautiful photographs of St. Albans. We had great fun working together.

I want to thank photographer Jack Zehrt for the use of his picture of Tavern Cave originally taken for National Geographic Society.

Carol Porter took time from her writing to proofread my book. Thank you, Carol.

Mary Noone, my dear daughter, has given great support and guidance in all phases of this history, from the writing to the production.

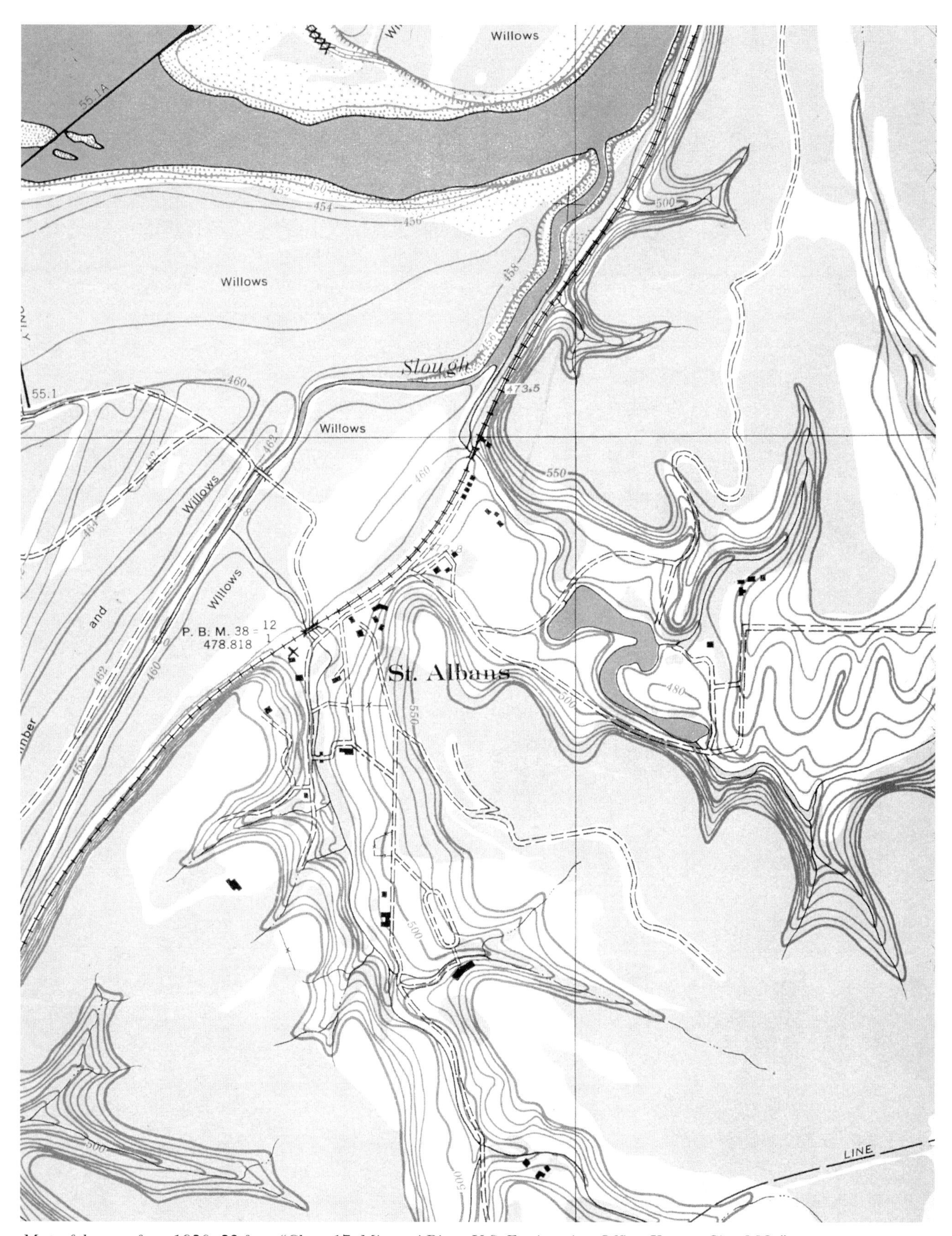

Map of the area from 1930–32 from "Chart 17, Missouri River, U.S. Engineering Office, Kansas City, MO."

LIST OF ILLUSTRATIONS

PROLOGUE

It was the kind of a day you would expect for a funeral. A fine mist completely enveloped the hills. It was a typical autumn morning. Herman Neuhaus had died of a heart condition at St. Francis Borgia Hospital in Washington, Mo. He was 75 years of age and a member of an old family around St. Albans. The funeral was to be from Theibes Funeral Home in Pacific to the family plot on the old Neuhaus place. This was then part of our property and it was the first funeral in the 20 years we had lived at *Fairfield.*

In order to get to the cemetery, one had to come in our entrance on Highway T and take the old "farm-to-market" road that cut in at the bottom of the driveway near the house. This old road used to connect with other roads crossing the ridges to Pacific. It was kept clear and used not only by our tractor and wagon, Jeep and pick-up truck, but as a walking and riding trail.

That Sunday, the men had come to dig the grave, driving a pick-up to get to the cemetery. Albert Schalke, a nephew-in-law of the deceased who had charge of the funeral arrangements, drove his tractor and brushhog to clear the area in the cemetery. Even though there had not been any funerals in recent years, the Neuhaus family had faithfully tended the cemetery. Every year during Memorial Day weekend, they brought a light lunch, the tools they would need and flowers to place on the graves. It was a nice family gathering that we always enjoyed seeing. They would stop to chat for a while before setting out. My husband was usually working in his flower garden and I would stop jelly making or whatever I was doing to talk family history and genealogy with them.

The day of the funeral, the pick-up was driven ahead with the baskets of flowers. Our farm man, Arb Bolin, had the tractor with the wagon attached waiting to carry the coffin. He had affixed strips of wood on the bed to keep it from sliding in transit. Jimmy Barnhart, who was just a little fellow when we moved to St. Albans, drove the hearse. His folks, Everett and Nellie Barnhart, used to work for us, so he had lived in our farmhouse and felt right at home.

The mist had turned into a gentle rain when the family and friends got out of their cars. We stood there under our umbrellas while the Reverend Mr. Millsap of the Methodist Church of Pacific read the prayers. A Jeep carried the elderly relatives and a few little children, but the rest of us walked behind the wagon and Jeep. I shared my umbrella with the preacher. Mary's horse was loose in the pasture but Wilbert Horn kept an eye on him, chasing him back until everyone got through the gates. At the grave site Reverend Millsap gave a nice prayer, bringing in the gentle rain in his thoughts on life and death. We invited everyone to come by the house for refreshments, but only a few came in to warm up before going to the family place for lunch.

In the early days, they used a horse-drawn hearse so there was no trouble getting to the cemetery. Fiddle Creek Road, or, as it is known, the "farm to market" road, ran through the Neuhaus place, over the hill, through our property and down to St. Albans. Minnie Stricker, nee Neuhaus, remembered walking from their house up over the hill and down to the store at St. Albans, carrying dozens of eggs to trade for sugar and other supplies. This was after the "hogback" in front of our house was cleared, around 1910.

In the 1970's, St. Albans and its surroundings had changed very little since we moved there in 1950. The bottom lands had filled in, roads had been built and the woods were still there. The town consisted of a few houses, Head's Store, the Post

Office and St. Albans Farms, which included the Old Barn Inn, the Village Green and cottages, the milking barn and other farm buildings. The total population was about 25 people. There were many small farms in the vicinity that had been owned by the same families since this area was first settled. A few estates had been formed but, generally speaking, it remained an area of virgin woods filled with most types of wildlife known in Missouri and a great variety of wild flowers.

Dr. Peter Kincaid, founder of the town of St. Albans, and his wife Martha Mueller Kincaid between 1856–1861. History has it that Peter is wearing a red wig. Photo courtesy of Evelyn Gilsinn.

CHAPTER ONE

Early History

St. Albans, Missouri, is located along the Missouri River west of St. Louis. The exact location would be described today as being located in Franklin County, Section 3 Township 44 Range 2 East; 40 miles west of St. Louis by railroad, 72.5 miles by two rivers, the Mississippi and Missouri, with an altitude of 478 feet.[1]

The original site of the village, located on Tavern Creek, was east of the present town. The first thing the settlers looked for was a supply of fresh, clear water. Spring fed, Tavern Creek supplied such a need.

The recorded history of this area begins with the Indian tribes living near the Missouri River. The State and River were named for the Missouris (known as the "Pekitanoui") who with the Osage, were the most prominent in the region. The Indians of Missouri were generally peaceful and helped the white explorers to settle, teaching them to cultivate and to cut trails through the wilderness.

The Spanish were the first Europeans to lay claim to the vast Mississippi Valley. Next came the French from Canada. Father Marquette, S.J., a French missionary, and his companion Louis Joliet, a French Canadian explorer, are credited with the discovery of the Missouri River.[2] The first recorded history of the Osage Indians is in Father Marquette's journal of 1673, which he kept on his voyage down the Mississippi River with Joliet. The journal places the tribe on the Osage River near the mouth of the Missouri River. The Osage, as well as the Missouris, were part of the Siouan Indian Oto tribes. Algonquin Indians, such as the Delaware, Shawnee, Sac, Fox and Kickapoo tribes also lived in Missouri.[3]

The French were interested in furs and trading and tried to stay on good terms with the Indians with whom they conducted business. They used various types of boats to haul their goods; keelboats or barges carrying about 30 to 40 tons, flatboats with 8 to 10 ton capacity and Indian birch bark canoes. Although often difficult, the river was a preferred route to the overland paths through the wilderness.[4]

The Indians, and later the French *voyageurs* plying the Missouri River, used a large cave on the northeast corner of what is now Franklin County as a shelter and stopping place, calling it the *"taverne."* The name *taverne* comes from the French meaning a lodging place. Pierre or Pedro Montardy is the first to be recorded as having a lodging place for boatmen in the old cave at Tavern Rock.[5] The Tavern Cave was subsequently first known as "Taverne de Montardis."[6]

Drawing of Tavern Cave for the National Park signs located in St. Albans honoring the visit of Lewis and Clark. Artist: Evangeline Groth, 1997.

Pierre or Pedro Montardy came from Fort de Chartres to St. Louis. He was a son of Pierre Montardy, a native of Montauban, France. In 1765, he married Marie Theresa Duchemin at St. Anne de Chartres. He was a merchant, and the lot he owned in St. Louis was subsequently acquired by Auguste Chouteau, who, along with Pierre Laclede, had founded St. Louis in 1764.[7] There is no record of where or when he died. He is listed as Sub-Lieutenant in the roster of St. Louis militia companies in the year 1780.[8]

Montardy was licensed in 1792 to trade with the Indians and listed as having nine employees.[9] Jacobo L'Yglisse wrote to Governor-General Carondelet, June 19, 1794, "...the deponent having proper permission for the usual practice of hunting on the Missouri River, ...met a trader, Don Pedro Montardy, ...from whom the deponent bought some goods for trading with the Indians." [10]

The first graphic description of Tavern Cave appears in *The Journals of the Lewis and Clark Expedition.* [11] On January 18, 1803, President Jefferson proposed an expedition into the Louisiana Purchase territory from the Mississippi River to the Pacific Ocean, outlining plans for it to Congress.[12] Congress passed a bill naming Capt. Meriwether Lewis to head the expedition. At Lewis's suggestion, a second officer of equal authority was designated, and Capt. Lewis selected William Clark. Lewis was Captain and Clark a 2nd Lieutenant, but both were called captain. The Expedition lasted from 1804 to 1806.[13]

The Lewis and Clark Expedition departed from Wood River, Illinois Country, May 14, 1804, aboard the keelboat *Discovery* and two pirogues (flat-bottom dugouts). There were 29 men on the permanent expedition, in addition to Lewis and Clark. There were also 10 Frenchmen hired to help carry supplies and repel Indians, and six soldiers. Their first stop was in St. Charles; three days later Lewis and his dog joined them. They were entertained in St. Charles with a ball in their honor and finally shoved off on May 21st. On the third day out Lewis left the keelboat to explore the shore. This was May 23, the day they stopped at Tavern Cave.

This 1953 photo shows the abundance of game in the area. Imagine the bounty in the early 1800's. Private collection.

Tavern Rock in the 1990's. Here Meriweather Lewis fell and nearly changed history. Author's photo.

In his entry for Wednesday, May 23, 1804, Clark writes the following:

> We passed a large Cave on the LbdSide (called by the French the Tavern) about 120 feet wide 40 feet Deep & 20 feet high many different immages are Painted on the rock at this place the Inds & French pay omage. Many Names are wrote on the Rock. Stopped about one mile above for Capt Lewis who had assended the clifts which is at the Said Cave 300 fee(t) high, hanging over the waters, the water excessively Swift to day. We incamped below a Small isld in the middle of the river. Sent out two hunters, one killed a Deer. Course Distance 23rd May s 75 w2 miles to Osage WomnR the Course of last Night s.52 w 7/9 mills to a pt on StSide. This evening we examined the arms and ammunition found those mens arms in the perogue in bad order a fair evening. Capt Lewis near falling from the Pinecles of rock 300 feet, he caught at 20 foot.

There is a precipitous bluff about 300 feet high, overhanging the river which took its name Tavern Rock from the famous Tavern Rock Cave at its base. It could well have been the end of the partnership right here in the St. Albans area when Lewis climbed this 300 foot cliff and fell. He caught at 20 feet by thrusting his knife into the side of the cliff. The creek flowing into the river, one mile above the cave, was called Tavern Creek. [14]

Just above the mouth of the creek was a difficult rapid known as "the Devil's Race Ground." On May 24, 1804, Clark recorded in his diary: "Passed a verry bad part of the River Called the Deavels raceground, this is where the Current Sets against some projecting rocks for half a Mile on the Labd. Side."

Lewis directed the sergeants to keep a journal.

> The sergts. in addition to those (other) duties are directed to keep a separate journal from day to day of all passing occurrences and such other observations of the country as shall appear to them worthwhile of notice.[15]

Seven men kept journals on the trip; the two captains (Lewis and Clark), three sergeants (Charles Floyd, John Ordway and Patrick Gass), and two privates (Joseph Whitehouse and Robert Frazer). Six of these are published today, for which five original manuscripts are known to exist. That of Frazer is lost, as is the original manuscript of Patrick Gass.[16]

It is interesting to note that Sergeant Charles Floyd and Private Joseph Whitehouse both mention the dimensions of the cave in their journals. The practice of "campfire editing" was common among the journalists. Sitting around the campfire at night, they often agreed on the wording of the events of that day. This practice was encouraged by the captain as a way of having more than one copy of the events in case some of the records got lost.[17]

> Wednesday May 23d 1804 — We set out at 6 oclock AM plesent day passed the wife of Osage River three miles and half we passed the tavern or Cave a noted place on the South Side of the River 120 Long 20 feet in Depth 40 feet purpendickler on the South Side of the River high Clifts one mile to a Creek Called tavern Creek and encamped on the south Side of the River our arms and ammunition inspected.
>
> Sgt. Charles Floyd[18]

> Wednesday 23d May 1804 a fair morning. We Set out 6 oclock A.M. and proceeded on verry well. passed Some Inhabitants called boons (Daniel Boone) Settlement. passed a noted (p)lace called cave tavern on a clift of rocks on (the) South Side, which is 120 feet long 20 perpinticular high (ms illegible) us inspected our arms and camped.
>
> Pvt. Joseph Whitehouse[19]

The American settlement just below this place was the Kentucky Colony recently founded on Femme Osage River about six miles above its mouth. Among these settlers was Daniel Boone, who in 1798 had obtained a grant of land there from the Spanish authorities, whereon he resided until 1820.[20]

> — we passed the Cave Tavern, a noted place on the S.Side of River. Our arms and ammunition inspected.
>
> Sgt. John Ordway[21]

> Wednesday 23rd. At 6 o'clock in the morning we proceeded on our voyage with pleasant weather. Passed the mouth of the Osage river on the south side, about a mile and an half below the Tavern Cove, a noted place among the French traders. One mile above this is the Tavern Creek. We encamped this evening on the south side of the river, and had our arms and ammunition inspected.
>
> Sgt. Patrick Gass[22]

In *The Journal of a Voyage up the River Missouri Performed 1811* by H.M. Brackenridge, we read:

> The bluffs disappear on the N.E. side and are seen on the S.W. for the first time since leaving St. Charles. They rise about two hundred feet and are faced with rock, in masses separated by soil and vegetation. These are called the Tavern rocks; from the circumstances of a cave in one of them affording a stopping place for voyagers ascending, or on returning to their homes after a long absence. The Indians seem to have some veneration for the spot, as it is tolerably well scratched over with their rude attempts at representing birds and beasts.[23]

The following is an account of another trip up the Missouri.

> A later traveler, the German Prince Maxmillian of Wied, who went up the river in 1832 has preserved the earlier French name for the Cave. He writes, "A cavern at this place is called the Tavern Rock (Taverne de Montardi). The walls of this cave contain many inscriptions of names and rude pictures of birds and beasts,

the latter of which are the works of the red men."[24]

The early history of this area was rich with accounts of French explorers who first traded with the Indians along the Missouri River. Pierre/Pedro de Montardis (Montardy) is first associated with the Tavern Cave or Taverne de Montardis.

FOOTNOTES

1. Kiel, H.G., *The Centennial Biographical Directory of Franklin County, Missouri*, compiled and published by Kiel, 1925, p. 210.
2. Nasatir, A., *Before Lewis and Clark*, Vol. 1, p.3., St. Louis Historical Documents Foundation, St. Louis, Missouri, 1952.
3. Pepper, Miriam, "Settlers Ended Missouri's Long Indian Era," *St. Louis Post-Dispatch*, August 8, 1971, p. 15J.
4. Flannery, Toni, "Fur Was the West's Lure," *St. Louis Post-Dispatch*, August 8, 1971, p. 21J.
5. Tavern Rock Cave in 35-45-2E is in Tavern Rock bluff which reaches the Missouri River and the cave is about 20 ft. above the water and is shaped like the fireplace much used when we had more wood and less style than now. The cave was once inhabited and is of very great interest – fame for over 100 years. Kiel, Op cit., p. 195.
6. Ramsay, Robert L., *The Name Places of Franklin County, Missouri*, University of Missouri Studies, Columbia, Missouri, 1954, p.36.
7. Balesi, Charles J., *The Time of the French in the Heart of North America*, Alliance Francaise Chicago, 1992, p. 280, p. 287.
8. Houck, Louis, *The Spanish Regime in Missouri*, in 2 vols., R.R. Donnelley & Sons Company, Chicago, Ill., 1909; Vol. 1, p. 183, footnote 2.
9. Nasatir, op cit., p. 162.
10. Ibid, p.234.
11. Thwaites, Reuben Gold, ed. *The Journals of the Lewis and Clark Expedition: Aug 30, 1803–Aug 24, 1804*, Compiled by the Center for Great Plains Studies at the University of Nebraska, Lincoln-published in 8 volumes as *The Journals of the Lewis and Clark Expedition*, Vol. 1, p.27.
12. President Jefferson for many years observed what was happening in the vast area known as Louisiana. This territory included the Mississippi River valley, New Orleans and land to the west. The territory was ceded by Spain to France in the secret treaty of San Ildefonso in 1800. France then sold the area to the United States with the Louisiana Purchase agreement dated April 30, 1803; signed May 2, 1803, and approved by Congress on October 20, 1803. With the Louisiana Purchase the United States acquired 830,000 square miles for $15 million.
13. Goodwin, Cardinal L., "Settlements of Missouri and Arkansas 1803-1822," *The Missouri Historical Review*, Vol. XIV April-July 1920, pp. 385-388.
14. Ramsay, op cit., p. 41
15. Thwaites, op cit., Vol. 1, Introduction.
16. Patrick Gass, when the Corps of discovery was disbanded, apparently contacted his friend David McKeehan to edit his journal. It was published in 1807 in Pittsburgh, Pa., by Zadok Cramer. This edition is the source of the Gass journal as the original manuscript is lost. MacGregor, Carol Lynn, ed. *The Journals of Patrick Gass*, Mountain Press Publishing Company, Missoula, Montana, 1997, p. 19.
17. Ibid.
18. Thwaites, op cit., Vol. 7, pp. 3-5.
19. Ibid, pp. 29-31.
20. Ibid., Vol. 6, p. 27, footnote.
21. Ibid, Vol. 7
22. Ibid, p.40.
23. Ibid, p. 35.
24. Ramsey, op cit., p. 27

These signs today mark the approximate route of the Lewis and Clark Expedition of 1804.

CHAPTER TWO

Early German Settlers

The Spanish and French explorers came to the Missouri River area in the 18th century. The Louisiana Purchase dated April 30, 1803 marked the end of their domination. The Lewis and Clark Expedition in 1804 opened the vast western country to settlement. United States authority in Missouri dates from March 10, 1804, when Captain Amos Stoddard took possession of the territory for the United States.[1]

In *The Centennial Biographical Directory of Franklin County, Missouri* by Herman Gottlieb Kiel, p. 13, there is a list of pioneer homesteaders before 1831.

> Those who homesteaded U.S. public lands before 1831. Patents or deeds to these lands bear the signature of the President of the U.S. and this signature is made by a special clerk.
>
> List shows name, neighborhood or P.O., section with Congressional township, date of entry.
>
> Bell, Daniel, St. Albans, 2-44-2E, Dec. 1, 1820
> Belt, Philip, St. Albans, 20-44-2E, Dec. 16, 1820
> Bowles, Ambrose, Oakfield, 12-44-2E, Nov. 20, 1821
> Reed, Edward, Oakfield, 27-44-2E, Aug. 22, 1821
> Ridenhaur, Barnet, St. Albans, 15-44-2E, Dec. 16, 1820

After 1831, the first permanent settlers in the St. Albans area were Germans, the "Followers of Duden."

Gottfried Duden was born in 1785 in the town of Remscheid, Prussia, Germany. He received the traditional classical education of the time, studied law at Dusseldorf, Heidelberg and Gottingen, where he received his law degree in 1810. During the Napoleonic War, he served in the Prussian Infantry Regiment (1813-1814). He returned to civil practice in Cologne. The social and economic problems following the war aroused Duden's sympathies. He saw America as the answer to these problems and decided it was his mission to sell the Germans on emigration to America. For this purpose, he himself came to Missouri and wrote letters home recounting his experiences. His published letters were a leading factor in the German immigration of the 1830's to the central Missouri and Mississippi River Valleys.[2]

In 1824, Gottfried Duden arrived in St. Louis with his companion Louis Eversmann. After procuring charts and accounts in St. Louis, they began inspecting the interior of the state of Missouri. They explored the country on both sides of the Missouri River. Duden purchased land near what is now Dutzow and lived there for three years gathering information for his *Report 1824–1827.* He wrote in such glowing terms of the abundance of game, rich grasslands, virgin forests, minerals and water supply that many Germans, dissatisfied at home, eagerly sought this land of plenty.

Among the first to come were Herman and Frederick Steines, natives of Rhenish Prussia.[3] They came to verify or contradict Duden's *Report.* They were well educated men who kept diaries and wrote long letters describing their conditions at home, their journey to America and life in Missouri. These letters give a first hand account.

Herman Steines. Photo courtesy of the Steines family.

Herman Steines was born at Kettwig, Germany, June 7, 1809. He was educated as a druggist and physician in Germany. He came with his cousin Adolph Greef, a master tailor, and Adolph's wife and five children.[4] They sailed from Bremen on May 18, 1833, and were eight weeks in crossing. They docked at Baltimore, went by train to Frederickstown, walked to Pittsburgh where they took a steamboat to Cincinnati, boarded another steamboat to St. Louis, and arrived there September 29, 1833.[5] The reasons for leaving Germany and following Duden are well stated in Herman Steines' letter to his parents inviting them to join him.

> There will be inconveniences for all of us to face, but if you wish to see our whole family living in the same country, a country where freedom of speech obtains, where no spies are evesdropping, where no wretched simpletons criticise your every word and seek to detect therein a venom that might endanger the life of the state, the church, and the home, in short, if you wish to be really happy and independent – then come here and become farmers in the United States. Here you will find a class of beings that think sensibly, and still respect the man in man. Oppressive military systems and exorbitant taxation are foreign to this country. Nature has blessed this land abundantly. Here one fully enjoys what one earns, here no despots are to be feared, here the law is respected, and honest citizens do not tolerate the least infringement or interference by human authority.[6]

Adolph Greef. Courtesy of the Steines family.

Adolph Greef was born in Kettwig, Germany, February 18, 1807. He lived in St. Louis for a year. When the Solingen immigrants arrived in 1834, he went to the country to live on the land he had bought on Tavern Creek. He died there April 7, 1883.[7]

Herman Steines came to St. Louis in 1833 with Adolph Greef and practiced medicine with a Dr. Craft. In 1834, he bought two tracts of land on Tavern Creek in Franklin County from William Bacon and his wife Parmelia. He married Louise Westholz in 1836; they had four sons and two daughters. He farmed, taught school for several years, practiced medicine, was Justice of the Peace for many years and served several terms as Assessor for St. Louis County. He died August 14, 1875.[8] The Steines House is located on Hwy. T just before the St. Albans Development property. It was the home of August Steines, son of Louise and Herman Steines. August married Hulda Heipertz; their daughter Amanda married John C. Maher and the house is now called the Maher House and is still owned by the family.

Frederick Steines, Herman's brother, was a teacher in Germany. He submitted his resignation to the school authorities on January 2, 1834, and decided to join his brother in Missouri.

> Since the year 1820 I have been a teacher of the school here. Now the hour has come when I must sever the bonds that officially bound me. As a citizen and in my official and military relations to the state, I have had so many bitter experiences, which in my opinion an upright citizen of the Prussian State ought not to have been subjected to, that I find myself compelled to make a change. Since I see no opportunity for betterment of conditions here, I have resolved to migrate to North America.[9]

Bertha and Frederick Steines. Courtesy of the Steines family.

The Steines family in front of their home. The house was built in 1886 by Walter Schlemper for August Steines and is still owned by his descendants. Left to right: Edmund A. Steines, Adela Steines, Mathilda Steines, Justine Hulda Heipertz Steines, Amanda Steines Maher holding James Steines Maher, John Maher. Photo courtesy Steines family.

He emigrated to Missouri in 1834; married Bertha Herminghaus on January 1, 1835 at St. Louis. They had one son Ernest Edmund, born in 1849. In 1838, Frederick became seriously ill and resigned his teaching position in St. Louis and moved to the country. He bought a farm on Ridenhaur Creek.[10] Here sickness troubled his family so he entered a tract of Government land between the Meramec and Missouri Rivers; he called it "Oakfield." He opened a school for boys called Oakfield Academy in 1839. It continued in operation until 1869. For five years he taught in the public school after his academy closed. When the Post Office was established at Oakfield, he became the first postmaster. During the Civil War, he organized a Company of Home Guard and was chosen captain. He died April 24, 1890, and his wife Bertha died July 22, 1892, at Oakfield.[11]

The eldest Steines brother, Peter, was born at Kettwig, Germany, May 6, 1805. He, too, was a teacher in Germany but resigned and came to St. Louis in 1834 with his wife and his parents, Anna Catherine Unterlahberg and Johann Frederick Wilhelm Steines. His wife died of cholera in the 1844 plague that took the lives of many St. Louisans. His parents had settled on a 160-acre farm on Tavern Creek and, after his wife's death, Peter moved to Tavern Creek to live with them. Six months later he was thrown from his horse and died of injuries. His father died in 1843, and his mother in 1844.[12]

When it became known that Frederick Steines and his family intended to migrate to America, a number of families, mostly from Solingen, joined with them. This group became known as the Solingen Emigration Society and numbered about

153 persons. Frederick Steines was the leader of the group. They chartered the ship *Jefferson* and sailed from Rotterdam on April 17, 1834, and arrived in St. Louis on July 2, 1834.[13]

Travel in America was difficult and dangerous. There were long delays, and extra lodgings were costly. Most of the German immigrants came across the country from Baltimore as that port of entry was less expensive than New York. Frederick Steines gives a very vivid description of his journey to St. Louis when he wrote to his relatives and friends on September 15, 1834.

> The highways were in a very bad condition. (Across the Alleghanies). We always spent the night in the places where the railroad employees stopped. There we also got fresh horses on the following morning. At noon, too, the horses were changed. —In America every meal costs 25c, regardless as to how much or how little you eat. This is very expensive. A very pecular custom obtains in the taverns. If one asks for a drink of brandy, the barkeeper sets a flask of the liquor on the bar and a small glass and a flask of water beside it. The customer puts as much of the brandy as he desires in the glass and then takes a drink of water after he has drunk the liquor. In Maryland, Pennsylvania, and other places where small coins are in circulation such a drink costs a picayune or 6 ¼ cents. If the customer serves himself twice, no matter how much or how little, a fact which the barkeeper carefully notes, he must pay double. At any lodging place where one may chance to stop, the traveler has absolute freedom to do his own baking, cooking, or frying. In case one does his own cooking, the night's lodging costs only from six to ten cents.
>
> As soon as the newspapers announce the arrival of immigrants every speculator sends his agents and helpers to the highways which the immigrants are said to travel. They are found in the inns and everywhere along the way. They insist upon accompanying you on your way for a distance. What are they trying to do? They want to get the money of the immigrant, that is all.[14]

The following is his account of his route.

> We chartered two railroad cars to haul our 7098 lbs. of baggage at $1.50 per 100 lbs. (from Baltimore to Frederickstown). At Frederickstown the cars will be placed on other trucks. From Baltimore to Frederickstown we travel in passanger coach. No fare. Included in the price paid for baggage. From Frederickstown to Wheeling ride on the baggage down the Ohio River in steamboat to Cincinatti, to Louisville, to St. Louis.[15]

Herman Steines stayed in St. Louis while he looked around for a place to settle. On February 17, 1834, he wrote to his brother-in-law, Frederich Dellmann, a teacher in Meurs, Germany, telling him where various people had bought land.

> Daniel Knecht, Florenz and William Kochs, Matthias Wahl from Aachen and Wirth from Remscheid have all bought land. This land is located thirty-two miles from here on the Tavern Creek. It is on the south side of Missouri and one and one-fourth miles from the river. On the eleventh of this month I went to the Tavern Creek myself. I was accompanied by Adolph Greef and Peter Knecht. Adolph Greef has now also bought land on the Tavern Creek.[16]

In the same letter to Dellman, Herman Steines notes that all of the above mentioned men bought "improvements," intending to enter the various 40 acre tracts at the land office, for which they made settlement with the "squatters" (men who set themselves down upon land). The land was called "Congress" or public land and was sold for $1.25 an acre.[17]

> On the twelfth we arrived at the Tavern Creek. The valley of this creek is wide, and is surrounded by high hills which extend along the Missouri River. On the thirteenth I saw the Missouri for the first time, and then beheld for the first time the far-famed oak forests of its great valley. The river is as broad as the Rhine there. Its banks are but sparsely settled altho the soil is extremely rich. At the mouth of the Tavern two farms have

> been laid out, on which a large tract has been cleared, where I am told, a town is to be laid out.[18]

Whenever a man was looking for a place to settle, he would usually buy from a "squatter" what was known as an "improvement." These squatters were the hearty pioneers who moved into the unbroken forests and made a clearing, near a creek, and built rude log houses. They had no legal title to the land but lived on it for a while, then sold it for a small price depending on the amount of improving they did, and then moved further west and started all over with virgin territory.

> The "improvement" consisted of a hut built of rough unhewn logs, the cracks "chinked" with small blocks of wood and then daubed with mud. A huge fireplace of stone, about six feet high was built on one side of the hut. Above this was a chimney made of split oak slabs laid crosswise and daubed on the inside with mud. The door was hung on homemade wooden hinges and had no lock, nothing but a latch. When there was a floor, it was made of split logs roughly hewn with an axe. The room was just high enough for a man to stand up upright, and when the building reached that height, the builders used poles instead of logs and drew them in to make the pitch of the roof. A double row of clapboards was laid on these poles and another pole laid over them and pinned down with wooden pins to the pole below to hold them on. Not a nail was used in the construction. The other part of the "improvement" was the lot, a small area enclosed with fence-rails. The oxen, cows and hogs were sometimes kept there, even in winter, without any shelter. There was also a small piece of land called a "clearing" consisting of about two to five acres. The clearing was made by deadening the timber by cutting around the trees through the sap-wood, then cutting the underbrush and burning it on the ground. No grubbing was done here. Here they raised some corn, potatoes, pumpkins, squashes and turnips. They lived mainly by hunting and fishing. Their wants were few and easily supplied. Money was scarce so they were glad to sell their claims for ten to fifteen dollars according to the size of the "improvement." [19]

Adolph Greef's "improvement" consisted of a one-room hut, a smoke house, a corn crib and an enclosure about the well, seven acres of cleared land which had been tilled for seven years. Greef paid $20 to the "squatter." Fencing the land cost him about $15. The price of the tract of land at the land office, $85. He then had to buy stock. A good horse was $30; a brood sow with five to ten pigs, from $1.50 to $3.00; a fresh cow with her calf, $10; chickens, ducks, geese, turkeys etc. cost a few dollars a pair. It was therefore possible to settle in a new area for the total cost of $150.00.[20]

FOOTNOTES

1. Billion II, dissertation by Alice Lida Cochran, p. 28.
2. Duden, Gottfried, *Report on a Journey to the Western States of North America*, editor's introduction, James W. Goodrich; The State Historical Society of Missouri and University of Missouri Press, Columbia and London, 1980.
3. Rhenish Prussia was a part of the Rhineland given to Prussia as a defensive movement against the French at the Treaty of Vienna in 1815.
4. Bek, William S., "The Followers of Duden," *The Missouri Historical Review*, Vol. XVI, October, 1919, No. 1, pp. 30-31.
5. Ibid, p. 61.
6. Bek, Vol. XIV, January, 1920, No. 2, p. 230.
7. Bek, Vol XVI, October 1921, No. 1, pp. 126-132.
8. Ibid, p. 132.
9. Bek, Vol. XIV, April-July 1920, No. 3-4, p. 457.
10. Ridenhaur Creek, Boles Township said to have been named after John Ridenhaur, who was killed by Indians. It is said that he owned a beautiful white horse that the Indians wanted for their chief. They made an offer for it but Ridenhaur turned it down. Later they shot him while he was watering his horse at a spring

not far from Labadie, taking the horse for their chief. Kiel, p. 194.

11. Bek, op cit., Vol. XIV, April – July 1 920, No. 3-4, p. 457.

12. Bek, op cit., Vol XVI, October 1921, No. 1, p. 132.

13. Bek, op cit., Vol. XV, April – July 1920, No. 3-4, p. 457.

14. Bek, Vol. XV, April 1921, No. 3, p. 532.

15. Ibid, p. 525.

16. Bek, Vol. XIV, January 1920, No. 2, p. 226.

17. The Preemptive Act of 1841 established the right of settlers to occupy and improve unappropriated public lands and later buy them at a minimum prevailing price without competition from speculators or other potential purchaser. Any person 21 years of age or older, if he had resided on it, had partly improved it, and did not own 320 acres of land could buy 160 acres at a price ranging from $1.25 to $1.50 per acre. From the *The Western Movement* by Ina Frye Woestemeyer, p. 45.

18. Ibid, p. 227.

Detail of the earliest known map of the area from circa 1834–1840.

CHAPTER THREE

The Founding of the Town

Although the area of Tavern Creek was settled by the "Followers of Duden," the town of St. Albans was laid out in 1837, by a Scotsman, Dr. Peter Kincaid.

The first record of purchase of land for the town of St. Albans was in 1829, eight years after Missouri became a state.[1] It is recorded that Dr. Kincaid bought from Wm. Orr 33.86 acres in Bowles, Township, Franklin County, April 5, 1829, for the sum of $42.30. On April 1, 1830, he bought 100 arpens (1 arpen = 0.85 acre) for $150, and on August 20, 1831, another 100 arpens for $164.00 from Colonel Justus Post. Dr. Kincaid bought 18 acres of land in Section 10 from the U.S. Government on November 23, 1835, for $1.25 per acre; part of Section 11, 80 acres, from U.S. Government, October 31, 1837.[2]

Herman Steines notes in his diary the naming of the town.

> Feb. 11, 1837, Ball and Kincaid are planning to plot sites for two towns. One of these to be named St. Albans.[3]
>
> March 2, 1837, Dr. Kincaid came back from St. Louis. He showed us a plan for the site of the proposed town of St. Albans. The plan was made by Kayser.[4]

The original land of the town of St. Albans was conveyed to Peter Kincaid as shown in Plat Book A.

> United States of America To Peter Kincaid Conveys:
>
> The Southwest fractional of Section 2, Township 44, Range 2 East containing 155.36 acres according to Gov't Survey is covered by this entry which is regularly and properly certified.
>
> Plat Plat Book A., p.24
> Dated March 7, 1837
> Filed March 11, 1837

ST. ALBANS
All the lots are 66 ft. by 33 ft.
The streets 33 ft. wide.
Scale of 66 feet to one inch.

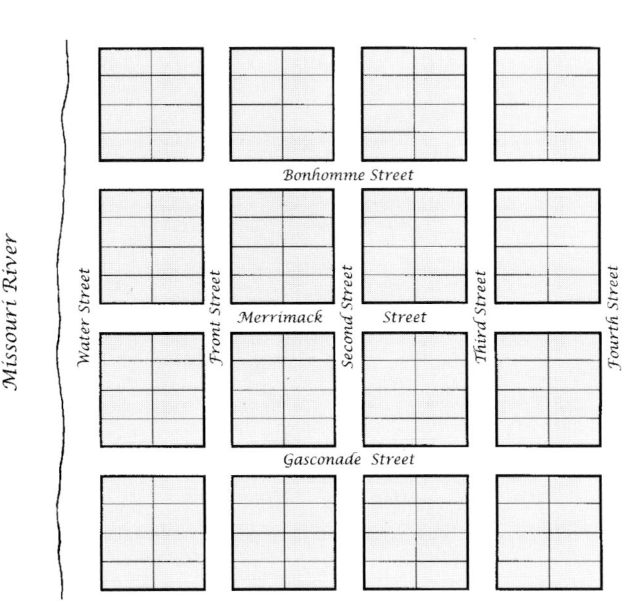

The town is laid out on the South Bank of the Missouri River in the lower end of Franklin County, in the Township of Bowles, being on the southwest fractional ¼ of Section 2, Township 44, North Range 2 East. This town is laid out on a liberal scale, the lots being 33 feet front by 66 feet deep all running at right angles. Water Street being 60 feet wide the other streets 33 feet, it contains 128 lots. This place is well known to all Navigators of the Missouri River as a celebrated landing place for steamboats and it is 1 mile above the Tavern Rock nearly opposite Missouri Town. It is about 30 miles distant from St. Louis and 25 miles from St. Charles and about 20 miles from Union and 13 from Manchester; 10 miles from the Merrimack river and about 15 miles from the New Lead mines; The Town of St. Albans contains many natural advantages being surrounded by fine never failing springs and fine timber and stone quarrys for building comprising 2 or 3 excellent sights for building machinery of any kind on a never failing stream being wholely fed by springs being in a thick settled and wealthy neighborhood being a fine high healthy situation; it being one of the finest sights for a town on all the Missouri River and offers many inducements for mechanics of all description and the county

> adjacent to this town is thought to contain large quantities of lead mineral. All persons wishing to locate themselves in the town of St. Albans will do well to call and examine for themselves.
>
> Peter Kincaid, Proprietor
> State of Missouri
> County of Franklin, ss:
>
> This plot of the town of St. Albans in the County of Franklin in the State of Missouri, hath been made by authority and under the direction of the undersigned proprietor of said Town and I do hereby declare that the said plot and allotment of streets alleys and landings are hereby granted to the use of said town, and public forever.
>
> Peter Kincaid (Seal)[5]

On April 11, 1838, an auction sale by Savage & Austin of 128 "valuable building lots" in the town of St. Albans was held. After this and until the flood of 1844, there are many entries of lot sales in St. Albans in the Records of Franklin County.[6]

H.G. Kiel gives the following description of the town:

> As a town, it was laid off by Dr. Peter Kincaid Sr. in 1836. It has four houses, and probably had never more than ten. In 1844 the land that was in the Mo. River bottom, including most of the site, was washed away by the very high waters of the river. The remnant of the place is located in Sect. 3, Twshp. 44 R2E on the Rock Island RR, where Little Tavern Creek flows into the Mo. River. It is said to have been named after St. Alban in England but may have been named after the town in Franklin County, Vt. Distance to St. Louis by railroad 40 miles, and by two rivers 72.5 miles. Altitude 478 feet.[7]

The town lay in the Big Tavern Creek Valley parallel to the Missouri River with streets named Water, First, Second, Third and Fourth. The cross streets were named Bonhomme, Merrimack and Gasconade. After the devastating flood of 1844, Peter Kincaid and other owners of lots in St. Albans remained in the area and reestablished the town.

Dr. Peter Kincaid was born November 15, 1785, at Larbert, Stirlingshire, Scotland. The family home was described as being "Garleaws near Falkirk." He was the son of James Kincaid and Jean Gillespie Kincaid. He had four brothers: John, James, Robert and Charles, and one sister, Elizabeth. He studied medicine at Leipzig and was graduated from the University of Edinburgh.[8] He served as a doctor during the Napoleonic War in 1813.

There are conflicting stories about his service. According to the *History of Franklin County* by Goodspeed, he served under Napoleon[9] but his granddaughter, Mrs. Edna Gilsinn, told me according to the tradition in their family he served under the Duke of Wellington.[10] The information for Goodspeed's directory was gathered from individuals and information available at that time, 1888. It was not always verified with written proof. I, therefore, believe the family tradition as given me by his granddaughter to be the truth. The fact that he sculpted a bust of Wellington, in uniform, supports this opinion. He was a Scotsman and the Scots presumably served under Wellington.

Evelyn Gilsinn, daughter of Edna, also recalled that one of Dr. Kincaid's hobbies was sculpting. There was a room in the old house with a stone floor where he worked on his sculptures and mixed his medicines. In the yard were two busts carved in native limestone: one of the Duke of Wellington and one of himself, both in uniform. These were placed on three-foot Corinthian-styled columns. Hazel Bower, a great-granddaughter, also remembers these carvings from visits to St. Albans between 1925 and 1930.[11]

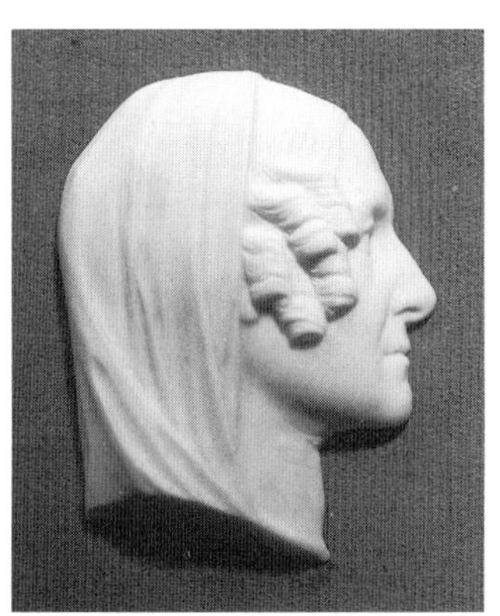

Sculpture by Kincaid. Photo courtesy Evelyn Gilsinn.

It is also stated that he came with his two children:

> Dr. Peter Kincaid came from Scotland with his children Peter and Jane to St. Louis c. 1820; practiced medicine in St. Louis; later settled on the Missouri River in St. Louis; later settled on the Missouri River in Franklin County; he named the settlement St. Albans.[12]
>
> "—He came to St. Louis between 1818 and 1820 with his children Peter and Jane—." [13]

According to the family records, he came to St. Louis in 1818 with John Muir, a Scotsman, and had property near the Old Court House. At the time of the cholera epidemic in St. Louis in 1832, he moved to Bonhomme, St. Louis County, where he practiced medicine before moving to the Tavern Creek area.[14]

He was married to Ann McKinnon but it is not known whether they were married before or after he came to Missouri. The census for 1820 was destroyed.

The census of 1830 shows Dr. Kincaid living at Bonhomme, St. Louis County.

Peter Kincaid (household) no slaves

1 male	age 40-50
1 male	5-10
1 female	30-40
1 "	15-20

That he married Ann McKinnon is shown in the following announcement in the Missouri *Argus*, June 24, 1836, published in Franklin County.

> Take notice – whereas, my wife Ann Kincaid (alias McKinnon) did on the 10th of this month desert my house, board and blanket without my knowledge or concent, and is now at large. I do hereby forewarn all persons (not) to harbour or credit the said Ann on my account, as I will not be responsible for debts or engagements of her contracting. P. Kincaid

On December 17, 1835, Peter Kincaid and his wife Ann sold to George Henderson 260 acres in Bonhomme Twshp. St. Louis County, for $750.

> 1840 Census – Franklin Co. Bowles Township.
>
> Peter Kincaid household – 3 whites, one of which is "Learned professionals & engineers"

1 male	age 50 – 60
1 male	10 – 15
1 female	5 – 10 no negroes

This shows that his wife Ann is no longer a part of his household and that he has two children. According to the census of 1850, Peter and (Mary) Jane were born in Missouri; Peter in 1826 and Jane in 1831. According to a great, great granddaughter, Rita Mae Morrison, Mary Jane was born in 1832 at St. Albans.[15]

He evidently had a falling out with his son in that on December 5, 1840, it was recorded in the Franklin County, *Missouri Argus*:

> Take notice that I forewarn all persons not to harbour or credit P. Kincaid, Jr. a minor about 12 year old, who is wandering about the country as I will pay no debts of his contracting.
>
> P. Kincaid, Sr.

In 1841, Dr. Kincaid, then 56 years old, married Martha Mueller, a younger woman. She was born in Germany and living in the Gumbo-Chesterfield area. Martha met Dr. Kincaid while he was treating her father for dropsy. According to her, he cured him. She was a beautiful woman who could not speak English very well. They had ten children: Charles, Robert, John, James, Alexander, Elizabeth, Julia, Caroline, Martha and George. As it is recorded in the Franklin County 1850 census :

> Peter Kincaid, Sr. Age 64, male, white physician Property evaluation $4,200; born Scotland.
>
> Martha Kincaid, 31 female, white, born Germany.
>
> Peter Kincaid, Jr. 22 male, white, farmer born in Missouri.
>
> Mary, 19 female, white, born Missouri.

Children of Dr. Peter and Martha Kincaid

Charles Kincaid

John Kincaid

Robert Kincaid

Martha Jane Kincaid Hardt

Eliza Kincaid Ossenfort

Alex Kincaid

Caroline Kincaid Niesen and Julia Kincaid on a bluff above the Missouri River. All photos from private collections.

Charles, 8	male,	white,	born Missouri
Robert, 7	"	"	" "
John 4	"	"	" "
James 2	"	"	" "

Arthur (Alex?) 1 male, white, born Missouri.

Peter left home when a young man to go to California. Sometime in 1851, Mary Jane eloped with Thomas Burns who was illiterate and not acceptable to her father. They had eight children and lived on a farm in Camden County.[16]

Census 1870		Camden County
	Age	
Thomas Burns	39	farmer born Ill. Cannot read or write
Mary J. Burns.	39	born Mo. Can read & write
Mary	18	cannot write
Charles	18	farm laborer Cannot write or read
Thomas	14	" " " "
David	12	" " " "
James	9	
John	7	
Malissa	4	
Sarah	1	

Dr. Peter Kincaid died October 12, 1861, and was buried in the family cemetery at St. Albans.[17] He died intestate. The estate of Dr. Peter Kincaid was probated December 26, 1861, with final settlement May 9, 1866, containing 408 acres. An affidavit of heirship filed September 20, 1912, by John Kincaid, son of Dr. Peter Kincaid, lists all the heirs and states that Peter A. Kincaid and Jane Burns were stepchildren of said Martha Kincaid.

In 1866, Mary Jane Burns, Camden County, sold to Martha Kincaid 1/12 interest in the estate for $230.00 and in 1868, Peter A. Kincaid of West Point, Calaveras County, California, sold to Charles A. and John Kincaid 1/12 interest in the estate for $233.00.[18]

Mary Jane Burns died October 21, 1914, at Osage Iron Works, Mo., and her husband, Thomas

Burns, born November 10, 1831, Northern Illinois, died April 7, 1912, at Osage Iron Works, Mo.[19]

John gradually bought the remaining shares of the estate. In 1880, Charles and his wife deeded to John all interest in SW fraction NW fractional ½ Sect. 2, 44, 2E including remainder of the town not washed away by the Missouri River, for $437. George Kincaid deeded to John Kincaid in 1895 his interest in the estate for $170.

In 1866, the remaining heirs conveyed to the St. Louis, Kansas City and Colorado RR a 100-foot-wide strip of land for $850[20], and conveyed a strip of land to the Chicago, Rock Island and Pacific RR; 1.95 acres for $125.[21]

In 1912, the St. Albans property was sold for $10,000 with arrangements made that the heirs would have a life interest in the house and an area of 20 acres on which the spring, orchard, garden and barn were located.[22]

Photo collection.

In 1915, John conveyed the family cemetery by warranty deed to his sisters and brothers and their descendants forever.[23]

John, Alex and Julia, who never married, took care of their mother until her death September 14, 1897. She is buried in the Kincaid Family Cemetery near her husband Peter. Their tombstones read:

"Weep not for me"

Dr. Peter Kincaid	
Oct. 12, 1861	Mrs. Dr. M. Kincaid
Aged	wife of
75 years, 10 mos. 27 da	Dr. Peter Kincaid
	died
Alex Kincaid	Sept. 14, 1897
Aug. 5, 1849	aged
Jan. 28, 1937	78 years 23 days

John, Alex and Julia are also buried there as well as Martha Wright Kincaid, wife of Charles, and two of their children. L.C. Allersmeyer was appointed guardian for John in June, 1927; John died in July, 1927, and was buried in the family cemetery in August, 1927; Alex in 1937, and Julia a short time thereafter. Eliza was buried in the Ossenfort family cemetery located at the intersection of Highway T and Ossenfort Road.

FOOTNOTES

1. The "Missouri Compromise" was adopted March 6, 1820, after a long debate between the House of Representatives and the Senate over the question of slavery. It allowed Missouri to enter the Union as a slave state and Maine as a free state. The debate still continued in Congress and was finally settled whereby Missouri was admitted to the Union. The admission of Missouri into the Union was announced on August 10, 1821, by proclamation of President Monroe, and the State from that day took rank as the twenty-fourth of the American Republic. *History of Southeast Missouri*, published by The Goodspeed Publishing Company, 1888, pp. 57-60.

2. Scharf, John Thomas, *History of St. Louis City and County from the Earliest Periods to the Present Day, Including Biographical Sketches of Representative Men*, 2 vols. Philadelphia; Louis H. Everts and Co., 1883.

3. St. Alban was the first martyr of Britain, suffered c. 304. His feast day is June 22. He has been continually venerated in England since the fifth century. Reference: *The Catholic Encyclopedia*, Vol. I, pp. 252-3. The Encyclopedia Press Inc. NY 1913. *The Lives of the Saints*, Vol. II edited by Herbert Thurston, S.J., and Donald Attwater; P.J. Kenedy & Sons NY 1956.

4. Bek, Vol. XIV, April - July 1920, Nos. 3-4, p. 444.

5. Plat Book A, Office of the Recorder, Franklin County Courthouse, Union, Mo.

6. Franklin County Records.

Block I lots 1,2,7,8 to Fred Steines $90 April 1837. lots 5 & 6 to Abraham Gottschalk April 1838.

Block III lots 1,2,5,6,7,8 to Christian Hardt 1840; Hardt to Henry Brensing $250 plus 40 acres tract 1854.

Block IV lots 1,2,7,8 to Frederick Stratman $70 1840 Stratman to Henry Brensing $40 1848

Brensing and wife to John August Steinernagel $375 including Block III 1864

Steinernagel to Chas. Kincaid $225 1868 (10 lots)

Chas. Kincaid and wife deeded to John Kincaid $375

Block VII lots 1 & 8 to Frederick Dings $40 1837

Block XIV lot 4 to Ferdinand Nohl $100 plus adjoining parcel 1840

Block XVI lots 3 & 4 to Ferdinand Nohl $20 1839. Lot 5 to Christian Hardt 1840

7. Kiel, p. 210

8. Stevens, Walter B., *Centennial History of Missouri 1820–1921*, Vol. 2, p. 108, University of Missouri Library, Columbia, Mo., says he was graduated from the University of Edinburgh.

9. "Dr. Peter Kincaid, a Scotsman, and a very prominent physician and surgeon, who served under Napoleon Bonaparte, settled on the Missouri River in 1818, and in 1837 laid off St. Albans which was washed away by the great flood of 1844."

Goodspeed's *History of Franklin, Jefferson, Washington, Crawford & Gasconade Counties, Missouri*, Ramfre Press, Cape Girardeau, Mo., 1958, p. 225. Originally published Goodspeed Publishing Company, Chicago, 1888.

10. November 5, 1965

As far as tradition in our family goes my grandfather, Peter Kincaid, served under the Duke of Wellington against Napoleon.

Mrs. Edna Gilsinn (signed)

Daughter of Caroline Kincaid.

11. In her "A Family History," Hazel Bower refers to various articles similar to Goodspeed's notation that Dr. Kincaid served under Napoleon and suggests that he may have been captured and thereafter ministered to French troops.

12. "Origin of Franklin County Names," *Republican Tribune*, Union, Mo., August 15, 1919.

13. Kiel, op cit., p. 30.

14. Bower, op cit., p. 29.

15. Rita Mae Morrison is a direct descendant of Sarah Elizabeth Burns, youngest daughter of Mary Jane and Thomas Burns.

16. Letter from Evelyn Gilsinn to the author.

17. Kincaid Cemetery, File 1060. H.F. Hansen, Union, Mo.

"6 chains or 40 feet square containing 37/100 of an acre said tract to be kept and reserved continuously without interference for a family burying ground for the said Kincaid family." Franklin County Records, Courthouse, Union, Mo., Bk. 74, p. 383.

18. "This address is the only indication we have of the later life of Peter Jr." Bower, p. 34. According to Evelyn Gilsinn he drowned in California, but no date is given.

19. Genealogy from Rita Mae Morrison.

20. Franklin County Records, Bk. 30, p. 21.

21. Ibid, Bk. 69, p. 189.

22. Ibid, Bk. 74, p. 383.

23. Ibid, Bk. 78, p. 361.

CHAPTER FOUR

Life in St. Albans 1830-45

The German immigrants who came to Missouri in the early 1830's were men and women of varied trades and professions. Regardless of what means of livelihood they had in Germany, of necessity they became farmers in Missouri. They had to raise all their vegetables and useful crops. Corn was to them what the potato was in Germany. Wheat, rye, barley, oats, broomcorn, tobacco, cotton, flax and hemp were the crops commonly grown. They hung tobacco in specially constructed barns for drying and made their own cigars. The broomcorn was seeded to make brooms.

Farming was done in a very primitive way, as in Biblical times. The following account written by Frederick Steines describes an American farm in 1835.

> Instead of a house you must think of a hut, behind it a still smaller hut for a smokehouse, farther back a still smaller hut for other purposes. All this is surrounded by a zigzag rail fence. Sometimes a spring flows right through the yard. The paths are unpaved. There is no trace of domesticated fruit trees, no garden shrubs, grape vines, or tame flowers; simply a plowed, fenced-in, little plot of ground, which in the early spring can scarcely be found on account of the weeds. There are no barns with threshing floors in them. Some times the grain stays out in the field all winter long in stacks. The grain is not beaten out but trampled out by animals. The grain is laid out on the ground in the field, on a place cleared of stubble and weeds, and then horses or cattle are driven over it till the kernels are trampled out of the ears. By winnowing the grain is then cleaned. On account of the cold, threshing is rarely possible in the winter months. One reason for this backwardness is the fact that the American farmer does not regard his farm as something that he as well as his descendants after him are to improve and enjoy, but as something to be but slightly improved, in order to be able to sell it at a small profit in the future.[1]

The following are some entries from the diary of Herman Steines:

> April 15 – Sowed oats today and dragged them in with the branch of a tree.
> July 14 – Mother and I cut our own rye with a scythe.
> July 28 – With my two horses I helped Gross and Paffrath trample out their wheat.
> Aug 5 – Threshed out peas at home after having hauled them with my ox team.
> Aug 10 – Mr. Bornefeld made me a lot of cigars from his homegrown tobacco.
> Aug 26 – Got twenty-four bushels of oats of which I put thirteen bushels into a "gum" that is a piece of hollowed out tree.
> Sept 9 – Hung tobacco in barn to dry.
> Oct 27 – Today we got 4 gals. of honey from our bee hives.[2]

Horses were essential and raising them was a profitable and easy sideline of farming. Horses cost from $30 to $50 a head. Saddles cost $6 to $20 in St. Louis and the rest of the riding equipment and harness were in proportion to this price. The pioneers were very clever in the use of woods for their harnesses. The bark of the hickory and all of the pawpaw made the strongest kind of cords. A greater part of the bridle was made from hickory bark, and the saddle had wooden stirrups. The trees were very large and there is the story that on one occasion when Dr. Kincaid was surprised by a storm, he rode into a hollow sycamore tree for shelter. Everyone rode a horse, though the Germans were often laughed at for all the walking they did.

Here is an entry in Herman Steines' diary for March 6, 1837:

> I rode to St. Louis today carrying about twenty-two dozens of eggs and eleven pounds of butter on my horse.[3]

Steins claimed he could make the distance from St. Albans to St. Louis, 32 miles, in five or six hours.

On May 24, 1837, Herman Steines tells about some of the farms that belonged to his friends.

> In company with Florenz Kochs we (Glaser and I) visited Dr. Terril on the Tavern Creek this morning. Then we looked at the farms that Kochs, Wahl, and Greef have bought. The land is very good; the water is excellent; the forest is average; the general aspect of the country is hilly; the farms are located in the valleys; the roads are bad, and there are no connecting roads as yet.[4]

Everyone worked together as neighbors to clear the land, build houses, harvest crops and help each other in times of need. Almost every farmer designated a plot on his farm as the family burial ground. In the case of death, a neighbor would dig the grave and render other assistance. A house raising was a special occasion. The men would start early building the log cabin while the women cooked all day to feed them. When it was finished, they had a big party with music and dancing.

When Frederick Steines built his house, his neighbors helped him. There were three rooms. #1 was about 20 feet long and was built by Rev. McKennon; #2 the hall, 12 feet built by Dr. Terril and #3 room was 22 feet long. It cost him $45 to build.[5]

Another entry by Herman Steines gives the following description of a house raising.

> Oct. 21, 1833. At our house raising today we laid up five logs on each of the long sides and four on each of the short sides of the building. Gross and Greef were the corner men — Jacob Ridenhour was here and he agreed to split 1000 fence rails for me at five bits a hundred. He will take his pay in wool at 37½ cents a pound.[6]

The farms of Adolph Greef, Mathias Wahl, Frederick Steines, Stump, Florenz Kochs, Johann and F.W. Steines, Dr. Terril and Dr. Kincaid were near the Missouri River and thus the people had the use of the river for transportation. There was a steamboat landing at Knecht's place. They used a hollowed-out log for a boat and paid 25¢ each to the owner. In case of high wind, this was a dangerous crossing.[7]

Oh, what a relief it is!

Dr. Kincaid took care of the people on both sides of the river. There is a story of a woman patient of his who lived on the north side of the river who continually complained of a stomach problem. She was convinced she had swallowed a tadpole in the drinking water and the tadpole had grown into a frog which she thought she could feel moving about in her abdomen. Dr. Kincaid got tired of rowing across the river to call on her for this ailment. He went to a spring and caught a small frog which he took with him when he went to see her. He gave her a strong physic and when she wasn't looking, he slipped the frog into the bucket. That cured her. She was convinced her diagnosis was correct.[9]

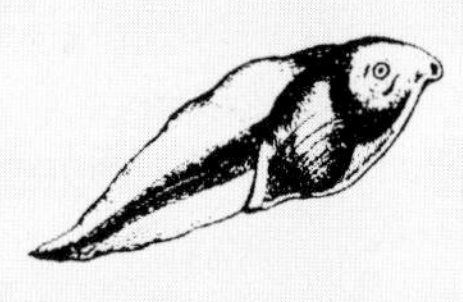

Though game was plentiful the people were besieged by insects and various sicknesses. They were afflicted with boils. "You see here that everything that is German must give way, even the skin is peeled off."[8] Ticks and mosquitoes were a real pest to them. Frederick Steines writes the following regarding the subject:

> A terrible plague from which we suffer. It is the American scab or itch, some call it the Brazilian itch. Every part of the body is affected by it to some extent, tho it attacks the abdomen seriously, and the feet worst of all. The Americans are not free from the itch either, tho they are not attacked as severely as the foreigners. The physicians here know no remedy against this plague. My friend Dr. Kincaid—has taught me a schottish, which he calls the itch dance. In executing this dance one hops and jumps about in even time and scratches and rubs quite lustily. I must confess this itch dance, in its most uncomfortable, affords me more pleasure than the most successful parade, which I have ever participated in, gun in hand.[10]

Along with these sufferings, there was the severe cold. The year 1835 was particularly frigid. In this same letter Frederick Steines gives this description of the cold.

> In the morning when we awoke, there was ice on the bedcovers. Boiling water with which we attempted to wash off the table, froze before it could be wiped off. The whole day long the table was covered with ice. Cups filled with hot coffee almost instantly froze to the table. We stood or sat about the fire while eating our meals, but in spite of this, the fat from our meat at once became thick and cold on our plates. Calves and young hogs died. I gave my livestock all the corn they could eat, and to this, I attribute the fact that I did not sustain greater losses. The weather is very inconsistent and is subject to the most extreme changes. All of February it was very cold and even now the snow lies more than a foot deep on the ground. The Mississippi was frozen over for six weeks, so that four-horse wagons could pass over it.[11]

Labor was high and hard to get. A good hired hand was paid $80 to $100 a year. "The common laborer wants to eat and drink well, draw good wages, but do little work." [12] Some farmers had slaves but this did not conform to the industrious German settlers' idea of freedom. Few Germans had slaves. They took great pride in working their farms.

> We are Germans and want to remain Germans, and one must be able to see by our farms that Germans live here.[13]

FOOTNOTES

1. Bek, Wm. G., "The Followers of Duden," *Missouri Historical Review*, Vol. XV, July 1921, No. 4, p. 663. I have used Bek's quotations from the letters of both Frederick and Herman Steines frequently to illustrate a point. Norma Cunningham gave me a copy of the *Letters of Frederick Steines* and *The Steines Papers*.
2. Bek, Ibid, Vol XIV, April – July 1920, Nos. 3-4, p. 445-446.
3. Ibid, p. 664.
4. Ibid, p. 436.
5. Ibid, Vol. XV, No. 3, p.535.
6. Ibid, Vol. XIV, April – July 1920, Nos. 3-4, p. 445.
7. Bek, op cit., Vol. XIV, April – July 1920, Nos. 3-4, p. 437.
8. Bek, op. cit, Vol. XV, No. 3, p. 537. This was probably smallpox.
9. Bower, Hazel Meier, "A Family History," p. 30.
10. Ibid, p. 544. These were probably "chiggers."
11. Ibid, Vol. XV, No. 3, pp. 542-543.
12. Ibid, Vol. XV, No. 4, p. 661
13. Ibid, p. 680.

Oakfiled Academy, built in 1839, and an interior view showing the old blackboard. Courtesy Washington Historical Society.

CHAPTER FIVE

Schools

The first school in the vicinity of St. Albans was called Oakfield Academy and was located on the Great State Road (now Manchester Road or Highway 100). It was established by Frederick Steines, who had been a teacher in Germany. (See page 6).

He bought a farm at St. Albans and later moved to St. Louis where he taught in a German-American school. At the end of October 1838, due to bad health, he resigned his position in St. Louis and returned to Franklin County. He bought a tract of government land on Ridenhaur Creek, which he called *Oakfield*. Ridenhaur Creek was commonly called "Fiddle Creek" because people living along there were very musical and used to fiddle to one another from their houses. One would start and the others would answer back and forth across the creek.[1]

Oakfield Academy was opened in 1839 as a school for boys and attended by most of the young men in the neighborhood. It continued in operation until 1869.

Frederick Steines' son Ernest Edmund[2] was assistant to his father for two years. The school was well planned. Classes started at 8 a.m. and ended at 5 p.m. with two hours for lunch at noon; each class lasted one hour. English, German, mathematics, general history, natural history, U.S. history, geography, singing and declamation, drawing and penmanship were taught. H.G. Kiel in his *Centennial Directory* notes that there were about 500 students at Oakfield Academy between 1840 and 1869. "It was probably the most widely known ever in Franklin County." [3]

By the year 1844, there was a need for an organized school district. A majority of qualified voters in the township petitioned the General Assembly of the State of Missouri to form a school township and hold meetings. This petition was granted March 27, 1845. A number of leading citizens then assembled to select the school directors.

> State of Missouri
> County of Franklin
> for Congressional Township
> No. 44 R2 East
> And in the School Township No. 15
>
> It is ordered by the Hon. County-Court of the aforesaid county that the first meeting is to be held on the 19th day of December, 1846.
>
> The undersigned directors appointed the following persons to notify the inhabitants of the township of the first general meeting, to be held at Frederick Steines' on the 19th of Decbr.
> 1. William Steele
> 2. James Whitset
> 3. Julius W. Kurlbaum
> 4. Hugo Lenz
>
> We the undersigned school directors, at Frederick Steines' residence assembled according to law for the purpose of organizing school districts in this township, appointed as township-clerk Frederick Steines.
>
> D.C. Tursley
> John Decker
> Fred. Steines

The meeting was held on December 18, 1846, but there was not a sufficient number of the inhabitants present so the directors adjourned the meeting to the second Monday in January. They appointed the following to notify the inhabitants qualified to vote at township meetings: James Whitset, those living on the south-side of the State Road; Alex Leathers; Julius W. Kurlbaum, those on Ridenhaur Creek and its branches; and Adolph Greef. The following notice was sent:

> The meeting will be held at the house of Frederick Steines on the 11th of January, 1847, at

eleven o'clock in the forenoon.

By order of the directors:
Frederick Steines
Clerk

The meeting was indeed held January 11th, 1847, at the house of Frederick Steines for the purpose of establishing schools. He called the meeting to order and read the act to provide for this organization, approved March 27, 1845. The assembly appointed James Whitset as chairman. He then called the qualified voters present to elect their township officers. The following were elected by unanimous vote as Directors:

David C. Tursley, School Commissioner
Francis Becker   Inspectors
Frederick Steines

They appointed James Whitset as Clerk. Three school districts were set out:

1st being the southeast quarter of this township;
2nd N.E. fractional quarter of the township, bound on the west by Ridenhaur Creek to its mouth;
3rd S.W. fractional quarter of Township 44 and the N.W. fractional quarter embracing the whole district west of Ridenhaur Creek from a point where the district line intersects the creek.

The next meeting was set to be held the third Saturday of September, 1847, at the house of Frederick Steines.

The next meeting of which there is a record was held September 8, 1849. At this meeting the directors thought it advisable to change the dis-

The original Little Tavern School was in use from 1846 to 1897. In this photo: Elizabeth Auchenbach, teacher. To her right, Sophie Niehaus, Lula Steuernagel, Amanda Steuernagel; (by the door) Lydia Pohlig, Rosa Lenz, Henry Rosenbaum; Otto Pohlig, Fred Mottert (with dinner bucket); Ben Pohlig, Paul Pfeiffer, Frank Lenz. Photo courtesy Ruth Campbell.

trict line between districts No. 2 and No. 3 to include John Ridenhaur, George Reede and John Calvin in district No. 3. There was a unanimous vote that schools' land should be leased out by order of the directors. They approved the lease already negotiated by the director and Charles Marsh.

In 1850, Franklin County had only 19 public schools and 19 teachers and an annual income of $1160 for all these and about 461 pupils in attendance. There were four academies in the county with a total of 75 students and only four teachers.[4]

The annual meeting was held September 11, 1850 and called to order by Chairman Francis Becker. There was no township business to be discussed, so the meeting was adjourned. They set the second Saturday of September 1851, for the date of the next meeting. The school district had a meeting January 18, 1873, at which Kochs, Birk, Kincaid, and F.W. Hartman were present. They entered into a written agreement for six months at $50 with the understanding that Christian Hardt should teach ten months. They backdated the agreement. Wilhelm Kochs donated forty acres of land for the school.

A one-room log schoolhouse was built by Wilhelm F. Kochs in 1846, when the school districts were organized. Kochs, an architect by trade, was born April 25, 1805, at Gelsenkirchen, Germany. He emigrated to America in 1833. He worked in St. Louis, Mo., and Dubuque, Iowa, building houses and churches. He returned to Germany in 1838, where he married Henriette Becker, March 23, 1838. She was born near Cologne, Germany, June 1, 1819. Returning to Missouri, they settled on Tavern Road across from the William Kierspe place. (The old Kochs house burned down while we were living out there.) They had 12 children: six boys and six girls. He was one of the first settlers to come to Tavern Creek settlement and the last of the first settlers to die.

The Kochs place in St. Albans. Photo: M.W. Keller, Glencoe, Mo.

He died October 1, 1898, at the age of over 93 years. His wife died December 14, 1900.[5]

Christian Hardt was the first teacher in the Little Tavern School. He was born March 16, 1804, in Ruenderath, Rhine-Prussia. He taught school in Germany before emigrating to America in 1833. He settled on Tavern Creek. He married Karolina Wilhelmine Adolphine Kochs, widow of Florenz Kochs who died October 12, 1839.[6] Christian Hardt died January 19, 1886.

Christian Hardt. Private collection.

The log schoolhouse was used until 1897, when the building was covered with siding and a second schoolroom, a coatroom and furnace were added. This work was done by John Kuelper, a carpenter, who lived on Big Tavern Road. With the addition of a second schoolroom, another teacher was added, Esther Kuelper. The school term was four to six months. The children had to walk two miles or more through fields and over a cow path to school. In winter they had to clear a path to make it passable. Some of the teachers in Little Tavern

Little Tavern School, renovated with clapboard siding, was used from 1897 to 1951. Photo courtesy of the Becker family.

School were Annie King, 1882–1891; Augusta M. Hanning, 1891; Elizabeth Auchenbach, 1892–1909; Emma Halbach, 1909–1911; James S. Maher, 1912–1917; Frieda Hoerle, 1922–1923; Nellie Hurdabee, 1924. I was told by Minnie Stricker that Nellie Hurdabee was just twelve years old when she was the only teacher for 32–33 children.

Anna Lee Glen, who lived in St. Albans, recalled what it was like in 1929–31, when she attended Little Tavern School. It was too far for her to walk so her mother drove her to school, picking up several children on the way. They drove past the St. Albans general store and across Tavern Creek. There was no road through the woods to the schoolhouse so she let them off at a farm at the edge of the woods. The farmer did not like the children crossing through his farm so he would "sic his mean dogs" on them. The children gathered around the flagpole in the schoolyard to recite the Pledge of Allegiance to the flag before going inside. Reading was always the first lesson. If a child missed a word, he or she had to stand in the corner until recess when the children of the directors were sent to get switches. In bad weather, a ruler replaced the switches. The offender had to hold out his or her hands to be switched.

Lucille Graves Schoelich taught at the Little Tavern School 1948–49. The frame schoolhouse was used until 1951. In 1949, four schools joined to form the Labadie R-5 School District. These were Bethel, Labadie, Little Tavern and Becker. At this time the children were taken to Labadie by public school bus.

Children wishing to attend the Catholic school had to be driven privately to Pacific to attend St. Bridget's or St. John's at Guildehaus. After the building of the railroads, they took the train to Washington, Mo., to attend St. Francis Borgia School. About 1914, there were two daily trains from Labadie to Washington. William Calvin[7] told me he took the train the year he made his First Communion in fourth grade. Sister Anthorella was his teacher at St. Francis Borgia School, Washington, Mo. Communications tickets cost five dollars per month. Later children were taken privately to Labadie where the school bus from St. John's Guildehaus transported them to school at Guildehaus.

In the days of the little log schoolhouse, the children attended school ten months. Part of the time they studied at home memorizing the dictionary and similar books. Each one had his own slate for school.[8] The grades went from first through eighth, but when a child was fifteen years of age, he could stop school. Some children were taught at home; Bernice Stricker was the teacher for her three children.

Wilhelm F. Kochs was chairman of the school board at one time. His son Albert wrote the following poem about the little log schoolhouse. "The hand that superintended, passed the age of 93" was his father, and "one who enjoys her 80th year" was his mother, Henriette Becker Kochs.

The consolidated school district was reorganized in 1961, and a notice was given regarding election of directors and tax increases.[10]

The Old School-House
By Albert Kochs

Over the hill to the school-house, I twenty-five years ago,
Was sent to learn the A.B.C's, a difficult task you know,
But since then the reason why, became so clear to me,
That I now take the liberty, to write some poetry.

Over the hill to the school-house, playmates I would meet,
We would run and jump so merrily, until to our books retreat.
After which I enjoyed, knowing full well the reasons,
Why I was sent to that school-house, for nearly thirteen seasons.

Over the hill to the school-house, a seat of education,
Where lessons are taught, that you'll not forget is a blessing of civilization.
Where Art and Science gets a start, continued by knowledge and wisdom,
Until our earthly journey, has ended in heavenly kingdom.

Over the hill to the school-house, some have found their treasures,
In wisdom, strength and beauty, while others sought for pleasures.
Thus comes the change of our thoughts, in a pride of glory,
That every one of us should try to reach the topmost story.

Over the hill to the school-house, a photograph to take,
A house built fifty years ago, a relic of this state. Yes!
Indeed an old remembrance, can be seen on paper here,
And the hand that superintended, passed the age of 93.

Over the hill to the school-house, various moments were spent
By one who enjoys her 80th year, is a blessing which heaven has sent.
Yes! Indeed a truthful heart, overflows with justice,
Was the motto of her thought, in her lifetime duties.

Over the hill to the school-house, recollections often wander,
From those who can recall a scene, when they were in danger,
Like the scenes on a teacher's face, sometimes kept them guessing.
And now to Him who rules on high, we ask you a blessing.

St. Louis, Mo.[9]

Wilhelm and Henriette Kochs and family. Becker family photo.

In 1965, the Labadie R-5 District became part of Washington School District.

The following account was given at "Old Timers Night" at the February 1974, meeting of the Labadie School P.T.A.

In 1895 Minnie Stricker, nee Neuhaus, attended Little Tavern School. She said she walked three and a half miles morning and night, leaving home at 7:30 and arriving at school by 8:45. Minnie said she thinks if the kids "got it bad now" they should have walked that three and a half miles in below zero weather. She recalls wearing copper toed shoes and wool stockings She said the school was heated with a box stove.[11]

It seems to have been the custom at the close of the school year for the teacher to have some little souvenir for the children to take home. I don't know what the souvenir was, but in 1910, Emma Halbach wrote the following little poem to accompany her gift.

My pupils dear, this souvenir small,
I dedicate to you.
And fondly hope that each and all
Will read the pages through.

In memory of the school days spent
Together sweetly here,
I give it with acknowledgment
Of all your love sincere.

Your Teacher

Another poem, for which I have neither date nor author, was entitled:

The Close of School

The school is out and now we part
And go our several ways,
To mingle in life's busy mart
And spend vacation days.

Left to right: Harry Hausgen, Cora Hausgen, Tillie Mae Tracy, Fred Krienkamp. Becker family photo.

Pupils of the Little Tavern School in 1914

7th Grade

Hazel Jones — Armine Jones
Leona Schopp

6th Grade

Katherine Meyer — Louis Meyer
Elmer Bell — Norman Stone
Lorne Shelton — Austin Shelton

4th Grade

Mabel Bell — Eugene Jones
Irvin Smith — Neil Wood
Willie Calvin — William Brinkmann

3rd Grade

Lizzie Burton — Areta Rutherford
Bertha Calvin — Albert Hellmann

2nd Grade

Sophia Brinkmann — Carrie Rutherford
David Wood — Archie Shelton
Charley Burton — Georgie Feldmann
Bessie Fitzsimmons

1st Grade

Effie Bell — Matilda Holman
Ester Shelton — Flora Poor
Edwin Lauxstermann — Claudie Stone
Georgie Holman — Dayton Phillips
Gaylord Phillips

As St. Albans Properties developed in the 1990's, many of the families building homes there found a real need for a private school for their children. The search for teachers resulted in the establishment of a second campus of the Chesterfield Day School.

The old George Gaehle House, formerly the Henry Brensing house built in 1848, was originally a log house later covered with weatherboard. This house was converted into a charming school. The interior was remodeled with some alterations to the original plan of a center hall and staircase with two rooms on each side. The yard was enclosed

Chesterfield Day School/St. Albans occupies the old Henry Brensing/George Gaehle House, built in 1848. Photo by author.

with a white picket fence and playground equipment added.

The school opened in September of 1994, with fifteen pupils, ages 3-8; preschool through second grade and two teachers, Barbara Rueter and Chris Blair. After Christmas, three more pupils were added, making a total of 18 for the opening year. The children came from St. Albans, Labadie, Pond, Ballwin, Ellisville, Glencoe and Chesterfield. The school is operated on the Montessori system of education. Tuition was $2650, preschool, half day; $4500 preschool, full day up to 6th grade, plus a few additional fees. Dr. Barbara Fulton is the head of the Chesterfield Day School and its second campus at St. Albans. Mrs. Tosca Hallock was the first Director of Admissions and School Administrator.[12]

1995–96 there were 35 children K to 4th grade.

1996–97 there were 65 children K to 5th grade.

1997–98 there were 125 children K to 6th grade.

1998–99 was the first year to have a graduating class of 6th graders.

Staff 1997–98: Dr. Barbara F. Fulton, Head of School, and Chris Blair, Assistant Head.

We are temporarily located in houses in the village. The houses were named in honor of the DAR ceremony as follows:

Meriwether Lewis—Large Victorian by Lewis and Clark marker—houses elementary children.

Sacajawea—Original Cape Cod—houses all day preschool.

Pomp's Chapel—annex attached to Sacajawea—morning preschool.

William Clark—Large Victorian—houses Kindergarten and first grade.

Next new building finished February 1998. It is a large train station building called the Thomas Jefferson Building.[13]

This history of St. Albans had to stop at some point in time. I chose the date of the dedication of the Lewis and Clark National Historic Trail wayside exhibit, October 1, 1997, as the cutoff date. But, as we go to press in the spring of 2001, I want to update the school history. The new Chesterfield Day School/St. Albans opened November 1999 at 123 Schoolhouse Road. Today's enrollment is 175 boys and girls from eighteen-month-old preschoolers to ninth graders.

FOOTNOTES

1. On New Year's Eve at about 12 o'clock, neighbors would get together with accordion, fiddle and banjo and wherever they visited they would be served coffee and cookies.
2. Ernest Steines maintained the only meteorological observation and weather station in Franklin County and prepared U.S. weather records. He performed this service, without salary, from June 13, 1892 to May 25, 1920.
3. *The Centennial Biographical Directory of Franklin County, Missouri*, compiled by H.G. Kiel, p. 208.
4. Ibid.
5. Bek, Vol. XVI, October 1921, No. 1, p. 135.
6. Florenz came to St. Albans with his brother Wilhelm and Francis Becker in 1833 and bought a farm near Frederick Steines.
7. William Calvin lived in a house, said to have been built by Gustav Wilming c. 1885, located on Hwy. T at the bottom of a double S curved hill known as "Calvin Hill." "Bill" worked for St. Albans Farms. His wife, Catherine, and daughter, Jackie, worked at the Old Barn Inn. Later Jackie worked for us at our home. His father, Isaac Calvin (12/11/1866–2/9/1956), known to us as "Grandpa Calvin," lived along Fiddle Creek. Isaac's parent were Perry and Missouri Calvin. On our way home from church, we often saw him walking along Hwy T and gave him a ride. He usually was carrying a bag of empty soda bottles to cash in at Head's Store. Our son Gregory wanted to sit next to him because "Grampa" wore buckskins when he was younger and that impressed our son.
8. John Pfeiffer told me about Little Tavern School at the time he attended.
9. I found this poem to be a parody on "Over the Hill to the Poor-House" by William Carleton in his book, *Farm Ballads*, published by Harper & Brothers Publishers, Franklin Square, New York, 1882, p. 51.
10. In compliance with Sect. 1655-330 RS Mo. Notice is hereby given to qualified voters of Labadie Reorganized School District #R-5, County of Franklin, of an election to elect 2 directors for a term of three years each; to authorize a levy of an increased tax rate in excess of One Dollar ($1.00) per One Hundred Dollars ($100) assessed valuation, the amount authorized by law to be levied without voter approval, for the following purposes:

    (1) For Teachers' Fund – 30 cents for a period of 1 year.

    (2) For Incidental Fund – 30 cents for a period of 1 year.

    (3) For Building Fund – 10 cents for a period of 1 year.

    This will make a total levy of $1.70 for school purposes. This does not include a levy of 5 cents for the Sinking Fund to retire bonds.

    This 16th day of March, 1961
    Miss Sadie C. Kissing
    Secretary, Board of Education
11. "Old-Timers at Labadie Have Their Night," by Mrs. Sandra Gurnow, *Washington Missourian*, Thursday, Feb. 21, 1972, p. 9A.
12. School information was given to me by Joe Pottebaum and Tosca Hallock.
13. Chris Blair furnished me with this information.

CHAPTER SIX

Post Office

Transportation in the beginning of the ninteenth century was by horse, stagecoach, or river steamboat. There was a mail route from St. Louis to Jefferson City with appointed stops along the way. Fox Creek Post Office, located on Manchester Road on this route, served the community of St. Albans. Herman Steines had the following entry in his diary for August 31, 1833:

> The mail carrier failed to come on the last two mail days. Harrison who had contracted to carry the mail from St. Louis to Jefferson City for $500.00 a year, has become bankrupt. They say we shall not get any papers and letters till a new contract is made for carrying the mail.[1]

In his diary for April 24, 1835, Herman Steines makes the following entry:

> From here to New York it costs 25¢ to send a letter—come directly up the Missouri on a steamboat and land at Dr. Kincaid's at the mouth of Tavern Creek, opposite Missouritown. My address is
>
> Fox Creek Post Office
> Franklin County, Mo.
> Via Havre and New York USA[2]

The postal money order system was established under the law of May 17, 1864, and inaugurated November 1, 1864, primarily to protect savings of the Unionist soldiers against the numerous mail robberies of that time. This service falls into two sections: Domestic and International. The dates given here indicate the beginning of the service.

Domestic
- Union, August 15, 1881
- Pacific, July 2, 1883
- Labadie, January 3, 1883
- St. Albans, July 1, 1902

International
- Washington, October 1, 1874
- Pacific, January 1, 1905
- Union, January 1, 1905[3]

The following post offices were established:

Oakfield, located about Section 26, Township 4, Range 2 East, was established June 2, 1847, and discontinued August 14, 1895. Frederick Steines was the first postmaster. He and his brothers Herman and Peter Steines all occupied public lands near here on July 31, 1834.[4]

Becker was established June 6, 1892, and on February 24, 1898, the name and probably the site was changed to Klondike, which is a post office and a station on the Missouri, Kansas & Texas Railroad in St. Charles County and about three miles up the Missouri River. Becker was probably named after Francis Becker and was located on the Rock Island Railroad about Section 16, Twshp. 44 R 2 E. The locality, a little west, is now known as the R.R. Station Oetters and the locality is also near Reeds Landing.[5] This was one of the four post offices moved out of Franklin County and the only one of them that changed the name when moved.[6]

Francis Arnold Becker was born January 21, 1807, at Strasserhof, Koln, Prussia. He emigrated to America in June 1832, arrived Baltimore in the fall of 1832, went on to Pittsburgh until the spring of 1833, thence to St. Louis. He moved to Illinois and then Iowa. He returned to Koln in 1838 and

Judge Francis Arnold Becker. Photo courtesy Becker family.

The Becker place on Tavern Creek. The barn was built near the creek with the tool shed between the house and the barn. The barn later became the Old Barn Inn. Photo courtesy Becker family.

married Cornelia Fetta who died and was buried at sea on the way to America. He returned to Dubuque, Iowa, and Galena, Illinois, until 1840, when he settled on his land grant farm at the mouth of Tavern Creek, near St. Albans. He married Wilhelmina Hausmann June 23, 1841. They had three children. Wilhelmina died in 1849. He married her sister Henrietta Hausmann October 10, 1849. She died November 22, 1849. He married Emma Helen Hardt, daughter of Christian and Karolina Kochs Hardt, on November 26, 1850, at St. Albans. They had five children.[7]

Francis Arnold Becker was a carpenter by trade. In 1840, he built his house above flood stage on the banks of the Missouri River where Tavern Creek meets the river. The barn was built near the creek with a tool shed between the house and the barn. The barn later became the Old Barn Inn. There was a bridge over Tavern Creek to get to the town. Soon after Becker moved to Missouri, he became interested in politics. In 1839, he became a United States citizen. He was Justice of the Peace from 1844 to 1850. He was elected County Judge from 1850 to 1864, and again in 1866 to 1870. Judge Becker was the banker, magistrate, and postmaster of the town. His wife, Emma, died July 12, 1862. Francis Arnold Becker died September 11, 1886, at Washington, Mo., and was buried in the family plot at St. Albans.[8]

St. Albans' Post Office was established November 6, 1889, and discontinued service March 30, 1907. The following were the Postmasters at St. Albans:

Charles Becker from November 6, 1889 to March 26, 1895. His highest annual salary was $53.80, paid in 1893.

Bernard E. Heipertz from March 26, 1895 to August 24, 1901. His highest annual salary was $157.08, paid in 1899.

Ed. Pfeiffer from August 24, 1901, to December 3, 1903. His highest annual salary was $82.57, paid in 1903.

Gustav McDaniel from December 3, 1903, to September 24, 1906. His highest annual salary was $110.06, paid in 1905.

August Hoerle from September 24, 1906 to March 30, 1907.

The mail was brought by train as long as there was a railroad station and stop at St. Albans. A timetable dated 1893 lists the following:

Port Royal	35.8 miles from St. Louis
St. Albans	39.7 miles from St. Louis
Becker	42.1 miles from St. Louis

Gertrude Becker Horn, granddaughter of Francis Becker, told me that she remembered "as a little kid" Fiddle Creek Valley where the railroad went through was Becker's Station, afterwards called Becker. "There was a post office down there near the old pump station used by the sand works; lots of houses for the people that worked there. Forsythe's place was called Oetters – later on, called it Oetters. Mr. Oetters' brother had a chicken ranch there. We had to go there to get our mail. The whole valley called Becker, then Oetters' Station."

After 1907, the mail was on rural route out of Pacific until 1922, when John Pfeiffer applied for a post office. He requested that it be named St. Albans, but at that time there was a St. Aubert's Post Office so the request was rejected. He then named it Becker after Francis Becker. When St. Aubert's Post Office was discontinued, he asked to have Becker changed to St. Albans. He had the post office in the general store and was Postmaster from 1922 to 1949. His daughter, Mae Loraine Head, bought the store in 1941; the Post Office was moved into a small separate building. This was an old boxcar alongside the railroad track. When we moved to St. Albans, this is where we picked up our mail.

The St. Albans Post Office was housed in an old boxcar for many years. Photo by Marie Pohlig during the flood of 1951.

The old boxcar would shake every time a train passed. The trains were very noisy. After the flood of 1951, the post office was moved into the west section of the St. Albans Farms office building, and the boxcar was removed.

Marie Virginia Pohlig became Postmistress at St. Albans April 12, 1949. She served in this capacity for 42 years and was given a service award upon her retirement in March, 1991.

The little post office was a popular meeting place where neighbors came to pick up their mail and to visit. There was always a very friendly atmosphere. Marie was often ironing the napkins for the Barn Inn when she was not attending to her postal duties.

Marie was born April 3, 1922, at St. Albans. Her great-grandfather, John William Pohlig, emigrated from Germany with his wife Anna Marie and their son Julius to St. Albans. They built a house along the St. Albans Road where their son Charles was born about 1845. Charles married Eliza Ossenfort and they had five children: Emil, William, Otto, Lydia and Benjamin, who was born April 17, 1885. They were all born and raised in St. Albans and attended Little Tavern School. Benjamin moved to Mascoutah, Illinois, where he married Mamie Gutjahr. Their eldest daughter Olivia was born there January 30, 1907. They moved to Labadie where their daughters Myrtle and Bernice were born. They later moved to Union and finally to St. Albans where Marie was born. Benny worked for St. Albans Farms. According to Marie, "My father worked mostly in the dairy at St. Albans—plus he did a lot of mowing in those fields and hills with mules pulling a mower. The last years he worked around the Studio on the grounds and ran errands before he couldn't work anymore." He died November 4, 1970.

After Charles Pohlig died in 1914, his widow Eliza built a new house for herself and her son Benny and family. Marie, their youngest, was born there. The old house with a barn and springhouse was located on the top of the hill. The Pohlig family cemetery was nearby. John William Pohlig and his wife Ann Marie and Charles Pohlig and his wife Eliza are buried there.[9]

The property located in Sect. 1 T44N R2E, containing 80 acres, was originally conveyed by the U.S. Government to Daniel Bell in 1820 for $250; next to Leonard Stump containing 80 acres; next to Frederick Steines and Bertha, his wife, 80 acres; next to Arnold Lenz and Johanne Marie, his wife; next to John Frederick Eymers for $385, 40 acres; next to Otto Janssen, 40 acres; next to John William Pohlig and Anne Marie, his wife, 40 acres; next to Charles Pohlig and Eliza, his wife. Eliza sold the 40 acres to James Buckner Fisher and Regina, his wife, in 1925. The Fishers named it *Long Meadow.*

The Fishers never lived there full time, but used it for weekends and vacations. They had four children: 1. Charles m. Mary Bruce Nichols, he died in 1968. They had three daughters: Peggy, Betty and Barbara. 2. James, m. Reka Nielson, he died 1994. They had two children, James Jr. and Alison. 3. Elizabeth, m. Norman Hinchey, she died 1995. They had one daughter Anne. 4. Jean, m. Harry Cochran Gibbs.[10] They had four sons: Christopher, David, Buckner and Scott.

James Buckner Fisher died in 1969, and his wife Regina died in 1976, leaving *Long Meadow* to their children and heirs. In 1989, the family sold the property to the St. Albans Land Development Company. Jean Gibbs represented the family in the sale. The old house was taken apart, piece by piece, numbered and put in storage by David Gibbs. The barn was also dismantled by someone else and moved to St. Charles County. The family cemetery has been preserved.[11]

When Marie was three years old, her family moved to St. Louis for a short time, then to Union, Mo., where she attended the Immaculate Concep-

Marie Pohlig, left, on her retirement as postmistress in 1991 with Dorie Oberhaus, current postmistress. Courtesy Washington Missourian.

tion School until 4th grade. They returned to St. Albans and she attended Tavern School, where she was graduated from 8th grade. She rode the bus to Washington to attend Washington High School, being graduated in 1940. After retirement from the Post Office, she moved to Wentzville, Mo., to a retirement center there.[12]

Dorie Oberhaus became the officer in charge of the Post Office. On October 30, 1993, Dorie Oberhaus was appointed Postmistress at St. Albans. The Post Office has been enlarged and the mail is still delivered by rural letter carrier from Pacific.

FOOTNOTES

1. Bek, Vol XIV, April-July 1920, Nos. 3 & 4, p. 445.
2. Ibid, Vol. XV, July 1921, No. 4, p. 664.
3. Kiel, Herman Gottlieb, *The Centennial Biographical Directory of Franklin County*, pp. 103-104.
4. Ibid, p. 198.
5. Oetters Station on Rock Island Railroad, 42 miles from St. Louis, was named after Henry Oetters who owned large deposits of white or glass sand at this place. Kiel, Op cit., p. 193.
6. Kiel, Ibid, p. 207.
7. Gertrude Horn was the one most helpful to me in permitting me to use the "Day Book" kept by her grandfather and continued by her father. Wilbert Horn shared with me family information after Gertie died May 9, 1985. He wrote a family history and genealogy, "Our Dear Gertie and Memories" by "William A. Horn and Gertie's Family 1986."
8. Bek, Vol. XVI, October 1921, No. 1, p. 136 and family records.
9. Three graves are marked:

   POHLIG

Sgt. J. W. Pohlig	Hanna Maria
Co. D	Wife of
Inns Batn.	John Pohlig
Mo. Inf.	Died May 25, 1882
	Aged about 66 years

   A small stone marked: A.M.P.
10. Harry Gibbs was well known in the 50s and 60s for his cowboy TV show, *The Wrangler's Club with Texas Bruce.*
11. This account was told to me by Jean Gibbs.
12. I am indebted to Marie Pohlig for the Pohlig family history.

The Beckers in front of their home in St. Albans. Left to right: Francis, Charles and Louise. Photo courtesy Ruth Campbell.

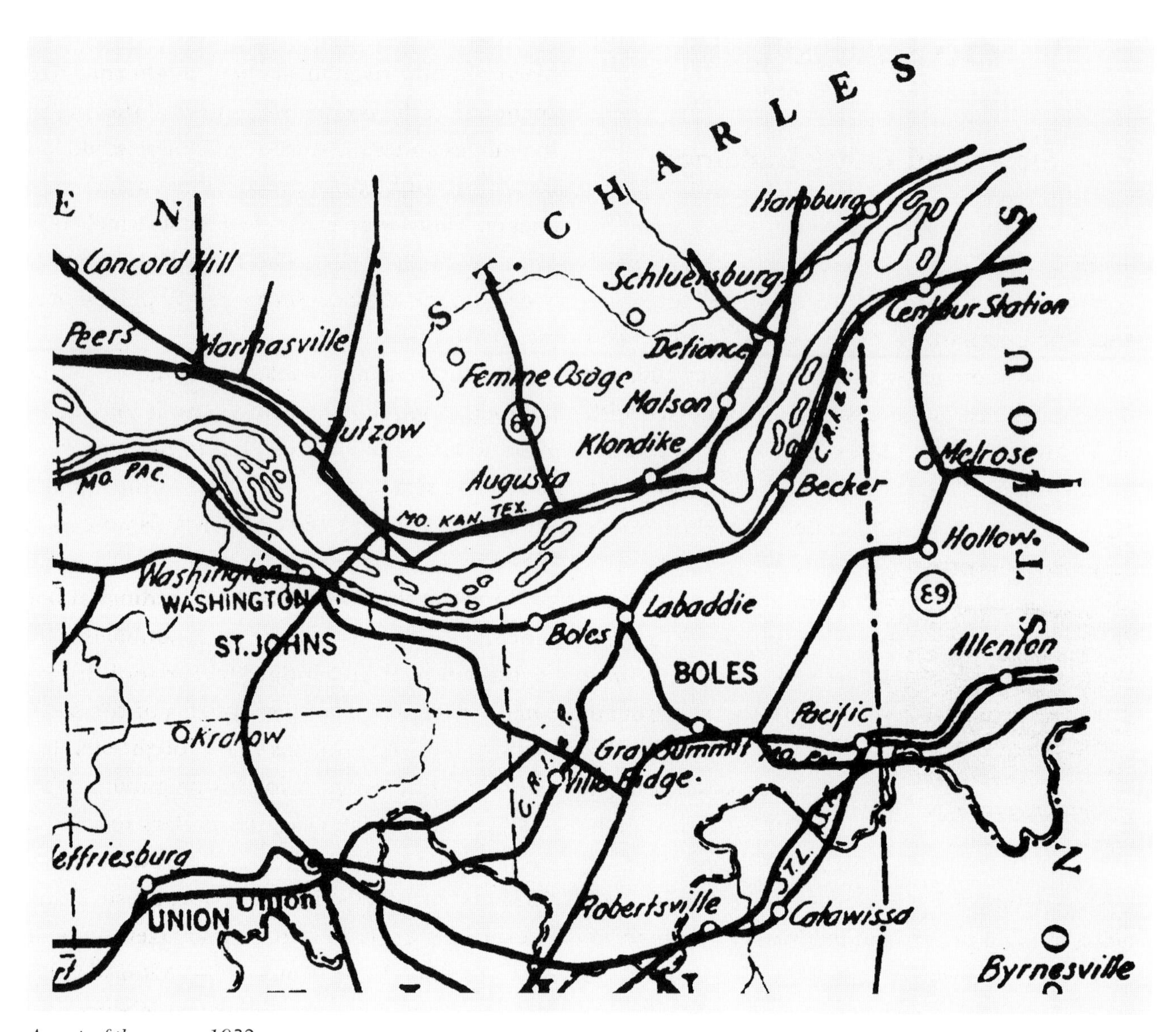

A map of the area c. 1932

CHAPTER SEVEN

Stores and Other Buildings

Before 1850, many St. Albans farmers rode horseback to other towns to trade or sell their produce and purchase needed supplies. The Franklin Road, now Manchester Road or Highway 100, was three miles east of St. Albans and connected with St. Louis and other places. The Farm to Market Road connected St. Albans with Pacific (originally called Franklin) where they could take the train to St. Louis.

Gustav Wilming. Photo courtesy Louise Stettes.

Gustav Wilming, the man who homesteaded the property where we lived, had a small house across from our entrance on Highway T. Gustav Wilming was a shoemaker. He made forms out of hardwood, using wooden pegs to put the leather on the form. Once a year he would walk to Pacific via the Farm to Market Road, a distance of about ten miles, to get the train to St. Louis. He would buy a year's supply of leather and return home the same day.

The steamboat was the principal means of transportation after 1850. They were all sidewheelers with full length cabins and were suitable for freight as well as passengers.

The Missouri was a treacherous river. It was swift and its channel was always changing. The banks were lined mainly with cottonwood and willow trees. The force of the current often undermined the roots of the trees, causing them to fall into the river. A river pilot was always on the lookout for snags or sawyers. The pilot kept notes on the condition of the river. The trees were carried downstream by the river until they caught and were anchored to the bottom with one end sticking up, sometimes under the surface. The pilot would look for a ripple or break in the surface as a warning of danger. There were many steamboats wrecked because of these breaks. The record of steamboat wrecks on the Missouri shows that 70 percent were due to this cause.[1]

Another serious problem was that of procuring fuel. Wood alone was used and it took lots of wood to keep the engines fired to produce steam to run the steamboats. The trees on the banks of the river were cut for this. Wood yards were established.

In 1835 there were steamboat landings at both Kincaid's and Knecht's places. Steamboats made regular stops there. Judge Becker took his son Charles along to meet the captains of the steamboats docked at St. Albans who brought merchandise the judge ordered for his neighbors. Wood was loaded on for firing the boilers to run the steamboats. Wood was often exchanged for staples, furniture, dry goods, farm supplies or cash. Francis Becker kept a record of the wood taken on board in a little notebook, *Cordwood—1856-1863.* This gives the date, name of steamboat, number of cords of wood taken, price, whose wood it was and amount.[3]

The coming of the railroad marked the end of steamboating as the principal means of transportation.[4] The last commercial boat that ever arrived at Fort Benton left that port in 1890; 40 miles a day versus 400 miles per day by railroad.[5] On the 13th of June, 1902, Congress passed an act abolishing the Missouri River Commission, and virtually abandoning the river as a commercial highway.[6]

As the community grew in population, it was found necessary to establish a general store. In 1893, 12 citizens invested $100 each in a company to build a store. Those contributing were Charles

The St. Albans General Store was established in 1893 by a group of residents. Names of the children are lost; the dog's name is Shine. Photo courtesy Mae Head.

Hardt, Charles Becker, Frederick Steines, William Kochs, Gustav Hausgen, William Stettes, John Kincaid, August Hoerle, Bernard Heipertz, Tillie Gasner, Alvena Hoerle and Frederick Berthold.

The building of the general store is recorded in the "Day Book of the St. Albans Store Building" by Charles Becker, son of Francis Becker.

> At a meeting held by the neighboring residents of St. Albans, Mo., on March 6th, 1893, the following members—Gustav Hausgen, Charles Hardt, William Stettes Sr., John Kincaid, William Kochs, Bernard Heipertz, Hulda Steines, Mary Becker and Alvina Rosenbaum—agreed to organize for the purpose to buy a parcel of land and build a two-story frame store house on the same, suitable for a general country store, and the following resolutions were adopted by the vote of the majority of the members.
>
> 1st That each one pay $60.00.
>
> 2nd That the site to build on was decided by all ten votes to be on the corner of Chas. Becker's field.
>
> 3rd There were ten votes in favor to buy one quarter of an acre of land of C. Becker for the sum of $15.00.
>
> 4th That C. Becker had four votes being the highest number of votes for the first director for a term of three years.
>
> 5th That Wm. Kochs had six votes for the second director for a term of two years.
>
> 6th That Bernard Heipertz had four votes being the highest number for the third director for a term of one year. That the said directors should buy the material at their earliest convenience and proceed to build and superintend the building in the manner hereinafter specified.
>
> May 6 Commenced carpenter work.

The following is an 1892 account of the volunteers who worked on the cooperative building of the store.

Mar 16	August Heipertz	broke rock	1 day
	Henry Rosenbaum	“	“ “
	Otto Hausgen	“	“ “
	Fred Stettes	“	“ “
	Ernst Mottert	“	“ “
	Wm. Steinernagel	“	“ “
	Chs. Becker	“	“ “
	Wm. Kochs	“	“ “
Mar 18	Ed Pfeiffer	hauled rock with team	1 day
	Chs. Hardt	“ “ “	“ “
	Willy Lenz	“ “ “	“ “
	John Kincaid	“ “ “	“ “
	Otto Pfeiffer	without team	1 day
	Fred Uhter	“ “	½ day
	Chas. Pohlig	“ “	1 day
	Geo Fries	“ “	1 day
	Ernst Grah	“ “	1 day
	Bernard Heipertz	“ “	1 day
Mar 19	Louis Oelgar	“ “	1 day
	Geo Schuhler	on cellar	
	John Mottert	“ “	
	Alex Kincaid	“ “	
Mar 7 1905	Working grading road and hauling rock		
	C. Hardt.	1 day pd.	$1.00
	J. Kincaid	“ “	“
	Wm. Koch	“ “	“
	F. Stettes	“ “	“
	Edmund Steines	“ “	“
	E. Hoerle	1 day with team pd.	$2.00
	C. Becker	“ “ “ “ “	“
Mar 13	Hauling rock & repairing roof		
	C. Hardt	½ day pd.	.50
	J. Kincaid	“ “	.50
	Wm. Kochs	“ “	.50
	F. Stettes	“ “	.50
	C. Becker	“ “	.50
	E. Hoerle	½ day with team pd.	$1.00
	Wm Kochs	roofing materials	$2.50
April 6	Inside painting done by C. Dotz		$40.00

In March 1893, at the 2nd Annual Meeting of the members of the Store Building at St. Albans, Mo., the following resolution was adopted.

> 1st That E. Hoerle was elected by the largest number of votes present for Director in the place of B.E. Heipertz for three years.

When St. Albans Store was organized, Charles Becker, a director, wrote the bylaws and was treasurer.

Bernard E. Heipertz was the original proprietor and managed the store until 1899 when Edward Pfeiffer took over and made consignment of the store and books to Charles Becker; invoice of store showed $1170.25. On July 17, 1903, Gus McDaniels rented the store and moved in. It was next managed by August Hoerle. John William Pfeiffer, son of Edward Pfeiffer, wishing to get control of the company, bought out the shares of stock in the store for $100 from some; $125 from others and $250 from Charles Becker who did not want to sell.[7]

John Pfeiffer moved into the store July 15, 1915, with his wife, Ida Farrell Pfeiffer. Their daughter, Mabel (Mae) Loraine Pfeiffer, was born there December 13, 1915.[8] Mae attended the Little Tavern School. As a young girl, she helped her father in the store. Starting when she was 17 years old, she worked at the Old Barn Inn as hostess from 1932 to 1939. In December, 1941, Mae bought the St. Albans Store from her father. She married Clyde “Biggie” Head and changed the name to Head’s Store. The lettering on the building was done by the artist Frank Nuderscher. Mae and Biggie lived upstairs; John and Idy, downstairs. Biggie was born May 17, 1915; died April 28, 1982. He worked for a construction company, driving heavy equipment; Mae tended the store.

Head’s Store has everything from farm fresh eggs, vegetables, meats, canned goods, soap, pet food, work gloves, etc. You name it, she has it . She is well known for her special sandwiches. I remember many weekends we would meet hordes of cyclists on the hills. They would stop at Mae’s for sandwiches. She had extra help those days. In October 1985 the St. Louis Bicycle Touring Society gave her a plaque "for the many years of kindness." Members of the McDonnell Douglas Motorcycle Club came out to St. Albans also.[9] When we lived there, the Rock Island RR used the line. The station was gone. It wasn't even a regular stop, but the train would stop around noon for the engineer to pick up his lunch at Head's Store; would advance a short distance and stop again for the workmen in the caboose to get their lunches.

Unfortunately, many city people think they are being kind to their pets by dropping them off in the country. These poor little animals were often seen sitting by the side of the road patiently waiting for their owners to pick them up. Many starved to death, but a number of them found their way to Head's Store. Mae fed them. Sometimes there would be a great number of strays she'd take care of. She loved them all, but especially her own little Pekingese "Tinker." Tinker was the boss around the store. Mae cooked tasty treats for him. He was indeed her friend and companion.

Mae's mother Idy helped in the store until she was unable to do much work. She moved to a nursing home at Hopkinsville, Ky., where her other

Alta Pate and Mae Head in 1975. Photo collection.

Head's Store in 1993. Author's photo.

daughter, Florence, her son-in-law, Wallace Turner, and their five children lived. Idy died June 2, 1990. Alta Pate was a faithful helper in the store for 30 years. Everyone knew Alta.[10]

Mae Head has the only piece of property privately owned not part of the St. Albans development. She is unique and a link to the past; the best known and loved member of the community.

The store has always been a meeting place and center of social life in the community. In the old days, the Beer Drinkers Club, about 15-20 members, met monthly at the store and on special occasions such as political rallies and holidays. Charles Becker reported the balance every month, usually $5 to $6. The McKinley Club (Republican) met once a month. Candidates for office at Union would come down and set up a keg of beer.

There are several entries in Charles Becker's records regarding this.

> May 1, 1904 Beer Club 5 kegs of beer $7.00 bal. in Treas. All candidates here.
> May 21, 1904, Primary Election.
> June 5, Beer drinking balance in Treasury $6.50.

Another club was noted in Becker's Day Book.

> November 5, 1905, went to Chas. Pohlig Horse Shoe Club.

The Community House, as its name indicates, was used for community interests. It was part of

"The Beer Drinkers Club," left to right: Charles Hardt, William Lentz, William Kochs, John Kincaid, Charles Pohlig, Charles Becker, Charles Brueckner. Date and source of photo unknown.

"Birthday Celebration," left to right: William Kochs, George Fries, a Mr. Tallon, Ben Kochs, Albert Kochs, Otto Pfeiffer, Goering King, Ernst Hoerle. Date and source of photo unknown.

St. Albans Farms and originally used as a chicken house. It was the polling place in times of elections. When we first moved to St. Albans, we voted there. To vote you showed your identification,[11] though the election clerks knew everybody, and you marked your ballot; no voting machines. It was one place where everyone could get together for any and all occasions.

There used to be celebrations for every event with feasting and dancing. This was especially true after houseraising, slaughtering or harvesting. There was always someone to fiddle, play the guitar or banjo. In here the Farmers St. Albans Club had their meetings. The club was composed of local farmers who met to discuss their problems and socialize. The County Farm Agent usually spoke at the meetings. The club would undertake various projects such as road work.

Highway T was surveyed in 1929 and built about 1931 or 1932. According to Everett Barnhart,[12] his father worked on building Highway T about 1932. A Canadian was in charge.

When we lived in St. Albans, the men who worked for St. Albans Farms met for a beer or soda in the store before going home at the end of the day. The potbellied stove in the center of the store was replaced by an oil burner, but men still exchanged stories and discussed politics.

The store as it stands today is the original building with some additions. It is one of the few old-fashioned general stores in the vicinity of St. Louis. People from the city enjoy seeing all the unusual items that can be purchased there. Head's Store still serves the community well and does a good business. The hitching rail is gone but one does see saddle horses tied up while their riders refresh themselves at Mae's.

In 1931, or 1932, Mrs. Oscar Johnson opened a new country store, known as St. Albans General Store, built by Jim Evans. It was located right in the center of town not far from the old store which was then called St. Albans Inn and operated by John Pfeiffer. Eight years earlier he was willing to sell his store and quarter-acre tract to Mrs. Johnson for $5000. Later he was asking $50,000 for it, claiming Mrs. Johnson gave him too much competition. The new store was managed by Earl Frick. He had a meat market and general store selling everything from hardware to shoes. He became temporarily insane and after treatment recovered but, in the meantime, his family moved to Washington. They auctioned all the contents of the store.[13]

The building was owned by St. Albans Farms. It had three parts. The center section was the store;

The history of a river town is directly affected by the flooding of the river. Photo by the author in 1951. Photo collection.

the left hand part was their living quarters, and the other section served as a library. The library was run by Mrs. Johnson's sister, Miss Lillian Walter, who was a librarian at the Cabanne Branch Library in St. Louis, and two other ladies, Mrs. George Porteus and Mrs. Glenn. The library was closed and the area was later serviced by a mobile unit from the Scenic Regional Library at Union. St. Albans Farms took over the entire building for its office. After the flood of 1951, the Post Office was moved into the right hand section. The left hand section burned down, and the center section housed the Farm office. It is now the office building for Chesterfield Day School/St. Albans.

The history of a river town is directly affected by the flooding of the river. The river has two floods every year, one usually in April and the other in June. The first is short, sharp and often very destructive. The second flood lasts longer and carries much more water, but does less damage.[14] Since St. Albans was founded in 1837, there have been four major floods. In 1844, most of the town was washed away including the twelve blocks between Water Street and Third Street. In 1903, land fell off the north side of the river and filled in on the south side forming the bottom lands, so today the town and Tavern Cave are about a half mile from the Missouri River. In 1951, the water rose as high as the flood of 1844, covering all the bottom land and the railroad tracks.[15] I remember the water reached the big tree that used to be in front of Head's Store, but it did not come up to the store. The flood of 1993 topped them all. Every man, many women and young people came out to fill sandbags to try to hold the river back. At Head's Store it took 3000 sandbags to keep the water out of the store. On July 31, the water rose over the gas pumps and covered the mailboxes. A pump was used to flush out the seep water. It required 9000 sandbags to save the restaurant Malmaison.

The saying, "God willing and the creek don't

In the flood of 1993, everyone filled sandbags to try to hold the river back. It took 3000 sandbags to keep the water out of the Head's store. Photo: Ken Gilberg.

rise," was the prayer of many early settlers. For instance, Ulmont Krausch told me when he and Cora Hausgen were married February 6, 1918, they had to cross Tavern Creek to get to their house. He recalled carrying his bride through the creek and over the threshold. That time honored custom proved a blessing as they celebrated their 50th wedding anniversary in the same house in 1968.

There never has been a bank in St. Albans. Men like Francis Becker and Frederick Steines would lend money at 10 percent interest. Francis Becker had lists for various years showing the amount he paid in taxes for people who repaid him later. He worked out a banking system of his own. Here is a typical list for tax payment.

November 7, 1868 I paid tax for 1868 as follows:

Godair Dav.	$7.52
Becker	73.00
B.F. Reed	57.72
Leon Reed	27.67
Greef, Ad.	54.09
Kochs	28.32
Hardt	27.88
Mottert	21.00
Iman, Wash.	85.02
Alkiri	1.00
Schwenke settled in Interest	6.21
Total Tax	$389.43

It is interesting to see the list for tax money as it gives the names of many of the people living at St. Albans at that time.

Ed Pfeiffer was a blacksmith in 1878. The garage behind the store was a blacksmith shop. Gus Lentz was also a blacksmith in the early days.

Bill Calvin's house belonged to St. Albans Farms. It is located on Highway T at the foot of the double "S" curve hill, known as "Calvin Hill," and Little Tavern Road. It was built in 1939, by Jim Evans, who was a carpenter for the Farms. Bill worked for St. Albans Farms, and his wife, Catherine, worked at the Old Barn Inn.[16]

The construction of the pumping station by Shell Pipeline Company near Labadie marked the first outside business in the vicinity. In 1917, the contract was made for the first pipeline, which was laid in 1918. In 1925–26 Oetters Station was built. A second pipeline was laid in 1948–49. There were seven men employed, with J.M. Bowen in charge, and in 1951, a new station was built. In 1958, the new station was operated by remote control out of Tulsa, Oklahoma. Only two men were required to operate the station; Mr. S.S. Lorenz was in charge in 1959.[17]

There were plans at one time for supplying the city of St. Louis with fresh water from the Missouri River. In 1907, Bidwell Young received permission to build a tunnel through the sandstone to get to the river.[18] He drilled a well south of the tracks at St. Albans and tunneled under the river. The railroad used the water tank and well. This was at the foot of Big Eddy Hollow; up further was another well at Little Eddy Hollow. There were two wells, one on each side of Little Tavern Creek near the pasteurizing barn of St. Albans Farms. Bidwell Young sent samples of the water daily to St. Louis. He took an easement through the valley to the Meramec River but finally gave up on this operation.[19]

Near Oetters Station where the water tank for

Bill Drewell and Shell pipeline workers. Photo collection.

Sandstone quarry near Oetters Station. Photo collection.

the railroad was located was a sandstone quarry. It was operated by the Tavern Rock Sand Company for many years. This quarry was located on Henry Oetter's property. He was paid $50 a month by Andrew Cummings for the right to take sandstone from the deposits there. When he tried to raise the price to $60 a month, the company closed operations and moved in 1895, to Klondike, where there was a more liberal supply of sandstone. Andy Cummings's son Archie managed the business.[20] The quarry was sold to the Johnsons in 1908 or 1909. Rock and square blocks of sandstone were used in the buildings of St. Albans.

Noah Calvin, Sylvester Dickens and Gus Stricker. Photo courtesy of the Calvin family.

Backward Musicians

In posing for this photograph, these St. Albans resident muscians believed that the photograph would reverse their images so they held their instruments backwards.

FOOTNOTES

1. Chittenden, Hiram Martin, *History of Early Steamboat Navigation on the Missouri River*, in 2 Vols. 1962, Vol. 1, p. 81.
2. Bek, Vol. XV, April 1921, No. 3, p. 535.
3. Becker, Francis, *Cordwood—1856-1863.* See Appendix for prices and names of steamboats.
4. The development of the railroads between 1835 and 1860 changed the pattern of Missouri commerce. Because the routes lay east and west, not north and south with the Mississippi River, Missouri allied with the industrial East and was released from dependence on the South.

   Missouri, American Guide Series, sponsored by the Missouri State Highway Department, Duell, Sloan and Pearce, New York, 1941, p. 80.
5. Chittenden, op. cit., p. 420.
6. Ibid, p. 448.
7. Most of the information on the store I got firsthand from John Pfeiffer and Mae Head; the rest from Charles Becker's "Day Book."
8. Mae was quoted as saying, "I was born here and it's as far as I'll ever go." "Country Store" by John M. McGuire, *St. Louis Post-Dispatch*, "Everyday" Sect. E, Monday, April 28, 1986, p. 1E.
9. Ibid.
10. Alta Mae Dossett Pate was born May 10, 1925, at Muhlenburg, Ky. She worked in Sacramento, Ky., and later moved to Evansville, Ind., where she met Thomas J. Pate, who was in the service. They were married

November 22, 1945, at Evansville. They moved to Missouri about 1960 and lived in one of the St. Albans Farms houses for two years while she worked at the Barn Inn. They had two sons, Larry Thomas and Gerry. In 1962, Alta started working for Mae Head at the store. They moved to Labadie and she continued working for Mae. Her husband died in 1980. She retired from Head's Store in 1992, due to health problems. She lives in New Haven, Mo., where her family also lives.

11\.

THIS IS TO CERTIFY THAT

Lucie Z. Huger

IS A LEGAL RESIDENT OF FRANKLIN COUNTY, MISSOURI, AND A QUALIFIED VOTER OF

St. Albans PRECINCT

Boles TOWNSHIP

EMMETT REED
COUNTY CLERK

12\. Samuel Everett Barnhart was born June 8, 1903, at Capps, and later moved to the Hausgen house on Little Tavern Road. At that time it was owned by Fairfax Funsten and was a part of *Fairfield*. We purchased the property in 1950. In 1954 Everett and his wife, Nellie, built a house on Little Tavern road across from our property. It was called "Gobbler's Nob." In 1974, their children gave a 50th wedding anniversary party for them at the Pacific Lion's Club, which we attended. Nellie died June 20, 1975. Irene Berry, his brother Elmer's widow, cared for Nellie before she died. Nellie wanted Irene to take care of Everett. Irene moved to Pocahontas, Ill., and Everett had his friend John Pipes drive him there on the weekends while he was courting her. In fact he drove him there the day they were married in September, 1975. Irene died about 1993, and Everett moved to Pacific where his daughter lives. Everett was 94 when he came with John Pipes to the dedication of the DAR marker on October 1, 1997.

John Pipes, Lucie Huger, Everett Barnhart and Mary Huger Noone at the DAR dedication. Photo collection.

13\. This information came from a newspaper or magazine article that I have not been able to identify.

14\. Chittenden, op. cit., p. 83.

15\. "The Flood of 1951. Like the flood of '03, most of this one rolled in along the Missouri River from Kansas City, where it is still remembered as "The Really Big One." *St. Louis Post-Dispatch*, July 25, 1993. P. 13J.

16\. In 1963, John Pipes and his wife Henrietta lived there. He worked for the Chrysler Company in St. Louis, and his wife was a waitress at the Inn until it closed in 1968. Henrietta then worked for Cherry Hills Country Club until it moved to St. Albans and became the Country Club of St. Albans. She worked there for one year and retired. They moved into the Hausgen house in 1975, and he worked for us part time as caretaker. He retired from Chrysler in 1983. He is our caretaker at this time, 1997.

17\. John H. Iman, Shell Pipeline, Houston, Texas.

18\. From handwritten copy of original document, courtesy of Mrs. W. Horn.

St. Albans, Mo., May 1907

> For ten dollars and other valuable consideration the receipt of which is hereby acknowledged I hereby give to Bidwell Young his heirs, assigns, servants, associates and agents the exclusive privilege to (to) construct and operate a tunnel in the sandstone formation under-lying my property in Sec 10 & 3 T44 continued from year to year upon the payment of ten dollars per annum, payable on or before June 1st each year. It is expressly understood that all mineral, coal and oil rights are reserved by the owner.

19\. Information from Mrs. Frank Stricker.

20\. In 1971, I received a letter from Mrs. Erwin Nienhuser, whose family owned the property at one time. She stated that the Tavern Rock Sand Company, Klondike, was operating at the time under the name of Pennsylvania Glass Sand Corporation, Augusta.

Photograph by the author.

The Angelus Bell at *Fairfield*

This old bronze bell was left by the Funstens when we bought *Fairfield* back in 1950. I started the ritual of sounding the bell to ring the Angelus every day, a Catholic prayer. *"The Angel of the Lord declared unto Mary..."*

The bell was rung three times with three single strikes, with a pause in between, then back and forth thirty-three times, representing the thirty-three years Christ was on Earth.

I would ring it at noon and six o'clock in the evening. The children and whoever was home would stop what they were doing and pray the Angelus. Our neighbors would often say they heard our dinner bell. They would not have appreciated my ringing it six in the morning when the Angelus should also be rung.

CHAPTER EIGHT

RELIGION

There has never been a church building in St. Albans. In the early 1830's, when a preacher was passing through, the townsfolk would assemble in someone's house for services.

The Community House was originally a chicken house built c. 1914 by Jim Evans for the St. Albans Farms. The Community House became the religious center of St. Albans. On alternate Sundays, ministers from Pond and Gray Summit held services and Sunday School there. After the Evangelical (Reformed) Lutheran Church was built in Labadie, services were discontinued but members of the community conducted Sunday School. There was a sign "Chapel" at the Community House when we moved to St. Albans, but in 1951, the building was no longer used for religious purposes.

The Steines family belonged to the Evangelical (Reformed) Lutheran Church, and when they established their school at Oakfield, they also built a

The Community House in St. Albans was used as a mission church for many years. Today it houses part of Chesterfield Day School/St. Albans. Photograph by the author.

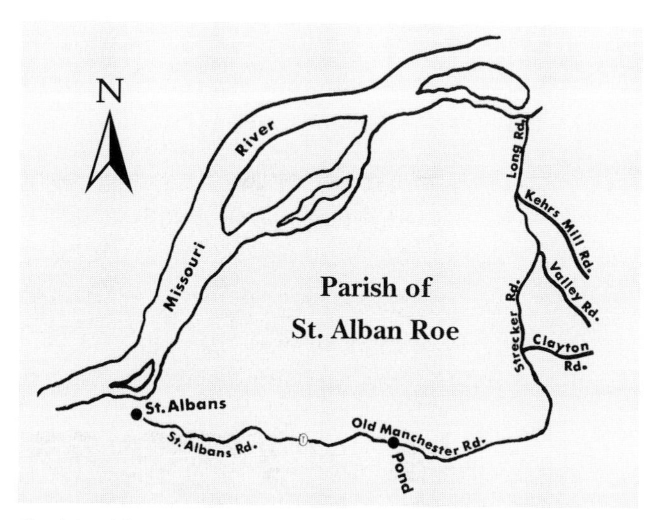

Parish of St. Alban Roe. From St. Louis Review, *June 1980.*

church and rectory around 1840. These old log buildings were still standing at the intersection of U.S. Highway 100 and Little Tavern Road when we lived out there, though they were not in use.

Catholics in the community attended St. Bridget's Church in Pacific. This parish was established in 1841. The little log church was used until 1850, when the foundation for the present church was laid by Father Miller. Later the parish boundaries were changed and St. Albans was included in the parish of St. John the Baptist Church, Gildehaus, at Villa Ridge. In 1980, Archbishop John L. May established the parish of St. Alban Roe[1] located at 2001 Shephard Road, Glencoe. The parish covers approximately a 60-square-mile area of West St. Louis County and a small section of Franklin County, including the village of St. Albans. Rev. Thomas J. Graham was the first pastor.[2]

Members of the Methodist church attended church in Labadie, about six miles away. The Old Bethel Church at Labadie is considered the "Mother Church of Methodism" in Franklin County. Judge Henry Brown and his brother Joseph were commissioned by the government to go to Missouri Territory to sectionize it into a state in 1814. The first place of worship was an open field near the Missouri River at Brown's Camp Ground. A circuit rider[3] minister who came on horseback held services. A conch shell was sounded to assemble the people. According to legend, Daniel Boone, magistrate at La Charette across the river, often attended. After a few years of outdoor services, the congregation built a log church on a piece of property donated by Judge Brown. When the church was completed in 1840, it was called Bethel Methodist.[4] It was deeded to the Methodist Episcopal Church. In 1867, the log church was sold with the proceeds applied to a new brick[5] building erected on property offered by C.C. Jones in the town of Labadie. This church was called Bethel Methodist Church and was dedicated by Bishop Marvin in 1868. The preacher in charge was Rev. John Emory Godbey. In 1889, the Rev. S.W. Emory took up the matter of building again and in the fall of 1891, the new Labadie Methodist Church was dedicated. The old Bethel Church was used thereafter for social services.

The Old Bethel Church is on the National Register of Historic Places. It was restored in 1987 by the Friends of Old Bethel, Labadie Area, under the guidance of Glenn Warnebold, president. His grandfather, John Warnebold, was one of its founding fathers. Today the church looks just as it did 125 years ago. The original pump organ is still in use. The structure was set on a field stone foundation and was complete with a slave gallery, even though it was constructed after the Civil War. The church is one of three left standing that includes such a gallery.[6]

FOOTNOTES

1. St. Alban Roe of the Order of St. Benedict lived in the 17th Century and was a member of the community that settled at Ampleforth, England, and in due course became Ampleforth Abbey. It was from Ampleforth Abbey in 1955 that the St. Louis Priory was founded in St. Louis, Missouri, and became St. Louis Abbey in 1995.
2. *St. Louis Review*, June 13, 1980; and "Religion," *St. Louis Globe-Democrat*, June 14-15, 1980, p. 11A
3. Because the pioneer preachers went from place to place holding meetings, they were called "circuit riders."
4. Bethel in Hebrew means "House of God."
5. Bricks handmade by freed slaves in the area.
6. Information on the Methodist church found in "Labadie" by Pamela Selbert, *St. Louis Post-Dispatch*, June 24, 1993, and "Mother church of Methodism in County" by Betty Trail, *Washington Missourian*, August 5, 1971, and "In Retrospect-Bethel Church-Labadie" by Sue Reed, *Tri-County Journal*, Wednesday, July 16, 1971.

Old Bethel Church.
Illustration by Eloise LeSaulnier.

CHAPTER NINE

Utopia

Theodore C. Link

Since the time of the "Followers of Duden," the area of St. Albans has been considered a unique "paradise," its natural beauty unmarred by progress. When Theodore Link and Oscar Johnson came out to St. Albans, they too were charmed by its beauty.

The renowned architect, Theodore Carl Link, second from left, often entertained his friends and members of the St. Louis Artists' Guild at his cottage. From Link's scrapbook.

Theodore Carl Link was a renowned architect in St. Louis. He was born in Wimpfen, Germany, March 17, 1850. He studied in Heidelberg, London and Paris between the years 1864 and 1869. He emigrated to the United States in 1870; married Annie C. Fuller in 1876 in Detroit, Michigan. They had three children: Karl Eugene, Edwin Cary and Clarence Vincent. He won first place in competition for his design of the St. Louis Union Station, the largest terminal station in the world, which was built according to his plans and under his supervision. He was a member of the commission of architects for the Louisiana Purchase Exposition in 1904. He was consulting architect for the St. Louis City Hall and many churches, public buildings and residences, including his friend Oscar Johnson's Portland Place home. His office was in the Carleton Building that he designed.[1]

It is not recorded when he first visited the St. Albans area, but Charles Becker's "Day Book" has the following entries:

August 5, 1903	Theo C. Link, 1000 Carleton Bldg., St. Louis out to look at Tracy Place.
August 8	L. and Sanger out.
August 15	T.C.L. and Sanger came out.
August 23	Edward D'Arcy 616 Roe Bldg. & Link & Sanger here made contract.
August 30	T.C. Link & Sanger
September 9	Made deed for Theo. C. Link at Pacific.
September 27	Theo C. Link gave me check for $1511.75.
September 31	Recorded contract of Theo. C. Link.

Theodore and his wife Annie built a summer place at St. Albans where they invited their family and friends to visit and enjoy the beauty of the countryside. There is a guest book or "Hotel Register" dating from 1903.[2] In the entries are signatures, greetings, sketches and photographs. Edwin Cary Link was their son, father of T.C. Link, Jr., the reporter. The old place burned down in 1905 and another place was built where they continued to have guests. The entry in the "Hotel Register 1909" had a tribute to Theodore Link, and in 1917, there was a tribute to Oscar Johnson after his death. (See Appendix 3)

Later Theo. C. Link and his wife Annie paid $3000 to Charles Becker for approximately 132 acres.

> Chas. Becker, Esq. moved to his new home near Labaddie – The farm they (the family) just left —— was owned by his father, Judge Francis Becker, and sold to Theo. C. Link, the St. Louis architect, last year.
>
> Franklin County Tribune, Mar. 12, 1909

In 1923, Theodore Link envisioned the St. Albans Colony as shown in the following instrument.

St. Albans Colony Prospectus

Three-hundred acres of broken country
with a frontage of a mile and a half
of limestone bluffs;
Overlooking the Missouri River;
Situated in Franklin County,
A few miles from the St. Louis County line;
Thirty-five miles from Grand Avenue,
Densely wooded, almost untouched,
With superb views into charming valleys
And over the Islands of the River,
With an abundant supply of pure water,
Rising three-hundred and fifty feet above
The level of St. Louis, and
Without a doubt, the finest scenery within many miles of the city,—such is the place offered to lovers of nature for a place of rest, recreation and pleasure.

The topography of this piece of land is so diversified and rugged that it suggests upwards of 20 logical building sites for week-end bungalows, hunting lodges, summer residences and even permanent country homes,—all so distributed and situated that perfect privacy and individuality is assured to each.

The owner of this property proposes to lease these building sites for a term of not less than ____ years at an annual rental to be agreed upon and varying according to the prominence of the location selected. A site means just enough ground as will be required for the improvements contemplated by a member and surrounded by an enclosed yard or garden, the enclosure following rather the logical topographical line for a fence or wall than a fixed number of acres.

The domiciled tenants on these sites shall constitute the

"St. Albans Colony"

and will have the right to vote upon the admission of all future applicants for membership. Such admission, however, must be by unanimous consent. These Colonists may adopt further rules, if it is found necessary to regulate matters pertaining to the general welfare of the Colony.

In general, however, it is to be understood that all members shall enjoy the utmost liberty, restricted only by consideration for their neighbors' peace and happiness.

Each member (and invited friends) shall have the free use of the entire property, which has already several miles of drives, bridle-paths, and trails through the woods. Each member shall be entitled to any fruit grown on the place in reasonable quantity, and for consumption on the premises only; but no fruit shall be taken away or used in large quantities for preserves, etc. (except wild berries) unless purchased at prevailing rates from the Keeper.

The Keeper will, without charge, keep the houses or cottages broom-clean from week to week; he will wash windows, make up the beds, and cut weeds within the yard or garden. In short, each house shall at all times be kept ready for occupancy. During occupancy, however, each member shall provide his own domestic service.

The Keeper will attend to the light laundry work required by the members at prevailing rates; calling for, and delivering, the laundry at their houses.

The keeper will be prepared to deliver and furnish to the members, at all times, and in quantities as ordered, the following supplies:

Ice	bread	coal oil
milk	poultry	gasoline
cream	vegetables	candles
butter	ham	canned meats
eggs	bacon	pickles

firewood and kindling, native wine, etc.

but in order that he may be able to properly adjust this service, the members shall agree to purchase all articles included in this list, and as far as they are needed during their stay, from the Keeper at prevailing rates.

The Keeper will maintain one or more conveyances for the use of the members between the station and their houses for which service he shall be permitted to make a small charge as agreed upon; he will also keep a number of saddle horses for hire to the members and their friends.

An automobile shed will be provided for the free use of members and their friends, and arrangements may be made with the Keeper to supply transient board and lodging to Chauffeurs.

Link's cottage overlooked the Missouri River at St. Albans.

Interior view of Link's cottage. The stone fireplace is all that remains after a fire in 1960 destroyed the building. Photos from T. C. Link's scrapbook, probably taken by J. W. Mack. Courtesy of Theodore C. Link, Jr., great-grandson.

> The members shall agree that they will not maintain a stable or kennel, or keep any live stock on their premises.
>
> Whenever the word "Keeper" is used hereafter it shall mean a tenant or other duly appointed representative of the Owner.
>
> Whenever the word "Member" is used hereafter it shall mean one of the persons who, together with the Owner, will constitute the St. Albans Colony.
>
> Colonists to date:
> 1. T.C. Link
> 2. Karl E. Link
> 3. Edwin C. Link
> 4. Edward D'Arcy

This Colony must have been abandoned as I cannot find any further reference to it. Theodore Carl Link, grandson, inherited the property and maintained a house on the bluffs while we were living across Highway T at *Fairfield*. Link's home was destroyed by fire in 1960. He died in 1974.

Irene and Oscar Johnson

Oscar Johnson was a frequent guest of Link's "Hotel Register" at St. Albans. He was a business man and his wife Irene was a southern belle used to plantation life. They loved the unspoiled beauty of the St. Albans area. The first record of Johnson's visit to St. Albans was also recorded in Charles Becker's "Day Book."

> July 9, 1907, Link and Johnson out.

Oscar Johnson was the son of James Lee and Helen Rand Johnson, born January 6, 1864, at LaGrange, Ala. His father died when he was an infant and he moved with his mother and older brother Jackson to the home of her brother Jackson Rand in Red Banks, Miss. This was in the period of hard times following the Civil War. When he was 14 years old, he worked full time for his uncle in his general store. A year later he and his brother Jackson went to Holly Springs, Miss., where they opened a small general store dealing principally with cotton. For ten years they operated as cotton commission merchants. They sold their holdings and moved to Memphis, Tenn., where they purchased a large shoe company. In 1893, they were well established as wholesale dealers. They expanded and moved to St. Louis in 1895. They merged with other shoe companies and eventually formed the International Shoe Company with Jackson Johnson as president and Oscar as vice president. In 1915, Oscar succeeded his brother as president.[3]

Oscar Johnson, Sr. Private collection.

While they were living in Holly Springs, Oscar met Irene Walter. They were married on February 19, 1889. They had four children: Harvey Walter, Fredonia Elizabeth, Oscar and James Lee. Irene was the daughter of Colonel Harvey Washington Walter and Fredonia Brown Walter. She was born July 7, 1867, Holly Springs, Miss. She was the first graduate of the Maura Institute in Mississippi.[4] Her father was a colonel in the Confederate Army and an outstanding citizen of Mississippi. They lived at "The Walter Place," a grand southern mansion. Colonel Walter opened their home to the victims of the Yellow Fever epidemic of 1878, and he and his three sons died ministering to them.[5]

Oscar started buying farms and bottom lands and in 1914 established the St. Albans Farms. He died at the early age of 52 in July, 1916. He was a moving force in the industrial, civic and economic life of St. Louis. He helped establish St. Louis as the shoe manufacturing center of America. In his

Irene Walter Johnson portrait by Frank Nuderscher. Original painting is in the lobby of the Washington University Medical School.

memory the Oscar Johnson Institute of Washington University was founded in 1931 by his widow, Irene Walter Johnson, and their two sons, Oscar and James Lee. This was established for the study and postgraduate teaching of diseases of the eye, ear, nose and throat. She also made a gift to the Washington University Medical School to establish a rehabilitation center known as the Irene Walter Johnson Institute of Rehabilitation.[6]

Irene Johnson further enlarged the holdings at St. Albans. Both she and Theodore Link envisioned the development of St. Albans as a haven of rest, recreation and fine country living. Irene Johnson had dreams of a community unique in American country life. There was a pamphlet prepared by Frank Nuderscher entitled *St. Albans and St. Louis,* copyright 1928. It starts:

> "Happy the man, whose wish and care
> A few paternal acres bound,
> Content to breathe his native air
> In his own ground."
>
> Alexander Pope

The pamphlet begins with an invitation to drive out to St. Albans to see the beautiful countryside and to see the development of the area.

> Investigate the Tavern Rock Road that is being built up to a spot, 400 feet above the Missouri River.
>
> You'll see preparations made to pool into a lake the water of scores of springs and streams now running in all directions. Examine the deep-well water system now building to augment the many springs that abound on St. Albans thousands of acres.

Included were directions and a map showing the roads from St. Louis to St. Albans.

> St. Albans is being got ready for you painstakingly. That is why you are being asked now to come see it, less than halfway through metamorphosis. When all is finished, the builders of St. Albans wish you to know just what it was that was done and against what odds it was.

Mrs. Johnson kept an eye open for additional property. She saw two islands in the Missouri River as necessary for her plans.

In 1931, it was reported in the *St. Louis Post-Dispatch*:

St·Albans invites St·Louis to watch a dream coming true. St.Louis some day will be very, very proud of what is still an infant, born on its doorstep only lately · St.Albans has nothing whatever to sell to St·Louis It is much too busy striving for perfection in growth.

It will be years - be-
fore St-Albans feels that
it has that dreamed-of perfection to offer St. Louis,
years before it will be prepared
to present - to the city a
consummate beauty spot for
homes that will be cherished.
Meanwhile, come to St. Albans
at your leisure and watch the
struggle going on in a great
forest atop towering and de-
fiant crags with stubborn
streams and huge, imbedded
rocks that yield only to dynamite
- warfare with the wild-
ness of nature to make this country, heretofore untouched since
the Creator put it there, an habit-
able place where you will
hope some day to have your
four walls. Come! - - - - - be
nature's guest.

A sample of the pamphlet prepared by Frank Nuderscher entitled St. Albans and St. Louis.

> The largest of the two islands, an area of nearly 3,000 acres which is technically part of St. Charles County but was enlarged until it borders Franklin County, by a stormy twist of this river, is being developed as a new landing field. A polo field will be made there also. Tennis courts and a racetrack will be constructed. The remainder of the island, like the smaller island, will be planted in corn.[7]

One of these islands was Brown's Island. Old John Brown, hunter and trapper, had floated down the river and anchored a houseboat on a sandbar in the river in 1913. In 1915 he and his family moved to a newly formed island nearby and built a shack on a high piece of ground. Three generations later, both the island and his family had increased. They were squatters who had never paid taxes on the property. That land became part of Franklin County after the flood of 1903, when land fell off the north side which was St. Charles County and filled in on the south side, Franklin County. Mrs. Johnson wanted that island and offered to buy it from the Browns. They refused, saying they had been living there and it rightfully belonged to them. Mrs. Johnson went to Union, paid back taxes and acquired official title to the land. Sheriff Lee Reed sent a deputy sheriff from Franklin County to the island while the Brown men were at work and evicted the families.[8] It took all of the deputies available to hold Mrs. Ida Brown, wife of John Brown, Jr., and her daughter, Mrs. Myrtle Christman, after they were carried away from their homes. Mrs. Christman, while handcuffed, managed to pick up a piece of wood and hit a deputy in the mouth, breaking some of his teeth. The deputies then put

From the St. Louis Star, *August 6, 1931, an artist's sketch "showing the relative location of the island formerly occupied by the Browns, and Mrs. Oscar Johnson's estate at St. Albans."*

the Brown's possessions on the railroad track, pulled their homes down with rope and tractors, and burned the rubble. There were guards all around, including some working for St. Albans Farms.[9]

John W. Brown, his son John W. Brown, Jr. and wife Ida, and son George Brown filed suits in December 1930, against Sheriff Isadore Grothe of St. Charles, claiming $79,500 damages for illegally evicting them from Brown's Island. The Brown family claimed title to the island under squatters' rights. The Browns also filed suit for an order permitting them to reoccupy the land; this was denied by Circuit Judge Woolfolk at St. Charles. After two years of litigation, Judge R. A. Breuer of the Circuit Court at Union, decided in favor of Mrs. Johnson, giving her title to 272 acres. In December, 1932, another son, Frederick Brown, filed a separate suit demanding $19,000 actual damages and $5000 punitive damages, bringing the total damages asked to $103,500.[10]

In February, 1934, the Browns filed suit for $23,150, alleging Mrs. Johnson and Jesse W. Schaefer of Washington, Mo., her former attorney, had wrongfully seized and converted to their own use crops and improvements in evicting them from the island in 1931, after they had been in possession for 18 years. They had successfully defended evictions sought by previous owners.

Final settlement was made April 6, 1935, over the ownership and possession of the Brown 2200 acre island in the Missouri River. The settlement, in cash to the Browns' three sons satisfied their claims and also quashed the litigation against former Sheriff Grothe of St. Charles County. John Brown Jr., Frederick Brown and George Brown signed deeds and releases, relinquishing all claims they may have had on the land. The Browns were represented by Walter A. Hayes; Mrs. Johnson by Guy A. Thompson.[11]

About 1930-31, Mrs. Johnson started "The Tavern Rock Development." There were house sites planned for more than 120 wooded knolls, each with a choice view on the 7500 acres then owned by St. Albans Farms. The sites ranged from 2 to 45 acres.[12]

Farming did not interfere with the scenic beauty.

"It took all the deputy sheriffs available yesterday to hold Mrs. Ida Brown, wife of John Brown, Jr., and her daughter, Mrs. Myrtle Christman, after they were carried from their home. Mrs. Brown, shown in the foreground, succeeded in scratching the face of one of the deputies and made several others howl by kicking them in the shins. Mrs. Christman later was released but Mrs. Brown was forced to wear handcuffs the rest of the day and last night was taken to the St. Charles jail with her father-in-law, on charges of threatening an officer." Caption and photo from the St. Louis Star, *August 6, 1931.*

Fields of oats, rye, corn, alfalfa, soybeans and timothy enhanced rather than detracted from the landscape. Prize winning Angus cattle and registered Southdown sheep grazed in bluegrass pastures. Fine poultry and Duroc-Jersey and Poland-China hogs were also bred.

Electricity, running water, fire protection, roads and bridges were established. In the early 1930s, the Franklin County Highway Department allotted money to build a new county road, Highway T. It ran from State Highway 100 to St. Albans, west to Labadie, and connecting again with Hwy. 100 further west. The right-of-way from Hwy. 100 to Fiddle Creek Road was to have a 60-foot width and from there west it was to be somewhat wider. The road itself was to be 30 feet wide and surfaced with gravel and maintained with a grader. Many times in bad weather, we skidded down "Calvin Hill," so called because the William Calvins lived at the bottom of the hill. We were hesitant to vote for blacktopping because we thought it might make it harder to drive in the ice and snow. Even with the resurfaced road, in snow and ice the back end of the car wanted to pass the front end sliding down the double S curved hill. Going up Calvin Hill was even worse. If you met another car coming down, you had to back down to the bottom; they had the right-of-way.

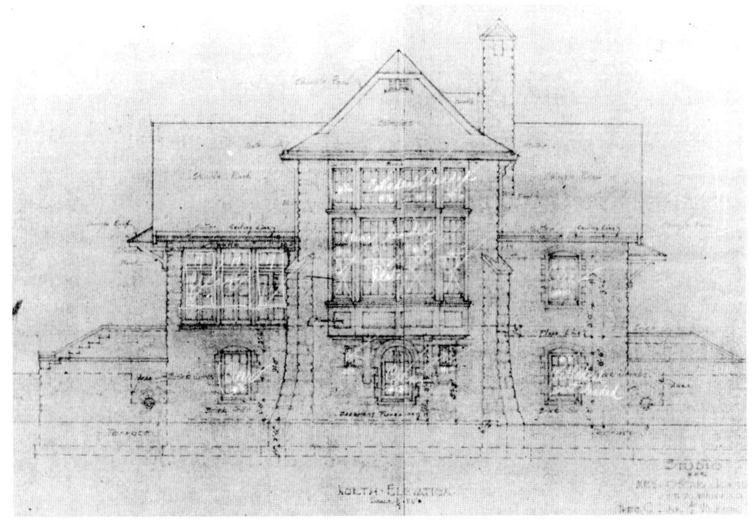

Original plan for the Studio in St. Albans for Mrs. Oscar Johnson by architects Theodore Link and Wilbur Trueblood. Courtesy Ken Gilberg.

Among the facilities available in St. Albans were the Post Office and the Rock Island train station. The trains had regular scheduled stops at St. Albans until 1948 or 1949.

Mrs. Irene W. Johnson with some of her peonies. From the Village Crier, *May 1931.*

Mrs. Johnson had about 3500 rose bushes planted along the ten miles of roads linking the buildings of the St. Albans Farms. The road radiated out from the village of St. Albans where the Farm office buildings were located. She held a peony festival with extensive plantings of peonies. Today there are beautiful peonies in the garden of Malmaison, formerly the Old Barn Inn.

The Johnsons' home at St. Albans was known as "The Studio" or "The Chateau." It was built on a hill overlooking the countryside with a commanding view of the Missouri River at St. Albans. It was first designed by Theodore Link and Wilbur Trueblood and later enlarged by the architectural firm of Jamieson & Spearl, and decorated by the well-known St. Louis artist Frank Nuderscher. On the ceiling in the salon were brilliantly depicted the signs of the Zodiac and the Milky Way. In the dining room were murals in gray and sepia of St. Louis scenes of the eighties. The Old Courthouse and the Old Cathedral furnished the background for two street scenes and Chouteau's Pond and a Mississippi riverfront were the subjects for the other walls. The card room was an English scene depicting a jousting match. He painted floral decorations on silver paper for Mrs. Johnson's boudoir.[13] In Louise Thaxter Wright's article on the Chateau published in 1930 she says:

> Mrs. Johnson's Utopian dream is fast being realized through her tireless energy and desire for perfection. What other treasures and beauties will it yield in years to come, and how many people will find rest and repose, zest and gay pleasure, in those old Missouri hills?

The Farm was completely self-sustaining. It employed 88 men, many skilled artisans, who built and equipped houses, constructed and maintained roads, built water systems, repaired machinery and cars. Houses were built to accommodate the farm workers.[14]

In 1945, the St. Albans Farms was incorporated and ownership passed to Irene Johnson's two sons, Oscar and James Lee Johnson. She died January 18, 1954.

There was a tribute to their mother in the *Missouri Historical Society Bulletin*, April 1954.

> **"In Memoriam" Mrs. Oscar Johnson**
> nee Irene Walter
>
> Early in the 1920s Mrs. Johnson became interested in developing the family farm of 7,500 acres around St. Albans, Missouri. Here she did scientific feed and grain farming, raised purebred hogs and prize winning Angus and Guernsey cattle, and operated a model dairy, the produce of which sold at a premium in St. Louis for many years. One of the largest dairies in the St. Louis area, it at one time supplied two per cent of all the milk used in the city. In the course of years, Mrs. Johnson added to the acreage of the farm, and purchased two nearby islands in the Missouri River. She built an elaborate inn, with a swimming pool, and constructed roads to open up the scenic bluffs. Her farm workers were furnished with trim white cottages, and gradually a group of lovers of country living built homes in the vicinity. Mrs. Johnson's own home there, the Chateau, was elaborately furnished with fine art and historical objects.

Hidden Valley, now Engelmann Woods. Photo: Ken Gilberg

To the Missouri Botanical Garden she gave a 150-acre tract of forest area at St. Albans for experimental forestry. It was known as Hidden Valley. Our family gave an additional ten acres to the Missouri Botanical Gardens which extended the tract to Highway T.

Now known as Engelmann Woods, the land is governed by Missouri Department of Conservation and is designated a natural area due to its high quality natural mesic upland forest. The woods host some potential Missouri champion trees and a gorgeous flowering of native celandine poppies every spring. According to naturalist Jim Bogler of the Missouri Native Plant Society, some of the huge trees date could date back to Precolumbian times. He says, "It may take a millennium of relative biological stability to produce the community that can be observed at this preserve today."[15]

FOOTNOTES

1. *The Book of St. Louisians*, edited by John W. Leonard, St. Louis, *The St. Louis Republic*, 1906, p. 359. *St. Louis, the Fourth City*, p. 392.
2. "Hotel Register" indicates that T.C. Link had a place at St. Albans where he entertained his friends.

   This place was acquired
   In August 1903
   Cornerstone laid with impressive ceremonies
   In September 1903 and finished for occupancy
   In October 1903 with the following staff:
   Theo. C. Link, lessor & Proprietor
   General Manager of Deficits
3. *The History of Missouri, Family and Personal History*, Vol. IV, pp. 615-617.
4. Bond, Christy Hawes, *Gateway Families*, p. 42.
5. *The History of Missouri*, Op cit, p. 615.
6. Bond, Op cit, p. 43.
7. McCulloch, S. R., "St Albans," *St. Louis Post-Dispatch*, c. 1931.
8. I was told by Magnus Graves that his father, Bill Graves, rented land on Brown's Island where he raised vegetables and pumpkins. When Judge Schaefer in Washington told the Browns to leave, he would not let Graves harvest his crop, which was ready. It all just rotted in the field.
9. *St. Louis Globe-Democrat*, September 8, 1933.
10. *St. Louis Post-Dispatch*, April 7, 1935.
11. McCulloch, Op cit.
12. Ibid.
13. Ibid.
14. Jim Bogler, "How Big Are the Trees of Engelmann Woods?", 1992.

CHAPTER TEN

St. Albans Farms

In 1912, Oscar Johnson purchased 135 acres at St. Albans. By 1914, he had increased this acreage to about 1500 acres and established St. Albans Farms. After his death in 1916, his widow, Mrs. Irene Walter Johnson, took over the operation of the Farm. She was responsible for the vision and success of the Farm. The following article describes the Farm in 1918 at the onset of World War I.

> The Missouri Woman for April 1918–
> **St. Albans Farms**
> St. Albans Farms, part in Franklin and part in St. Louis County, belongs to Mrs. Oscar Johnson of St. Louis, and she is preparing its fifteen hundred acres for a sheep farm, but as it takes several years to clear the pastures and get the soil in the right condition to yield forage, Mrs. Johnson is in the meanwhile, raising wheat and garden produce; and she is having her surplus canned for the winter. College girls and boys are doing the work.
>
> The moving spirit is Mrs. Johnson herself, a veritable 'grand dame' in appearance, with a keen sense of humor to help everyone over the difficult places, and a broad vision to keep things moving forward harmoniously. Then comes little Miss Nora Jaimeson – the farm manager – a graduate of Columbia College of Agriculture, poised, superlatively intelligent and energetic and fascinating in her 'Land Army Garb.' Miss Jane Watkins is in charge of the 'canning,' while Miss Hadley Richardson and Miss Caroline Blackman keep her well supplied with fresh vegetables from the garden. Miss Isobel Scott drives the motor truck, and Miss Marion Jaimeson has charge of the dairy.
>
> The buildings are grouped around a courtyard at the foot of a hill, one side of which is a massive white stone retaining wall covered with vines. There is one cottage for the girls and for the boys — at present there is only one boy — and far up the hill, overlooking the farm, is a studio where heat and work and practical things can be forgotten amidst tapestries and paintings, and one of the most beautiful views in the county can be seen.
>
> Mrs. Johnson is trying to make St. Albans Farm 100 per cent patriotic in several ways. First, she is increasing the food supply; second, she is using girl-labor, thus releasing men for government service; third, she is canning all her surplus vegetables; fourth, she is preparing to increase the supply of wool by raising sheep.

Mr. Doane was the first farm manager. The "Community House," as it was known, was originally one of the chicken houses, with the Farm offices located there. The Farm raised chickens, pigs, sheep and saddle horses, and practiced scientific feed and grain farming. After several unsuccessful years, Mr. Doane left St. Albans and went to St. Louis where he built up the Doane Agricultural Service later used by St. Albans Farms.

The farm managers following Doane were Ed Bair, Fritz Brown, Mr. Beckelheimer and Charles Danforth. In 1921, Danforth started the herd of Aberdeen Angus cattle with George Porteous in charge. *Erie Revolution 404 801*, first prize calf at state fairs, was bought at the International Sale in 1927, as the first Aberdeen Angus herd bull for St. Albans Farms.[1] In 1931, the herd numbered 116 head including calves.

Erie Revolution 404 801, *Aberdeen Angus herd bull. Photo by Smith and Morton, Kansas City, Mo.*

This was during the years of the Great Depression. Mrs. Johnson invested in fancy livestock, built roads and other improvements, spending large sums of money. She took great pride in her Southdown sheep, Duroc hogs and prize winning Aberdeen Angus cattle. She remodeled the old Becker barn into a fancy country inn but none of these enterprises showed a profit. Her lawyer and financial advisor, Mr. Guy Thompson of Thompson, Mitchell, Thompson and Young, and her family agreed to appoint Richard D'Oly Hughes as manager of the Farms.

It was in 1931 that D'Oly Hughes and his wife, Frances, moved from St. Louis to St. Albans. They were personal friends of the Johnsons. Mrs. Johnson felt that he, an Australian, would know how to manage an estate. Hughes was an American-born citizen who had served in the British Army in WWI. After the war, Congress passed legislation whereby his citizenship was reinstated by swearing allegiance before a Federal Judge.

Hughes knew nothing about farming or estate management. He wisely sought the advice of the professors at the Missouri State Agricultural College at Columbia, Missouri. Hughes wrote a journal of his life in which Chapter VII covered his years in St. Albans. The following history is based on his own story.

> It had quickly become apparent to me that everything which was being produced at the Farms, at great expense, was being sold in direct competition, in the open market, with similar products produced, much cheaper, by the dirt farmers all around. Yet, here was a beautiful 'show' farm situated only 28 miles from a city of nearly a million population. My problem appeared to be to find something for St. Albans Farms to produce which the surrounding dirt farmers could not duplicate, and which could be sold in the City of St. Louis at a substantial premium over market prices. The answer to which I came was Golden Guernsey Milk.

ANGUS CATTLE SOUTHDOWN SHEEP

SAINT ALBANS FARMS

POST OFFICE

BECKER, MISSOURI

Farm Located on the Rock Island Railway, on the South side of the Missouri River, 35 miles West of St. Louis. near Highways 50 and 66.

CHARLES R. DANFORTH, Manager GEORGE A. PORTEOUS, Herd Supt.

Hughes contacted Mr. Lide, president of the St. Louis Dairy Company, and surveyed the milk situation in St. Louis. He found that there was a need for a really first-class, low bacteria count, quality milk. He explained the plan to Mrs. Johnson and Mr. Thompson and obtained consent to sell the sheep, pigs, chickens and even the Aberdeen Angus cattle. They were sold in 1937. George Porteous left in 1938. The Farm converted the beef cattle barn into a dairy barn and built a pasteurizing plant.

The St. Albans Golden Guernsey herd was started in December 1932, with the purchase of one bull and ten cows from Sunnymede Farms, Bismarck, Mo. In that herd were included *Sunnymede Beauty Spot* and her dam, *Elm Farm Beauty*. They became the foundation of the "Beauty Spot" family. Sometime in 1933, the Farm went into the premium quality milk business. The first shipment to the St. Louis Dairy Company was 47 quarts. By 1940, they were sending between 4000 and 5000 quarts a day and still could not keep up with the demand for the St. Albans milk. The herd was increased by purchasing purebreds and grades from farmer-breeders in Wisconsin and other states at Depression prices. The herd reached its peak size about 1941, when over 650 head had been acquired. To feed this ever-increasing herd, bottom land on the banks of the Missouri River was cleared and planted in corn and alfalfa. Lawrence R. Rainey was herdsman for the Guernsey herd from February, 1933, until 1949, when he became farm manager.[2] Hughes was manager from 1931 to 1941 when he left to join the Air Force.

Wayne S. O'Neal, DVM, was the doctor for the Golden Guernsey herd from 1932, when it started, to 1945, when he moved away from St. Charles. He was the first in the state to perform artificial insemination in the development of a strong herd. He spent every Tuesday at St. Albans Farms taking care of this herd. Dr. Wayne O'Neal lived in St. Charles where he practiced veterinary medicine caring for large animals. Besides the St. Albans Guernsey herd, he cared for other dairy herds including the D.I. Meyer herd of Jersey cattle and the Anheuser herd of Holstein cattle, which had been carefully selected and imported from Jersey and Holstein. He was also Mayor of St. Charles from 1932 to 1935. He was elected on the slogan, "A one-horse town needs a horse doctor."[3]

Fredonia Johnson, daughter of Irene Walter and Oscar Johnson, married Malcolm Moss, a flying instructor in the Army Air Corps, WWI. After the war, he maintained his standing in the Air Corps Reserve as a Captain. In the fall of 1940, he was called to active duty and appointed Chief of the Air Corps in the War Department, Washington, D.C. In February 1941, he and Air Corps Capt. Hansel invited Hughes to apply for a commission in the Army Air Corps. In the spring of 1941, Hughes left St. Albans Farms to join the Air Force. He turned over the management of the Farms to Charles Mahin, who had been the bookkeeper since 1929.

The farm was incorporated in 1945, and ownership was passed on to Johnson's two sons, Oscar and James Lee.

Oscar Johnson Jr. was born August 18, 1905, in St. Louis. He was educated at private schools and attended St. Louis Country Day School, Haverford School, Dobbs Ferry School for Boys and Washington University. He had many interests.

He was a patron of the arts. He was elected president of the St. Louis Symphony Society in 1933. He remained president until 1955, and continued as vice president until his death in 1983. In 1966, he donated $500,000 to the symphony for the purchase of the St. Louis Theater building, which helped make it possible for the symphony to have a permanent home for the first time. The building was renovated, renamed Powell Symphony Hall and opened in January 1968. In 1936, he received the St. Louis Jaycees Civic Service Award for his devotion to the St. Louis Symphony and was given the key to the city in 1941 for distinguished service to the symphony.[4]

Oscar Johnson, Jr. in a 1953 photo. Private collection.

He was a gentleman farmer. He spent much of his life at the family's 5280-acre St. Albans Farms, which he operated with his brother, James Lee. He usually stayed at his mother's house on the Farm over the weekends, driving back to St. Louis just before noon every Monday taking the Melrose Road to Manchester Road. His big 16-cylinder Cadillac was well known in the area. In 1935, an attempt was made to kidnap young Oscar Johnson. D'Oly Hughes was farm manager at this time. Here is his account of the near tragic event, as noted in his journal.

Hughes had stopped at the Old Barn Inn to talk with the manageress about some business and overheard two men talking. They had seen three men fighting in a cornfield about one mile on the St. Albans side of Manchester Road and a big Cadillac parked nearby, unoccupied. Hughes knew at once that Oscar Johnson was in trouble.

> I ran over to the Farm Office and just as I got there, the telephone rang. It was the storekeeper at the Melrose Store phoning us that, shortly beforehand, Oscar Johnson's car had passed the store with three men in the front seat and Oscar Johnson in the middle, shouting for help.

Hughes rounded up all the readily available men on the Farm and drove out the Melrose Road towards the highway. They found Oscar's Cadillac. The men scattered through the cornfield trying to find Oscar. In the middle of the field was a large area where corn stalks had been trampled and there were great pools of blood between the rows. No Oscar. They followed the bloody trail into a wooded ravine filled with dead oak leaves. Here one of the men found, concealed under some leaves, a sawed-off shotgun, a pistol, two rolls of adhesive tape and a pair of goggles with tape over them. Still no sign of Oscar. The blood trail ended.

Returning to the Melrose Store, Hughes phoned Sheriff Lill in Clayton and the St. Louis County Sheriff. Sheriff Lill and his deputies arrived. Word came that three St. Albans farm men had captured two men skulking out of the woods trying to break through the cordon set up in a two-mile wide and three-miles long area. One was attempting to trample something into the ground with the heel of his shoe—$50 in small bills. It was the exact amount Oscar had in his wallet. Sheriff Lill took the two suspects into custody. Still no sign of Oscar. Here is the rest of the story pieced together by Hughes, Mr. Thompson and witnesses.

As Oscar Johnson was driving Melrose Road, he came upon a black Model A Ford crosswise on the road. As he stopped, three armed men jumped out of the underbrush. Two got into the front seat of his car, forcing him to sit between them. The third man drove the Model A Ford away. One of the kidnappers drove the Cadillac towards Manchester Road; the other held a sawed-off shotgun into Oscar's side and told him to keep quiet or he would shoot him.

Oscar realized he had to do something quickly so he shouted out for help as they passed the Melrose Store. He leaned forward, turned off the switch, then picking his feet up off the floor, kicked the switch, breaking off the ignition key. The car was immobilized immediately.

The two kidnappers became furious and pulled him out of the car into a cornfield and beat him with the sawed-off shotgun. They knocked out all of his front teeth, split his scalp in numerous places, slightly fractured his skull and left him for dead. Shortly thereafter he came to, staggered through fields until he happened upon a farm house where two young boys were cutting wood. He managed to ask them to take him to Barnes Hospital in St. Louis as fast as they could.

Mr. Thompson called Hughes on the phone at the Melrose Store. He called to say that Barnes Hospital had called him to tell him that Oscar Johnson had been admitted with serious multiple injuries, and that two farm boys had driven him in, in their old jalopy, but could only give the hospital a very confused account as to what had happened.

According to an unidentified St. Louis newspaper article, "The men tumbled out with Johnson, and struck him with a sawed-off shotgun and a revolver, weapons which were later found near the road. He fled from them into a cornfield, and got through the field to the home of R.F. Stern. After telling the Stern family who he was and what had happened to him, Johnson was driven to the city and to Barnes Hospital by Harvey White of Alton, Ill, who was visiting relatives in the neighborhood; Johnson told White the story of the attack on him." I think Hughes' account to be plausible. Oscar was

Oscar Johnson Jr.'s photograph of the bridge over Little Tavern Creek. The bridge was destroyed in the flood of 1993.

so badly beaten and left for dead, he could hardly have been able to relate the events two times. Also, the hospital told Mr. Thompson that two farm boys brought him in.

Hughes drove Sheriff Lill and the two suspects, guarded by two deputies, to Barnes Hospital. Oscar was heavily bandaged but still fully conscious and able to identify the two men as the ones who had attempted to kidnap him. The sheriff called a police car and took them to the County Jail. While they were in jail and awaiting trial, the police feared that other members of the gang would attempt to kill Oscar or kidnap other members of the family to interfere with the testimony. Private detectives were hired as bodyguards, and Hughes and other Farm men were armed with shotguns to escort their cars to and from the Farm. This ended when the kidnappers were finally sentenced to fifteen to twenty years in the Missouri State Penitentiary.[5]

Oscar was a yachtsman. In 1938, he competed on his 66-foot ketch *Nam Sang* in the San Francisco-to-Honolulu Yacht Race. He finished 16th.

He was interested in the sciences. He was a member of

the St. Louis Astronomical Society and the American Meteorological Society. He was an excellent amateur photographer and kept a darkroom at the Studio. Several of his photos illustrate this book.

He was a veteran. In 1941 he was drafted into the Army. He served in the Army until 1942, in the Pacific Campaign of WWII and then joined the Naval Reserve where he received the rank of lieutenant and then lieutenant commander. He served until the end of the war in 1945.[6]

He returned to St. Louis after the war. He married Eloise Long Wells Polk in Boston, Mass., July 12, 1946. She was a graduate of Pine Manor College and Cambridge School of Landscape Architecture. Oscar and Eloise had one daughter, Irene Walter, born December 19, 1947. Irene married James Craig Barnes on December 28, 1969. They divorced in 1984. Irene died August 2, 1995 in San Antonio, Texas. Eloise had two children by a former marriage: Samuel Wells Polk, Jr., born February 13, 1932, died August 12, 1997; and a daughter Eloise Wells Polk, a well-known concert pianist who married Dr. Dixon Spivy. Oscar died August 28, 1983, at St. Louis. Eloise died in 1992.

James Lee Johnson, Jr. Photo courtesy of Mrs. Richard S. Hawes, III.

James Lee Johnson, Oscar's brother, was born October 17, 1906 in St. Louis. He attended St. Louis Country Day School, was graduated from Haverford School (preparatory), attended the University of Virginia but left in 1926 to work for the International Shoe Company. He started at their Hannibal plant as a leather cutter and worked at many other plants owned by International Shoe Company. He became familiar with life in a factory in the 1920's. On January 14, 1930 he married Eleanor Clark Church, born May 2, 1909. They had three children: Marie Christy, James Lee Jr. and Eleanor Chouteau.

Just before World War II, James Lee, Sr. joined the Missouri National Guard and was commissioned second lieutenant. He enlisted in the Army Air Corps and was commissioned second lieutenant. After training at Fort Bragg, he was assigned to the 52nd Troop Carrier Wing. He fought in the African campaign and the European invasion including Italy, England, northern France and finally Belgium, where he was wounded. As a result of these injuries, he was given an honorable discharge from the Air Corps with the rank of lieutenant commander. During the war, his wife Eleanor was head of the Community Chest and worked as a Red Cross volunteer.

He returned to St. Louis and International Shoe Company. He and his wife and family lived on Squire's Lane, Huntleigh, Mo. They also had a house they built at St. Albans on the family-owned St. Albans Farms. It was designed by Jamieson and Spearl and built in 1926. It was a summer and weekend place for them. In 1963, it was converted into a shooting club, "The Wings of St. Albans," where members hunted ducks, quail and pheasant and used a skeet range. James Lee was also instrumental in the establishment of a stable at St. Albans Farms. His wife was an excellent horsewoman. He loved horses and was a good marksman and hunter. James Lee Johnson died November 22, 1985.[7]

Oscar and James Lee reorganized the Farm and continued the development of the herd. The Guernsey herd under Rainey's management was carefully developed. The St. Albans herd was a testing program which was a major factor in the development and proving of the two cow families, *Beauty Spot* and *Hale Spot.* As noted in the *Guernsey Breeder's Journal,* February 21, 1951:

Drawing from a brochure by Frank Nuderscher.

Major portions of the credit for the St. Albans herd should go to Mrs. Irene W. Johnson, owner of the farm at the time the Guernsey herd was started, and Lawrence R. Rainey, formerly herdsman and now superintendent of St. Albans Farms, Inc. Mrs. Irene W. Johnson established the foundation herd and maintained it during the difficult 'first years.' Her cooperation and leadership, provided through St. Albans Farms, has been a great assistance to many beginning breeders, to the State of Missouri and the Guernsey breed. The Missouri G.B.A. recognized this contribution by making Mrs. Johnson a lifetime honorary member in the State Association, an honor reserved for a few who contribute materially to the Guernsey breed and progress in Missouri.

The Golden Guernsey herd of St. Albans was the largest Guernsey herd in Missouri, and the largest single supplier of milk in the St. Louis area. The Golden Guernsey milk contained 5 percent butterfat. This was sold exclusively through the St. Louis

Dairy. Arthur Birge was in charge of these sales and scheduled tours of the St. Albans Dairy. Don Henry was the salesman for the St. Louis Dairy in charge of the Guernsey sales. St. Albans Dairy also supplied 2 percent soft curd that was sold to Highland Dairy.

The Golden Guernsey cows were driven in three times a day to be milked in the stone milking barn. They were milked by hand.[8] The grade cows were milked by machine twice a day. It was a major operation to maintain the herd and a lot of feed was required. Most years, the bottomlands produced a great crop, but too often the Missouri River flooded the area. Many years the flood waters came over the railroad tracks, covering the bottomland crops. Such losses made the operation unprofitable. In 1951, after ten years of such flooding, it was decided to sell the herd.

> St. Albans Farms, 5400 acres in Franklin and St. Louis counties, 305 Guernsey cattle sold because of frequent crop destroying floods have made operation unprofitable; 25 bulls, 160 cows, 120 heifers.
>
> L.R. Rainey, farm manager, said 100 acres of the farm's bottom land, planted in corn and other feeds, had not produced a complete crop since 1940, because of high water. The herd whose milk is sold through a Kirkwood dairy, was established in 1932 by the Johnsons' mother, Mrs. Oscar Johnson.[9]

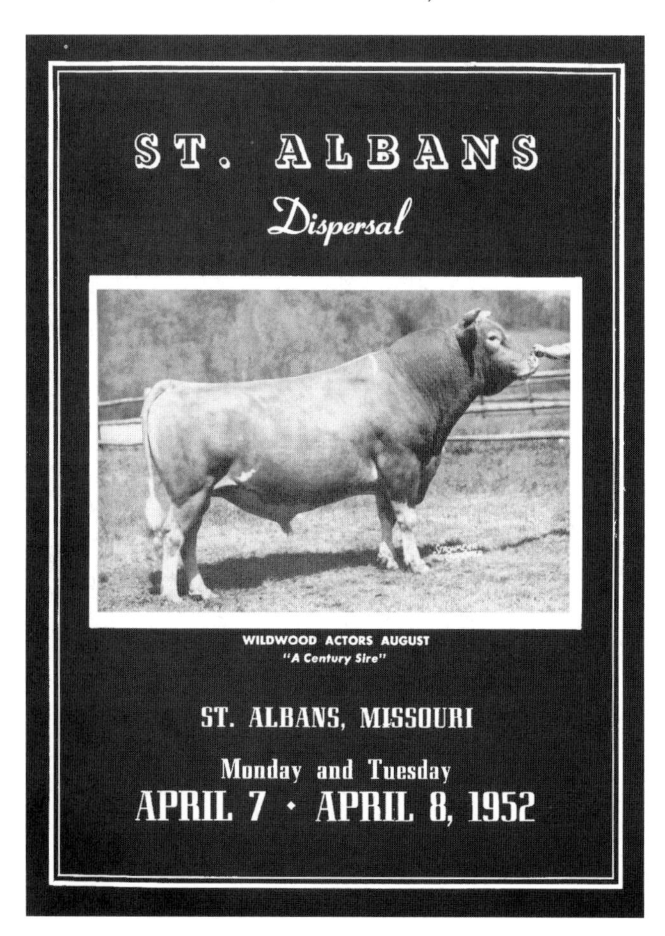

The literature for the sale read:

Complete Dispersal St. Albans Guernseys
305 Head – 25 Bulls – 160 Cows 60 Bred 60 Open Heifers

Sale Managed by
The Louis McL. Merryman & Sons Inc. Sparks, Md.
The Missouri Guernsey Breeders Association
H.A. Herman, Secretary, U. of Mo. Columbia, Mo.

It included a letter signed by L.R. Rainey:

> We have tried to develop a cow that can, and will, work under farmer conditions, and feel that we have succeeded. They have done well here and elsewhere. Our feed and forage conditions here never have been of the best. But, with working cattle, we have been able to develop and hold together a top herd of cattle for almost twenty years, the last ten of which have been in conflict with the Missouri River.
>
> It is with extreme regret that we offer the herd for dispersal. It is, however, with extreme pride that we offer the herd. We feel that the cattle are the kind that will carry on for their purchasers and keep the name of St. Albans in the forefront of Guernsey breeding for many years.

The herd, valued at $250,000, was sold at public auction April 7 & 8, 1952. It was the largest sale of a privately owned herd of Guernsey cattle ever held west of the Mississippi River. The sale was held at the stone milking barn where large tents were set up for cooking and dining. About 800 guests of the farm management were served. Altogether there were over 1000 people attending the auction. The top price of $14,000 was paid for *McDonald Farms P. Monarch*, the prize Guernsey bull, by Francis McCann of Bridgewater, Conn. He also paid a top price of $2300 for *St. Albans Monarch's Pretty Spot*. I was at the sale and it seemed to me almost every cow or heifer was "Bred to Monarch." "Monarch" was a huge animal and certainly the pride of the herd. An average price of $706.48 was brought by the 162 head sold. A large number of the herd was sold to the J.C. Penney herd at Columbia, Mo., where Mr. Rainey transferred. He left St. Albans for Columbia June 15, 1952.[10]

Cows in the pasture at St. Albans Farms. Ken Gilberg collection.

Mr. Wilson then became farm manger after Mr. Rainey until Mr. Philip Kilpatrick took over in 1953.

There were a few remaining cows not included in the big sale. To these were added some good stock to utilize the crops on hand. Maintaining this small herd proved to be impractical, and it was finally decided to sell all the animals and milking equipment. The following notice was sent out in a small catalogue:

> Sale of St. Albans Guernseys
> Wednesday, May 27, 1953
> To be sold at auction by
> St. Albans Farms, St. Albans, Mo.
> and
> Emery Vieten, Cove View Farm, Leslie, Mo.
>
> When the St. Albans Guernsey herd of 275 head was dispersed April 7th & 8th, 1952, there was left on the farm a few old brood matrons, unsalable, but carrying calves. There were also a few choice calves and one young sire kept. In order to utilize the feed and labor available on the farm, about a dozen good cows and heifers were purchased in the summer of 1952 and added to the nucleus. The decision has now been reached to discontinue all milking operations at the farm. The old cows are gone, but their splendid calves are available. Only good sound cattle are offered in this sale.
>
> Mr. Emery Vieten is adding about a dozen head–he has followed the St. Albans bloodlines.
>
> P.S. Kilpatrick, Manager
>
> Sales managed by the Mo. G.B.A.
> Bert Powell, Auctioneer, Topeka, Kansas

When Philip S. Kilpatrick became manager, he started a program of feeder cattle buying Aberdeen Angus and Herefords. The following article appeared in the newspaper.

> The famed St. Albans Farms is going to be converted into the raising of beef cattle. The switch to feeder cattle will not affect the present physical setup of the farms, which has close to 6500 acres.

Mr. Kilpatrick bought and sold throughout the years of his management, 1953–1975, about 5000 head of cattle. This allowed him to average the buying and selling prices. When he first came to St. Albans, there were about 500 acres of farming land in the river bottom. He had about 1000 additional acres cleared for farming and had a 35-foot levee built to help protect them from flooding. In really heavy flooding, the water would seep in the bottom of the land. I remember seeing the farm men down there filling sand bags to help reinforce the levee. Very often the river came up to the railroad tracks.

Mr. Kilpatrick left in 1975, when Dave Smith became manager. He continued in this positon until 1988, when the property was sold to the St. Albans Partners.

FOOTNOTES

1. St. Albans Farm literature entitled, "Views of St. Albans."
2. "The 'Beauty Spot' family at St. Albans Farms, Inc." by Fred W. Madden, Guernsey Breeders Journal, February 21, 1951.
3. I met his son, Dr. Lawrence W. O'Neal, a retired surgeon working at Mercy Center, St. Louis. He gave me this information. As a teenager, he often accompanied his father on his weekly visits to St. Albans Farms.
4. *St. Louis Globe-Democrat,* August 30, 1983.
5. Later the police found out this was to be a second kidnapping planned by a Mrs. Nellie Muench. The first had been the successful kidnapping of Dr. I.D. Kelly, who was held for ransom, but released without payment of the $100,000 demanded. Mrs. Muench owned a fashionable dress shop in St. Louis. She was the wife of a Dr. Muench. In her spare time she was the "finger woman" for a bunch of notorious gangsters and hoodlums. Mrs. Muench was finally caught in the well-known Muench baby case.
6. *St. Louis Globe-Democrat,* August 30, 1983.
7. Bond, Christy Hawes, *Gateway Families: Ancestors and Descendants of Richard Sumrall Hawes III and Marie Christy Johnson,* and *The History of Missouri, Family and Personal History,* Vol. IV.
8. Three of the milkers were Bill Graves, Emil Barnhart and Bryan Lail; 1934-1951. Each milked 18-20 cows.
9. *St. Louis Post-Dispatch,* April 2, 1952.
10. *St. Louis Globe-Democrat,* April 8, 1952, and in the *St. Louis Post-Dispatch,* April 9, 1952.

Frank Nuderscher's map from St. Louis to St. Albans c. 1930.

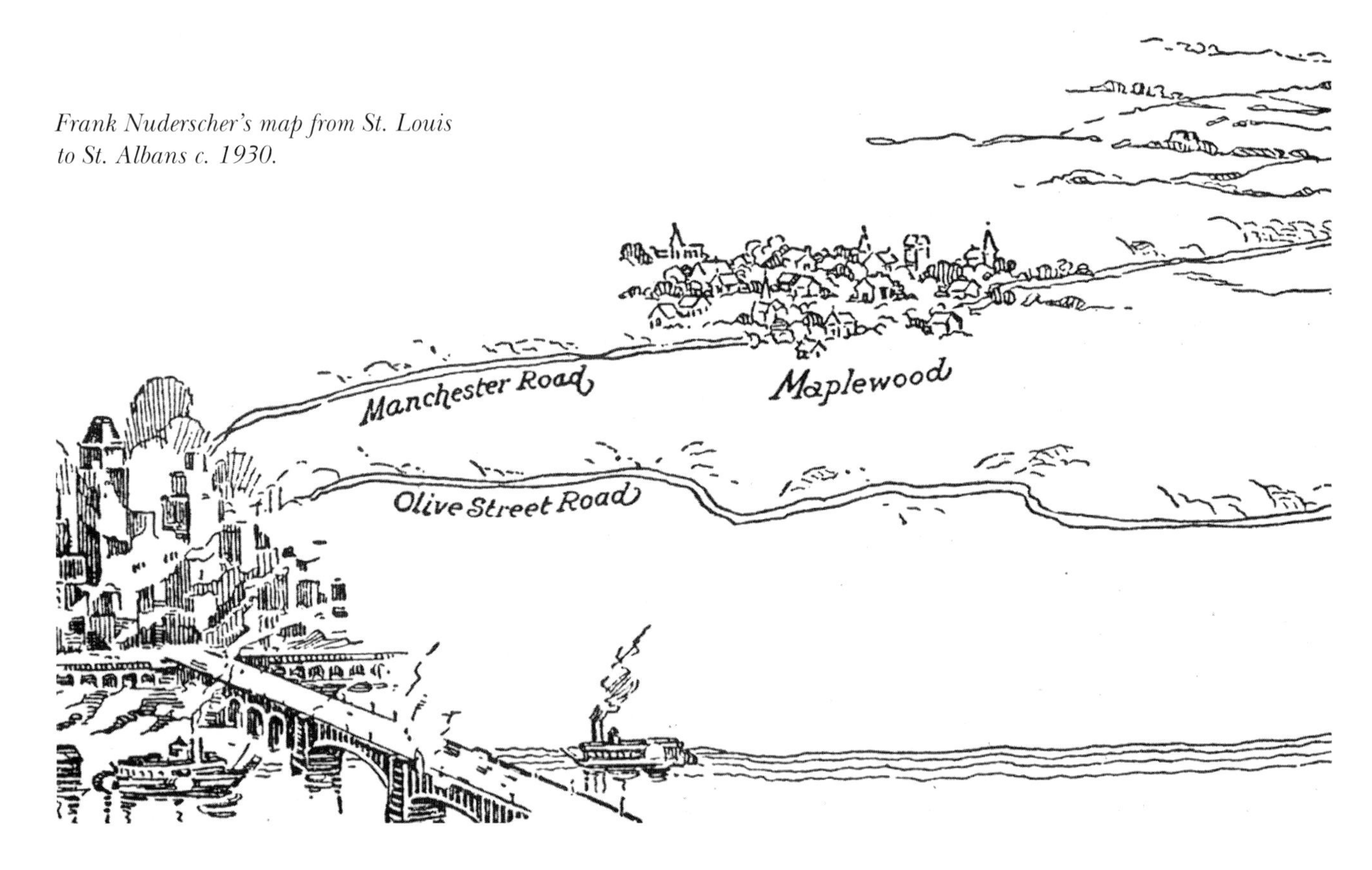

CHAPTER ELEVEN

St. Albans Farms Buildings

The Old Barn Inn

For many years the name Old Barn Inn was synonymous with St. Albans. It was a very popular eating place for St. Louisans—just a pleasant drive from the busy city to an excellent restaurant. When it opened on Thanksgiving Day 1928, it was called the Barn Inn because it was originally Judge Francis Becker's barn built in 1840. Some time prior to 1954, the name was changed to Old Barn Inn.[1]

Mrs. Irene Johnson in developing the St. Albans Farms saw the potential of the old barn as a restaurant. St. Albans Farm conducted tours of their dairy and a restaurant would be a place to welcome special guests. In 1928, the barn and hayloft were converted into a country inn by the esteemed architectural firm of Jamieson and Spearl of St. Louis. The machine shed became the restaurant area, seating about 75 persons. The other section of the barn, with its original beamed ceiling, was made into a lounge. Chimneys, massive stone fireplace and

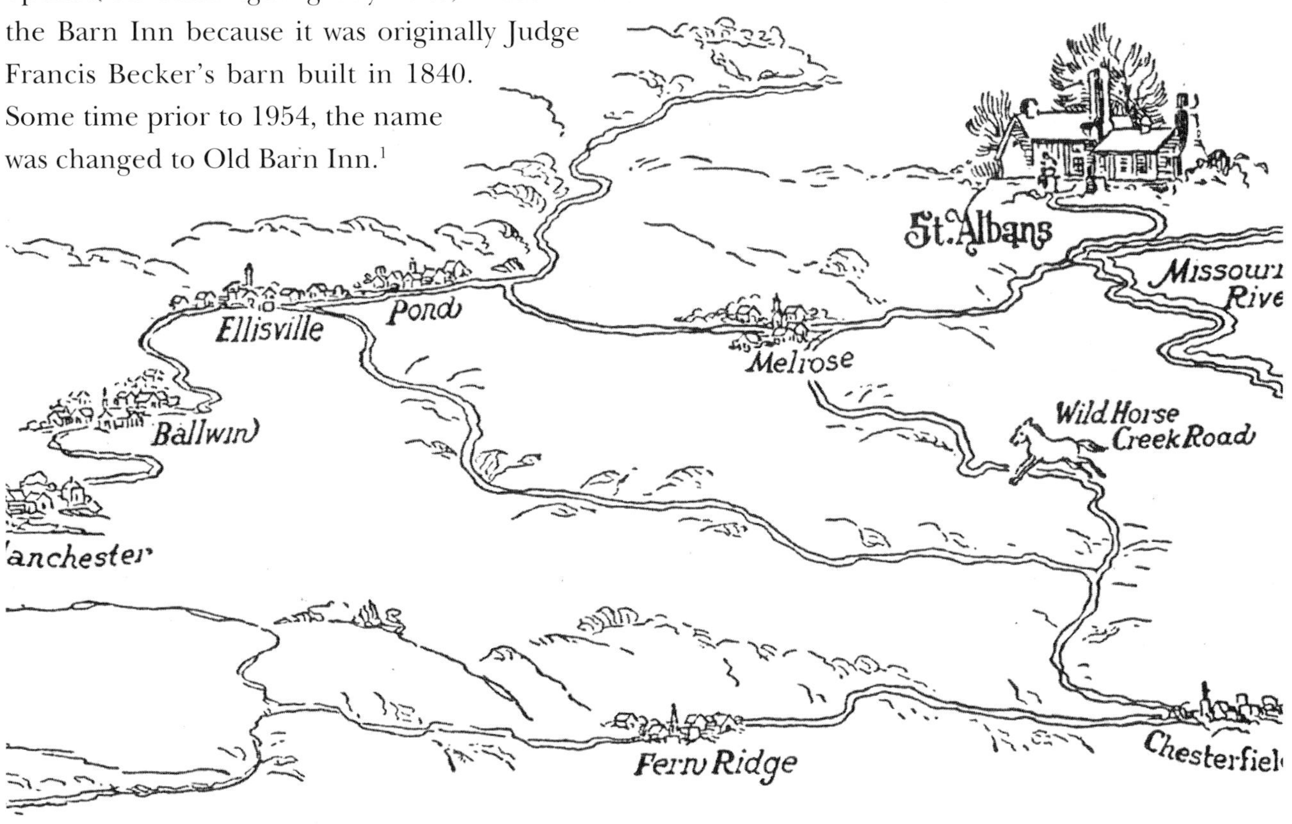

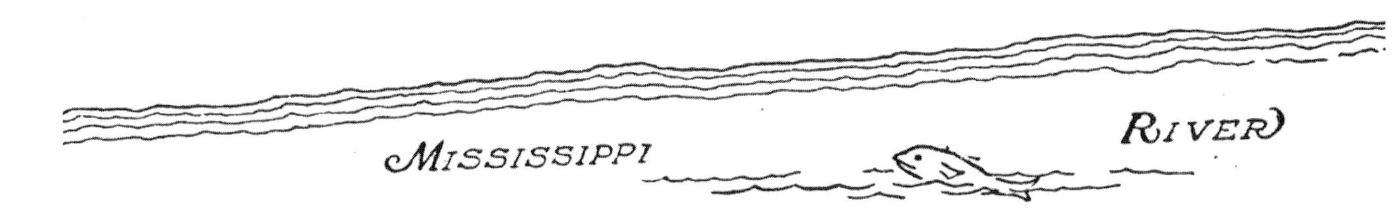

entranceway were added. It was truly a country inn. The menu featured country fried chicken, broiled steaks from St. Albans Farms' prized cattle, frog legs, home baked breads, rolls, cakes, pastries, country style salad dressing and sauces—all cooked by farm women.

There was a small booklet[2] printed about 1932, when the dairy was giving tours and the Barn Inn was in operation. This little booklet is so interesting and descriptive that it is herewith printed in its entirety.

The Old Barn Inn, photo from Food Service News, *November 1950.*

Cover

Please Keep This Booklet

The Barn Inn

ST. ALBANS, MO.

Inside Cover

FOR
RESERVATIONS
Call
"LONG DISTANCE"
And Ask For
THE ST. ALBANS INN
or CHestnut 6400
American Hotel
Ask for Mr. H.H. O'Neill

Page 1

St. Albans
What Is It...

St. Albans is a seven thousand acre farm of exquisite beauty and peacefulness. After several years of planning it is now reaching that perfection to which it has always aimed. Roads have been built, vistas cleared through the forests, spent farms reclaimed to fruitfulness and the necessities of electric power and pure water introduced.

Page 2:

Yet all this has been so carefully carried out that nature still reigns supreme. The result: one of the most beautiful places in Missouri is saved from unworthy exploitation.

St. Albans offers through its Inn temporary peace and refreshment of mind and body alike and a refuge from the noise, the confusion and the ugliness of a great city.

Page 3

The Barn Inn

A beautiful restaurant with all the catering facilities of a large modern hotel under the management of an expert caterer. For reservations simply call the long distance operator and ask for "St. Albans Inn" or call CHestnut 6400 and ask for Mr. O'Neill.

TARIFF

Breakfast and Lunch	$1.00 - $1.25
Dairy Luncheon	.75
Dinner	1.25

Also a la carte service

Page 4

THE TAVERN ROCK ROAD

Visitors to the Inn have the privilege of using this private road and from it seeing the wonderful views over the Missouri River from the bluffs. A pass is necessary and can be obtained at the Inn from the hostess without charge.

Along those bluffs will, in the future, be many lovely homes owned by St. Louisians. You yourself may be one of those fortunate ones.

Page 5

THE SWIMMING POOL

This beautiful pool is for visitors to the Inn. It is available for their use at all times except on Mondays. An attendant is present at the pool to whom swimming tickets obtained at the Inn for fifty cents each must be presented. This is essential so as to confine the use of the pool to Inn visitors only. Those intending to swim should bring their own bathing suits and towels.

Page 6

TENNIS and BADMINTON

Near the swimming pool is a first class tennis court available at a charge of fifty cents per player. Visitors should bring their own racquets and balls.

Badminton can be played at the Inn at any time without charge. Any attendant will supply the racquets and shuttles on request.

Page 7

HOUSEPARTIES

The six-room cottage, "Open Arms" on the grounds above the Inn is for overnight parties of six or eight guests, properly chaperoned. You are invited to inspect these guest rooms with all modern conveniences.

In mid-summer, when the city heat and noise become unbearable, let the Inn be your country house! Its exclusiveness, its comfort, its fine food as well as its swimming pool and tennis court, give all that

The dining area in The Old Barn Inn. Photo from Food Service News, *November, 1950.*

Page 8

the most exacting could ask and at such reasonable rates.

Those who are prevented from going to the East or West coasts for their usual vacations will find much needed rest at St. Albans and a weekend party of several friends is delightful relaxation.

TARIFF

$5.00 Per Day

(including meals)

Back inside cover

St. Albans Farms

GUERNSEY MILK

This milk is pasteurized, bottled and capped on the farm and is trucked in refrigeration to the St. Louis and Highland Dairies for distribution. It is exceptionally high in butterfat content and of outstanding quality. Of course all men employed in the dairy are medically examined and all cows tuberculin tested.

A regular supply of the milk can be ordered at the Inn by calling either the St. Louis or Highland Dairies.

CEntral 3900 or FRanklin 3980

There were tours through the dairy every two weeks. From 1932 to 1939, Gene Jantzen was the tour director and Mae Head the hostess of the Inn. After a tour, the guests could fish or take a ride in a hay wagon driven by Ben Pohlig, who worked for the Farm, and have lunch or dinner at the Inn.

Miss Dorcas Robinson was the hostess-manager from 1946 to 1953. She ran the Inn with "an iron hand in a velvet glove." In 1950, the Barn Inn was acclaimed one of the nation's top country restaurants by one of the most widely read restaurant magazines, *Food Service News.*[3]

In it the following description is given:

> Seating capacity of The Barn Inn is 90 and patrons are accepted by reservation only. The volume is not large, ranging from 600 a month in winter to 1,500 patrons during the summer months. Offsetting the low volume is the relatively higher check average of $3.50.
>
> Besides Miss Robinson, there are but five employees in the kitchen and two waitresses (at the Inn they are called maids). Luncheon is served from 12:00 to 2:30 and dinner from 5:00 to 8:00 o'clock. Tea is served from 3:00 to 5:00 every afternoon.[4]

Amanda Jabin was the head cook in charge when we went to the Inn. Over the years, the following served in various capacities in the kitchen: Cora Krausch, Catherine Calvin, Ida Pfeiffer, Shirley Travis, Gertrude Kerns, Henrietta Wilming, Grace Stettes, Edna Dutton, Betty Mueller and Wilma Spickelmier.[5]

Amanda Jabin, at the stove in the Old Barn Inn. Photo from Food Service News.

The Inn became a popular luncheon place for ladies, who often stayed to play cards. Dinner guests enjoyed the country menu. There was a strict dress code: dresses for the girls and ladies, coat and tie for the boys and men. Liquor was allowed but could not be sold by the drink or bottle, only setups were sold. Since this is usually the most profitable part of a restaurant operation, the Inn was never a "money-maker."

When Philip Kilpatrick became farm manger in 1953, his wife, Josephine, took over the operation of the Inn. More cottages were added. Guests could rent the cottages and enjoy the swimming pool and tennis courts. While there were some kitchen facilities, the guests usually took their meals at the Inn. Corporations often rented the cottages for a week to house their seminars or meetings. They would eat all their meals at the Inn.

> Monsanto Chemical Company came to the Inn for their seminars. They stayed about twelve years. There were 12 divisions which included the Overseas. Each division would stay one month. They were held in the Village Green, a beautiful house across from the Inn. They lived in some of the cottages.[6]

A notice was mailed each year to patrons announcing the opening of the Inn at Easter, and another announcing the season's end on Thanksgiving Day.

Blacks were not allowed at the Inn, as guests or employees. This policy eventually contributed to the closing of the Inn. When the time came to close, the following postal card was sent:

> Old Barn Inn Saint Albans, Missouri
> Old Barn Inn
> Will Not Open Until Further Notice
> Telephone WOodland 1-3600[8]

At the time of the closing of the Inn in 1968, Oscar Johnson, Jr. recounted the reasons for closing:

> In the beginning the losses were written off as a public relations expense for the dairy farm. The Inn was a sentimental matter for Lee and myself. It was a gesture of welcome for those who came to the farm.

> In the early years, our losses were minimal —about $300 a year. I won't tell you the amount this past year (1967), but it was in the five figures.[7]

The St. Albans Farms office moved into the building and operated from there until it was leased as a restaurant in 1988, to Gilbert and Simone Andujar who had operated "Le Bistro," a restaurant in West County, St. Louis. The Andujars came from Marseilles, in southern France. When Simone saw the flower gardens surrounding the Barn Inn, she thought of the famous Malmaison outside of Paris. Napoleon Bonaparte gave the Chateau de Malmaison to his wife Josephine who loved its serenity and beauty. The Andujars renamed the Barn Inn Malmaison.[9] It was decorated in French country style and featured fine French cuisine.

Malmaison continues to uphold the fine reputation as one of the nation's top "off the road" restaurants. Zagat's Survey "America's Top Restaurants, 1993" lists it as follows:

MALMAISON	F	D	S	C
	25	26	24	$30

F-food D-décor S-service C-cost

0-9	poor to fair
10-15	fair to good
16-19	good to very good
20-25	very good to excellent
26-30	extraordinary to perfection

> "A little known gem" is the general consensus on this lovely French restaurant reminiscent in its pastoral ambiance and décor of a French country inn, thanks to its setting in a 1920's country club; fans willingly drive about 45 minutes from Downtown for the "beautiful location," "excellent menu," and "enchanting evening."

The Restaurant Issue of *Gourmet magazine*, October 1997, lists Malmaison #3 in the St. Louis area by "Our Readers Top Tables." It is also chosen for "Top Ambiance" and "Tops for Romance."

The formal flower gardens surrounding the Old Barn Inn/ Malmaison. Photo by Ken Gilberg.

The Stone Dairy Barn

The dairy barn was designed by Theodore C. Link in 1918, as a horse barn, and was converted to a milking barn in the 1930's. It was at this time that the Farm went into the dairy business and the Fleet Mount stables were built near the maintenance shed.

It was constructed of limestone quarried on the property above the Cedars. Magnus Graves remembers helping his father, William Graves, and Carl Stettes in the construction. As a young boy, he hauled sand for mixing concrete. Forms were made, stones set in place and concrete poured, making a section at a time. He and Ray Pendleton, another young man living at St. Albans, worked on the shingles for the two silos, cutting them with a penknife to make them fit.

Magnus was born April 11, 1918, in northern Missouri, son of William and Minnie Alice Cannon Graves. When he was eleven years old, he moved with his parents and his two-year-old sister Lucille from Conway, Mo., to St. Albans. This was the year of the "Great Depression", 1929. They packed all their belongings into their car and drove to St. Louis, looking for work. His father, Bill, was told the only place they were hiring was at St. Albans.

The Stone Dairy Barn in 1956. Photo taken from the old road into St. Albans. Photo collection.

They drove out there and parked their car in a field and spread a blanket on the ground under a tree for sleeping. Bill's brother had given him $400, which was a lot of money in 1929, to help him get started. That night he put the four $100 bills in a paper bag and buried it in the ground. The next morning he discovered that field mice had chewed the money in half, but the serial numbers were still there so he was able to redeem it at a bank. They were sleeping under the tree and it was getting into winter. A man who worked at St. Albans cleared a room in his house, located at the top of Ossenfort Hill, for them to use. The temperature got down to 29 degrees below zero that winter.

Bill got work on the river at Matson. Lucille was just a little girl, but she remembers driving with her father to Matson to pick up his paycheck. The Captain he worked for invited them to stay for dinner. She still remembers what a feast that was. The Captain gave her five dollars and that was a lot of money in those days of the Depression. On the way home they took the ferry to Washington and shopped at Penney's. She got two new dresses: a blue and white striped and a red and white striped. Her mother made her clothes from whatever remnants of worn clothing that was handy so this was indeed a memorable occasion. Bill worked on the river for a few years then was hired by St. Albans Farms in their dairy.

Bill saved enough money to buy a tent. He went to a lumber yard in Chesterfield and bought a 14 x 16 tent. He wanted to make a wooden floor and the owner of the lumber yard gave him enough material for a floor and 4 feet high walls. He also got a cover to go over the tent to make it warm in the winter and cool in the summer. He bought two beds, a stove, table and chairs. The tent was set up on the other side of Tavern Creek across the railroad bridge. The family lived there for five years.

Magnus and Lucille walked to Little Tavern School, a distance of about two miles. They walked with the Pendletons or got a ride with Mrs. Frick and her daughter Shirley Mae. Shirley Mae was a bright girl but she was unable to walk. The Fricks hired Margaret and later Virginia Pendleton to help her. For a while, the Graves lived in a house on Johnson Island and when that was torn down, moved it piece by piece near where they had lived in their tent.

There were two milking barns and a calf barn at the Cedars. The prize Guernsey cows were hand milked three times a day. Bill Graves, Bryan Lail, and Hiram Barnhart were some of the milkers. Bryan Lail was the chief herdsman for the 144 head at the stone barn, and Charlie Salidine was herdsman for the 60 head at the Cedars. Bryan Lail, who had been with the farm since 1934, stayed with the Guernsey herd when it was sold to the J. C. Penney herd and moved to Columbia, Mo.

Magnus trucked the milk from the Cedars to the pasteurizing barn near the maintenance shed. Here it was pasteurized and bottled then stored overnight in a cooler in the hillside in back of the Barn Inn before shipping it to St. Louis. Magnus left St. Albans in 1939. He married Doris Fleer on January 29, 1940, and moved to Washington, Mo., where I met him.

Lucille taught at the Little Tavern School 1948-49. On May 23, 1948, she married Edward Schoelich. He was born July 9, 1923, at Union, Mo. Lucille had to take a year's leave of absence when her daughter Mary Frances was born on March 8, 1949. She returned to teaching 1950-51, the last year Little Tavern School was open. Eddie and Lucille moved into the "Missouri House" in 1951. Their second daughter Judith Ann was born December 3, 1954. Judy married Christopher Bocklage. Eddie died August 25, 1985. Lucille and Mary moved to Union in 1988. Their house was torn down and a Victorian house was built on the site. It is part of the Chesterfield Day School/St. Albans.

Bill Graves and his wife lived in a small house near the maintenance shed belonging to St. Albans Farms. He retired in the 60's. We often saw "Old Man Graves", as we called him, at St. Albans. He died November 13, 1969, at St. Albans and is buried in the Bethel Cemetery near Labadie.

Hiram Barnhart, married to Mina Pendleton, moved from St. Mary's County, Mo., to Wild Horse Creek Road in 1924. They had three children: Alton David, Emil Dewey and John Merrel. His son Emil, who was twelve years old when they moved, attended Little Tavern School. Emil worked at the "Studio" cultivating the rose garden and chauffeured "Miss Irene" in a Model T Ford. He carried mortar to the stone masons building the Old Barn Inn where he later helped in the kitchen washing dishes, mopping the floors etc. [10]

FOOTNOTES

1. "Old Barn Inn, St. Albans, Pilgrim 2-2182," listing in Gray Summit, Missouri Telephone Directory, October 1954, Southwestern Bell Telephone Company, p. 6.
2. This little booklet does not have the date or printer's name.
3. "Barn Inn," *Food Service News*, Electrical Information Publications, Inc., Madison, Wisconsin, November, 1950, Vol. 12, No. 11, pp. 8-9.
4. Ibid.
5. Joan Heisel, who worked in the Farm office, supplied me with the list.
6. Letter from Josephine Kilpatrick, June 29, 1993.
7. Powers, Ronald D. "Old Barn Inn closed, Once Top Restaurant," article, *St. Louis Post-Dispatch*, April 11, 1968, p. 8W.
8. Such a card addressed to us was postmarked March 15, 1968.
9. Pollack, Joe, "Malmaison: A Touch of France in the Country," article, *St. Louis Post-Dispatch*, September 14, 1989.
10. In 1931, he left to work for a man in the Gumbo bottoms who raised melons. He also worked for a construction company building dikes on the Missouri River. He married Ollie Barnhart in 1932. They had four children: Marcella, LeRoy, Carl Wayne and Connie. He returned to St. Albans to work for the farm at the dairy until it closed in 1951. They lived at the Cedars. His father, Hiram Barnhart was a milker for the Farm for about seventeen years. Charles Mann was followed by Lawrence Rainey as manager of the dairy at that time.

Anna Lee Glenn in 1923 in front of the Fleet Mount Farms stable.
Photo courtesy of Anna Lee Glenn Grone.

CHAPTER TWELVE

Fleet Mount Farms

In 1929, a group of horse lovers in St. Louis, George M. Berry, Mrs. Edward J. Walsh, Sr., Herman J. Sternberg, Paul Bakewell, Jr., and James Lee Johnson, son of Irene Johnson, got together to establish a horse farm at St. Albans. The group leased some property from Mrs. Johnson and established Fleet Mount Farms where they bred fine saddle horses for pleasure and show. They had outstanding brood mares, colts, show horses and royally bred stallions.[1] The horses were housed in a beautiful 60 stall, fireproof stone stable with a large paddock and training track.

Robert Paul Glenn was hired as the manager of Fleet Mount Farms. He and his wife, Catherine, and six-year-old daughter, Anna Lee, moved into the manager's house next to the maintenance shed across the road from the stable.[2]

> He was well-qualified for this responsible position. He came from Columbia, Mo. from a family of horsemen. Miss Rex, the celebrated Five-Gaited Champion, was bred at the Glenn Farm. He originated a fine breeding, show and training establishment for Fleet Mount Farms.[3]

The first notice I could find for Fleet Mount Farms was in the May 1930, issue of *Saddle & Bridle* magazine.[4] It lists "Paul Bakewell, Jr., Secretary, and R.P. Glen, Manager. The address is St. Albans, Missouri, Railroad Station, Becker, Mo. On Rock Island Lines. Telephone, St. Albans Inn." The Inn had been opened in 1928.

In the July 1931 issue of *Saddle & Bridle*, a set of pictures of some prize Fleet Mount Farms colts was shown.[5]

The May 1932 issue of *Saddle & Bridle* was dedicated to the 1932 foals of the country with a cover

A view of Fleetmount Farms stables. To the right is the outdoor ring. Photo by Taylor, courtesy Saddle & Bridle.

picture of "Edna Louise and her baby colt." This picture was taken at Fleet Mount Farms with the lead article entitled, "Fleetmount, Fine Saddle Horse Nursery." This names many of the fine colts, mares, stallions and geldings on the Farms.

> Fleetmount is a formidable factor in the breeding activities of Missouri saddle horse establishments and will continue to be known as one of the most progressive.[6]

Periodically they advertised individual horses in the magazine; five in 1931, and three in 1932.[7] In 1932, they also placed an ad in the "Dealers' Director and Buyers Guide" for the months of February, March, April and May.

In 1932, the Glenn family moved to Hillsboro, Mo. and Fleet Mount Farms followed Mr. Glenn.[8] The following notice appeared in the November and December issues of *Saddle & Bridle.*[9]

ANNOUNCEMENT
FLEETMOUNT FARMS

We Wish to Call the Attention of
Our Friends and Patrons to
Our New Location

All of our show horses, pleasure horses, stallions,
broodmares and colts are now located at the
HOLEKAMP FARMS
HILLSBORO, MO.

A cordial invitation is extended to all
to visit us at our new location
Directions:
Drive south on Highway 61 to Highway Z (just
one mile north of Pevely) then turn west 10 miles.

FLEETMOUNT STABLES
HILLSBORO, MO.

Lawrence Rainey, St. Albans Farms manager, lived in the horse barn until it burned by spontaneous combustion of alfalfa hay. The remains of the barn were torn down and a pasteurizing barn was built on that site.[10]

"Joy Bells No. 17162. R.P Glenn up." From Saddle & Bridle. *Photo by Taylor.*

FOOTNOTES

1. "Fleetmount, Fine Saddle Horse Nursery," *Saddle & Bridle*, May 1932, Vol. V, No. 5
2. Interview with Anna Lee Glenn Grone.
3. Op cit, p. 36.
4. Op cit, May 1930, Vol. IV, No. 5.
5. Op cit, July 1931, Vol. IV, No. 7.
6. Op cit, May 1932.
7. June 1931, p. 7 — December 1931, p. 62
   July 1931, p. 37 — February 1932, p. 30
   August 1931, p. 27 — March 1932, p. 32
   October 1931, p. 46 — April 1932, p. 34
8. Grone, op cit.
9. Op cit, November 1932, p. 35; December 1932, p.54.
10. Letter from Ruth Schultz.

CHAPTER THIRTEEN

Fire Department

Before any Fire Department was established in the St. Albans area, Irene Johnson had her own fire protection for St. Albans Farms. The following newspaper article describes her plan.

> Another stone building conceals a hose reel, which may be attached to an automobile and brought to concealed fire plugs located throughout the huge place. Water pressure is so high that no pumps have been deemed necessary. —— Water pipes leading from six reservoirs are placed underground.[1]

The earliest Fire Department in Boles Township was established in 1935 at Gray Summit. When James McDaniel became chief of the Gray Summit District, the department consisted of seven men and one piece of equipment. This fire truck was sold to the Labadie Fire Department when it was established in 1953. James McDaniel served as Fire Chief in Gray Summit from 1955 to 1971 when the Boles Fire Protection District was established.

The Boles Fire Protection District takes in the Villa Ridge, Labadie, Gray Summit and St. Albans areas covering 79 square miles. It was the first fire protection district in Franklin County. The first directors were Mike Casey, Lloyd Harfst of Labadie and A. R. Holthaus of Gray Summit; James McDaniel, Fire Chief. In 1974, Gene Harfst was elected Boles Fire Protection District Chief. At that time the Boles District operated with 65 men and 11 trucks. Fire calls involving any building were answered by all four stations.

St. Albans is part of the Boles Fire Protection District. St. Albans' fire house was built in 1972. Photo by the author.

I remember a big brush fire on our property in the early 60's. I came home to find our driveway filled with fire equipment. The tenants living on what we called the Dutton place had thrown out a bucket of live coals on the dry hillside. One hundred acres burned. Mr. Kilpatrick, farm manager at St. Albans Farms, was using a walkie-talkie to communicate with a helicopter hovering overhead. All four Boles District fire departments plus St. Louis County responded.

In 1972, the total assessed valuation of the district was $29,077.23. The district received its first tax money from the 30-cent levy per $100 assessed valuation. Taxes paid in 1971 and apportioned to the district in 1972 totaled $92,259.03. Most of this income of $77,861.80 came from utility taxes, chiefly from the Union Electric power generating plant between St. Albans and Labadie. One of the responsibilities of the district is to provide fire protection for the $400 million power plant.

At this time, 1972, the department had eight trucks: five stationed at Labadie and three at Gray Summit. Bids were being taken on a metal firehouse to be erected on property owned by the district at Villa Ridge. Two trucks were to be stationed at Villa Ridge as soon as the building was ready. The firehouse was built at St. Albans in 1972. Marvin Eberwein came from Gray Summit to be assistant chief at St. Albans and continued in that capacity until 1982, when Kenneth Meyer took over.

In the September 23, 1974 election, Gene Harfst was elected district chief; assistant chiefs were Lloyd Harfst at Labadie, James Duda at Villa Ridge,

Officers of the Boles Fire Protection District. Right to left: Fire Chief James McDaniel, Gene Harfst, Ralph Caldwell and Llloyd Harfst, all assistant chiefs; Carl Winistoerfer, Captain; Mike Casey, Jr., Assistant Chief; and Don Becker, Captain. Photo courtesy The Washington Missourian.

Marvin Eberwein at St. Albans and James Hendericks at Gray Summit.

The St. Albans Fire District covers about 19 to 20 square miles starting at the St. Louis County/ Franklin County line to the east; Manchester Road to the south; about the Union Electric plant to the west and the Missouri River to the north. It is a volunteer fire department with ten volunteers. Whenever there is a big fire, all four stations respond.

FOOTNOTES

1. McCulloch, S.R., article, *St. Louis Post-Dispatch*, c 1931.

CHAPTER FOURTEEN

Railroad

The railroad came to St. Albans after the Civil War. Francis Becker's "Day Book" gives the best account of the building of the railroad.

1870 February 15 – Survey of RR by John G. Joyce, 5131 S. 14, St. Louis

June 15-21 – Engineers (John G. Joyce, Finney, Pembleton, Bauer and others) were here and made survey of St. Louis & Fort Scott RR.

August 27 – St. Louis & Fort Scott RR Engineers & hands 10 came to supper.

August 31 – St. Louis & Fort Scott RR to here in front of my house Station 1759-30 39/54 or 30¾ miles.

Union or Washington Road has no. 2752, 18 5/8 miles; Island no. 80, mouth of creek to slough no. 1987.

September 15 – I to Washington about Union RR subscriptions.

1874 February 21 – J. G. Joyce, Surveyor, 1310 N. 8 St., St. Louis, surveyed Fort Scott. June 10-12, 1870.
surveyed August 27, 1870.
Took right of way for D.R. Garrison, Pres. P.RR.

1881 July 1st – Creve Coeur RR prolonged his right of way for 12 months.

July 3 & 4 – RR engineers came here.

7th Right of way to Central Mo., RR, A.M. Maupin RR Agent.

10th Engineers & Surveyors came back.

11th Maupin pd for right of way $75.00.

October 26 – C.C. R. R. survey made here by Coppedge Head Engineer

Waiting for the train back to St. Louis around 1910. From Theodore Link's scrapbook, courtesy Theodore C. Link, Jr.

(Link no. 746) Port Royal Stake no. 757 Fiscus House St. Albans (my house) no. 974½ to 974. Creve Coeur is 18 1/20 miles, Freem Bluff no. 1047½, Eddy Hollow, 1017.

December 5 to 7 Mo. Central RR surveyed by Ths. M. Long of Alton. Engineer in charge G. Loverett Edwville assistant Frank Loehr Rodman, Eng. West flagman Same Tracy chain man.
Freemans place
Eddy Hollow
St. Albans
Port Royal
St. Louis Co. line

1882 April 24 – Mo. Central RR contractor & agent were here examining RR ground.

J. Truin & W. H. Swift, Truin & Co., 805 Pine St., St. Louis, contractors. A. Wall of James Edwards & Co., Stock & Bond Brokers, 307 N. 3rd St., St. Louis

1883 May 29 – Central RR man Hall & Klein came here – left next day.

July 1 – 2 for bkfst, lunch, dinner, lodging.

July 26 – Mo. Central RR Surveyors Schrader and 2 workers came at 5 PM, stayed and

July 27-30 the same went to Eaton Hollow and sent wagon to Glencoe & brought Richard Klemm to Eaton and for Labadie.

Engineer Corps: Richard Klemm
Schrader
Othausen
Viervoeger
Feldmann
Van Dam
Catinane

Left for Port Royal.

(Through July and August worked here board and lodging with Becker) Becker went around and got the rights from Pohlig & Oetters and others.

1886 February 13 – St. Louis, Kansas & Colorado RR – For Right of Way came Judge Seg. Bolte Wiesel, Wood, North & Reinhardt Noble & Derik RR attorneys, 315 Olive St. St. Louis.[1]

In 1886, the heirs of Dr. Kincaid conveyed to the St. Louis, Kansas City and Colorado Railroad a small section of land.[2] Franklin County Records show a strip 100 ft. wide for $850.[3]

In 1909, the heirs again convey a strip of land to a railroad; this time it is the Chicago, Rock Island and Pacific.[4] Franklin County Records show 1.95 acres for $125.[5]

Many loads of rock had to be blasted from the high bluffs and transported by a special work train. Charles Becker was in charge of the train engine and serviced it each night and kept the fire stoked so it was ready when needed. The train was kept right behind the Becker home on a side rail at night. The big well provided water for the steam engines. Roadbed filling, pile driving for the trestles and grading were done along the right-of-way using the worktrain.[6]

Rock Island Lines

‡ Meals. + Coupon stations; ♁ Telegraph stations.

Table No. 54—ST. LOUIS AND KANSAS CITY.

27	23	Mls.	*June* 5, 1910.	24	28
P M	A M	.....	LEAVE] [ARRIVE	P M	A M
*10 25	*8 59	0	+ ..**St. Louis** (Union Sta.). ♁	7 20	7 25
10 32	9 07	2.6	.... Vandeventer ..... ♁	7 08	7 18
– –	9 15	5.3	....**Forsyth Junction**.. ♁	7 00	– –
h –	9 22	8.3	.... Clayton .... ♁	6 54	*h* –
– –	9 27	11.0	.... Olivette	6 47	– –
– –	9 31	12.8	.........Lackland.........	6 43	– –
– –	9 37	15.3	.... Maryland Heights	6 38	– –
– –	9 42	18.0	...........Vigus......... ♁	6 33	– –
– –	9 49	21.6	.......**Creve Cœur**.......	6 26	– –
– –	9 54	23.5	...........Hine...........	6 22	– –
g11 19	10 02	26.8	.... Chesterfield ..... ♁	6 15	g6 26
– –	10 12	31.9	.... Monarch.........	6 04	– –
g11 30	10 16	33.4	.... Centaur .... ♁	6 00	g6 13
– –	10 30	39.9	.... St. Albans	5 48	– –
g11 52	10 43	46.0	.........**Labadie**....... ♁	5 36	g5 52
g12 03	10 55	51.2	........Villa Ridge........	5 25	g5 43
12 19	11 14	59.5	+........ Union .... ♁	5 09	5 28
– –	11 25	64.9	.... Jeffriesburg	4 54	– –
– –	11 40	71.6	.... Beaufort	4 40	– –
g12 46	11 45	74.0	.... Leslie .... ♁	4 34	g5 03
g1 00	11 59	80.7	.... Gerald .... ♁	4 20	g4 50

A train schedule from June 5, 1910. Leave St. Louis at 8:59 a.m. and arrive in St. Albans at 10:30 a.m. Courtesy of the Mercantile Library, St. Louis.

The "Missouri House" was a boarding house in the late 1800's. The Schoelichs lived here until it was torn down for the 1990's development. Photograph by the author.

While the railroad was being built, some of the workers stayed at the "Missouri House." It had been a brooder house originally and became a boarding house for the farm workers and railroad workers. Dasha Lee Pendleton was the housekeeper. It was divided into two sections: one for farm workers, the other for the railroad workers. This was located behind the store and blacksmith shop.[7] Other workers got room and board with Francis Becker. When the railroad was finished at St. Albans, a camp was set up between Eddy Hollow and Oetters Station for the workers, and the surveyors stayed at William Stettes' place.

It is interesting to note the price of tickets.

> 1873, February 6 – P RR tickets – I bought 25 trips for $19.90.
>
> February 14 – Chas. A. Kincaid 2 Glencoe RR tickets for $1.65.[8]

In 1893 there were various types of tickets available between St. Louis and Union on the St. Louis, Kansas City & Colorado RR.

- Regular single trip tickets
- Working Man's single trip ticket
- Round trip tickets
- 10 ride Visitor's tickets
- 30 Ride Family tickets
- 50 Ride individual tickets
- 100 Ride individual tickets
- 44 Ride School tickets – Good for period covering the school term for which the ticket was sold.[9]

Railroad stop in front of the St. Albans Store. Also from Theodore Link's scrapbook, courtesy Theodore C. Link, Jr.

In 1896, the Rock Island RR began expansion; St. Louis to Union and west. Charles Becker helped with construction. Men often ate at Becker's home—20¢ a meal. Some executives stayed overnight. The railroad track was completed to Union in 1900 and a big celebration was held in Union when the first train arrived.[10]

The Rock Island stops at St. Albans in the 1920's. Courtesy Mae Head.

In the 1920's there were a number of boxcars along the tracks for workers at St. Albans. The Pendletons, the Joneses and the Smiths were some of those living there. Mr. Smith was in charge of the work; Alonzo Pendleton was night watchman for the railroad, and Lewis Jones was Section Foreman for the Rock Island RR. Lewis Jones lived in the old section house just beyond the stone barn.[11] At this same time, there was a Rock Island RR Station at St. Albans with regularly scheduled stops. Many St. Louisans used the train to go out to St. Albans. This was discontinued about 1948 or 1949.

When we lived at St. Albans, the Rock Island RR used the line. There were no longer regular stops or even the station. The Southern Pacific and Cottonbelt replaced the Rock Island. One of the principal users of the line was the Union Electric Plant at Labadie. Carloads of coal were shipped from southern Illinois to operate the plant. There were two lines carrying coal to the Labadie plant: one from Gray's Summit and the other passed through St. Albans. The first train through for Union Electric had 100 cars of coal and six engines; shipped on the Southern Pacific & Cottonbelt. There were two or three coal trains a week.

After the flood of 1903, St. Albans was no longer on the river and boats did not stop there. The building of the railroad was an important development for the community. Freight and passenger trains were vital to the area but today only an occasional train goes through. Goods are trucked out and people commute to the city by car.

FOOTNOTES

1. Becker, Francis, "Day Book."
2. Bauer, Hazel Meier, *A Family History*, p. 34.
3. Franklin County Records Book 30, p.21.
4. Bauer, op cit.
5. Franklin County Records Book 69, p. 189.
6. Campbell, Ruth Horn, Becker family papers.
7. Mae Loraine Head.
8. Becker's "Day Book."
9. — "Schedule of Suburban Trains and Communication Rates" sent to me by Dr. William D. Small.
10. Campbell, op cit.
11. He came to St. Albans from Meta, Mo., about 1921. His son Dempsey Jones was born in 1923, at St. Albans and later married Virginia Pendleton, Alonzo's daughter, also of St. Albans. Interview with Virginia Pendleton Jones.

CHAPTER FIFTEEN

Participation in Wars

The first war involving the United States after 1837, when St. Albans was founded, was the Mexican War in 1846. There is no record of anyone living in St. Albans having taken part in this conflict.

The Civil War

In the Civil War, 1861–64, Franklin County as a whole was in comparative peace except for Price's Raid made in 1864. General Sterling Price was a native of Virginia, but became a Missourian by adoption. He served Missouri in the Mexican War and later became Governor of the State. At the outbreak of the Civil War, he was placed in command of the State troops and from that time to the end of the war was the military leader of the Confederates in Missouri.[1]

General Price was a Secessionist. His army consisted of about 10,000 to 16,000 men well armed and equipped. He hoped to revolutionize Missouri again and re-establish the Confederate State Government. General Price's army entered Franklin County September 30 and remained in the county until October 4. On October 1, he took over Pacific, burning bridges, supply depots, the railroad depot and buildings. On October 2, he moved on towards Union and Washington.[2]

The German people living in St. Albans had come to America because they considered the Federal Union as the best form of government where there was real freedom. They were, in principle, opposed to slavery and anything connected with it. They could not be anything other than Unionists. Therefore, when Price's army came through they were the ones he sought out and whose property was looted. Fortunately there were a number of Indian caves in the area the location of which was unknown to outsiders. It was in these caves that they sought refuge. There is a large cave, now covered over by the building of Highway T, on the old Hausgen property which was used to store trunks filled with valuables, guns and ammunition. Between St. Albans and Labadie is the "Grand Army Road" where Price's army passed through.

Robert Kincaid at 18 years of age, in 1861 at the outbreak of the Civil War. Private collection.

There were the Missouri Volunteers under Capt. Christian Idel, Company D of the Battalion of U.S.R. Corps of Missouri Volunteers, Army of the U.S., Major Wm. C. Iaks commanding from the ninth (9) day of June 1861, when last mustered to the — day of September 1861.[3] Frederick Steines organized a company of Home Guards known as the Steines Company.

Steines Company

Barthold, Christian, Pvt.	Mottert, Chas. Sr.
Breuer, Albert, "	Niesen, William
Breuer, Charles, "	Muller, Wm.
Grah, Gustav, "	Ossenforth, Henry
Hardt, Christian, Sgt.	Paffrath, Charles, Sgt.
Haug, Wm., 2 Lt.	Paffrath, Henry
Heipertz, August	Paubel, Valentine
Henke, Henry	Paubel, Veit
Hoerle, Gustav	Pauls, Ferdinand, Corp.
Heynemann, John	Pauls, Ferdinand, Jr.
Hostermann, William	Scanty, Wm.
Kochs, John	Schmitz, Chas.
Kochs, William	Steines, Frederick, Lt.
Kochs, Florence	Steines, Herman, Corp.
Kregenkamp, Clamor	Thiebes, Nicholas
Kregenkamp, Herman	Uhert, Henry
Kregenkamp, Jost	Winkeloh, Christian
McDonald, James Alfred	Zitzmann, George

Other Unionists soldiers in the vicinity

Alt, Christopher, Oakfield, P.H.G. (Pacific Home Guard)
Alt, Michael, Oakfield, Mo. Inf.
Alt, Henry, Oakfield, Mo. Inf.
Becker, Francis, Oakfield, Sgt. P.H.G.
Bohres, Herman., Oakfield, P.H.G.
Berthold, Frederick Wm., St. Albans, Mo. Inf.
Brensing, Henry, Mo. Inf.
Grauer, Gustav, P.H.G.
Grauer, Gottleib, P.H.G.
Grauer, Louis, P.H.G.
Hartman, Chas. F., St. Albans, Lt., Mo. Inf.
Hausgen, Gustav, LT., P.H.G.
Hoerle, Justus, P.H.G.
Kincaid, Robert, St. Albans, Mo. Inf.
Kincaid, Chas. A., St. Albans, Corp. P.H.G.
Kochs, Albert, P.H.G.
Kochs, Henry, Mus. P.H.G.
Lenz, Robert, P.H.G.
Pfeiffer, Charles, E.M.M.
Pohlig, John Wm., P.H.G.
Pohlig, Julius Sr., Mo. Inf.
Rosenbaum, Henry, P.H.G.
Rosenbaum, Wm., E.M.M.

TO ALL WHOM IT MAY CONCERN:

Know ye, That, under the provisions of the Act of Congress approved May 15th, 1886, Gustav Hausgen a 1st Lieutenant, Co. "D", Pacific Battalion, Missouri Home Guards, Volunteers, who was enrolled June 9th, 1861, is hereby discharged the service of the United States to date September 18th, 1861

Given at Washington City, this 7th day of June, 1890.

MAY 28 1891

By authority of the Secretary of War:

Capt. & Asst. Surg. U.S.A.

Record of Union Army discharge for Gustav Hausgen.

Scheer, Oscar J., P.H.G.
Schueddig, Chas. E., P.H.G.
Stettes, William D., P.H.G.
Stricker, Adolph, P.H.G.
Stricker, Gustav, Surgeon
Vollmer, Ferdinand, P.H.G.

Missouri Home Guard

Company C, 4th Missouri Infantry
Bick, Bernard, May 29, 1861 to July 3, 1861

Company D, Pacific Battalion
Hausgen, Gustav, 1st Lieutenant
June 9, 1861 to September 18, 1861

Spanish American War

No soldiers from St. Albans are listed in Kiel's Directory for participation in the War with Spain in 1898. However, at right is a photograph of Howard Kincaid, son of Charles, in his uniform of the Spanish-American War.[4]

Howard Kincaid, son of Charles, at 19 years of age, in uniform for the Spanish-American War. Private collection.

World War I

Kiel lists the following for World War I:

Active American participation April 6, 1917 to November 11, 1918.

Army:	Bowler, Clifton A.
	Brown, Fred S.
	Pfeiffer, Chas.
	Krausch, Ulmont
Navy:	Maher, Harry
	Maher, James S.

No Marines

No Nurses

Harry and James Maher. Courtesy of the Steines family.

"First Call for World War I, 1917." Front row, l to r: Allen Ried, unknown, Rich Mueller, Johnny Iman. Top row, left to right: Emil Schultz, unknown, Julius Gabbin, Francis Kissing, unknown. Courtesy of Louise Stettes.

World War II

In World War II there were not many young men living at St. Albans. Those working at St. Albans Farms were exempt from service. Those whose records I found were the following:

Joseph Calvin, Electrician's Mate 1st Class.

Forest Francis Krausch, 7th Fleet, U.S. Navy, South Pacific. Awarded: American Area Ribbon, Asiatic Pacific Ribbon, 6 Star Philippine Liberation Ribbon, 1 Star Purple Heart.

Raymond E. Meier, Army. 29th Div. British and European Theater.

Military Registrants not in Martial Services

Alt, Christian	Mathews, James A.
Alt, Daniel	O'Brien, James
Alt, Edmund C.	Pennington, Loran
Alt, Michael	Pfeiffer, Frank
Beckerath, Wm.	Pfeiffer, John W.
Beier, Jos.	Pillmann, Geo. W.
Brown, George	Pohlig, Benjamin
Douglass, Daniel	Pohlig, Otto
Gilcrease, Anton E.	Schalk, Martin A.
Grauer, Wm.	Schueddig, Chas.
Halback, Richard	Seymore, Robt.
Hensler, Russel E.	Smith, Ralph A.
Isler, Wm. J.	Stovall, Chas. J.
Kissing, Louis	Strecker, Harry J.
Kreienkamp, Fred	Stricker, Chas.
Kulpter, John	Wilkenich, Lawrence A.
Lehmann, Geo.	

Post World War II

Gene Stettes, Army Reserve, 1958-1964.
Edward Schoelich, Army Reserve, Korean War.
Edward Schoelich, Infantry, 13 months.

FOOTNOTES

1. "How Missouri Commemorated," *Missouri Historical Review*, Vol. XVI October 1921, No. 1, p. 37.
2. "Rebel Raid Here 100 Years Ago," by Jack Shultz, Managing Editor, *Meramec Valley Transcript*, October 7, 1964, Second Section, p.1B.
3. *The Centennial Biographical Directory of Franklin County, Missouri*, compiled and published by Herman Gottlieb Kiel, 1925, pp. 112-136.
4. Photograph taken by C.F. Wheeler, Pendleton, Ore.

Photograph of St. Albans by Oscar Johnson, Jr. in the 1930's. Detail below. Ken Gilberg collection.

CHAPTER SIXTEEN

Theodore C. Link II

Who was Ted Link? "Suave and handsome with dark features that advertised his Cabanne ancestry, Link was probably the closest thing St. Louis ever had to a TV-type private eye...In his investigations Link could be capable, intelligent, courteous and most diligent (according to Verle W. Stafford, special prosecutor at Peoria), or when those methods failed he could be damned tough."[1]

Ted Link hadn't started with the idea of becoming a criminal investigator or even a newspaper man. In the beginning he wanted to be an architect, to emulate the grandfather for whom he had been named, the man who designed Union Station. Theodore C. Link, the architect, was Ted's hero.[2]

In the early 1920s he was a traveling salesman selling stoves on the road in Michigan and Indiana. He occasionally managed night courses in architecture at Washington University, St. Louis. Then one day he met Frank Sullivan who made newspaper work sound quite glamorous. He had found his calling. He was hired in 1924 by the *St. Louis Star* to run copy for Harry Brundidge, the *Star's* crime reporter. In time he became "legman" for Brundidge checking details of investigations. It was valuable experience and he developed the instinct of a policeman. He got along well with policemen. He had access to inside information in many police departments and in investigative arms of state and federal governments.[3]

Ted got his information anywhere he could, never sharing it with any other reporter. His job was dangerous and often life threatening. I remember his story about one time in a Chicago hotel he answered his bedroom doorbell, to find a man pointing a gun at him. He usually had a dog with him for protection, and this time the dog probably saved his life. He was renowned for his work with the Shelton Gang of Southern Illinois. Active until his death in 1974, he looked the part of a crime reporter of a generation earlier, wearing a broad-brimmed felt hat and wide trousers.

Ted Link II looks on as a highway patrolman looks for evidence. Time *magazine, July 15, 1960.*

Ted joined the staff of the *St. Louis Post-Dispatch* in 1938. He joined the Marine Corps in 1942, as a sergeant and combat correspondent. He served on Guadalcanal, New Georgia, Guam and Bougainville, where he was wounded in 1943.[4] As the *Post-Dispatch's* tough, tireless crime reporter for more than 20 years, Ted Link had coolly padded through the back alleys of the underworld, and probably written more about crime than any other U.S. newsman.

On July 11, 1960, violence was reporter Ted Link's companion. This time it was his doing.[5] Here is the story...

Ted Link was summoned home to St. Louis from New York Friday, July 8, 1960, by a telephone call informing him that his country home at St. Albans had burned to the ground. He returned home the next day and for two days looked for his part-time worker, Clarence Calvin.

Clarence Calvin, 38, lived with his parents about two miles from Link's place at St. Albans. In March, 1960, Link had hired him as a caretaker two days a week. Prior to that time, guns, food, etc., had been taken from Ted's place. Clarence had a reputation as a roughneck. Sheriff Bill Miller was often called to St. Albans to take Clarence into custody for disturbance of the peace, drunkenness and disorderly conduct. At this time, he was released on probation for having threatened to kill his father, William Calvin. Link said he hired him because he knew him to be a troublemaker and thought the work would keep him from bothering others.

On Sunday night, Ted finally reached Clarence by telephone. He fired him and told him to stay off the property. Ted believed the fire had been set deliberately, and he wanted to question Clarence about it.[6]

The next morning, Ted and his 11-year-old son, Theodore C. Link, Jr., drove out to St. Albans, stopping at a hardware store in Grover to buy a 12-gauge shotgun and some ammunition. He was "afraid" of Calvin and felt he had to protect himself. "I knew somebody down here didn't like me," he explained, and he purchased the gun "to protect myself from being ambushed by anybody." His son said he too carried a shotgun—a .410 gauge model—because he "just wanted to carry it - - - Dad said we might run into trouble."[7]

When they arrived at their place, they found Clarence Calvin digging in the ashes with a three-pronged garden tool. While they were sitting at a picnic table discussing the fire and early burglary, Ted accused him of setting the fire. "You did it."

"I didn't do it," Clarence shouted back.

Later Link testified that "Clarence suddenly became mad. He jumped up with a terrible expression, the three-pronged hoe in one hand and reaching into his pocket with the other, coming toward me. He came at me with the knife and the hoe, and I ran for my shotgun, which was propped against a tree. I yelled to my son to run. My first shot with the shotgun, from about 20 feet, struck Calvin in the abdomen. He kept coming and I fired again. He was still on his feet and I shot him three times with a .38-caliber revolver I drew from my pocket."[8]

Link sent his son to the home of a neighbor, who arrived a few minutes later. He and the neighbor went to the home of Calvin Steffens, about one mile away, where Link telephoned Sheriff Miller and the Highway Patrol and reported that he had shot Calvin, who appeared to be dead.[9] Link surrendered his guns to the sheriff.

The switchblade knife, found at Clarence's right side, was identified by Link as one taken from his place in a burglary the previous February.

Authorities Monday night reported that an 11-year-old neighbor boy stated he was with Calvin when he set fire to the house about 3 p.m. Friday. He stated that Clarence took him to the Link's house to get a drink of water. He said Clarence went into the shed and obtained a can full of kerosene and carried it to the house. Then he went into the house and got a candle. He poured the kerosene on the back steps, placed the candle under the steps, lit it, and the two walked away. The can was located near the scene late Monday.[10]

A Coroner's jury convened Tuesday, July 12, in the Circuit Court room in the courthouse at Union at 2:15 p.m. and after hearing the testimony, deliberated 40 minutes before bringing its verdict at 6:45 p.m.

Dr. H.D. Steinbeck, Franklin County Coroner, stated that Calvin received two shotgun wounds in the abdomen, and bullet wounds in the left arm, left temple and on the right side of the skull. The temple wound caused Mr. Calvin's death.

Ted's son was witness to the shooting. He said his father fired the first shot while Calvin was sitting at the picnic table, and the last three as he lay on the ground. He said he never saw a knife.

A verdict of "homicide by gunshot wounds by a .38-caliber pistol by Theodore C. Link, Sr." was returned.[11]

An arrest order was issued Wednesday night, July 13, when Link failed to surrender on a warrant is-

Farm Hand Dies In 2-Gun Blast By Ted Link

Post-Dispatch Crime Reporter Says Laborer Threatened Him

Ted Link Charged With First-Degree Murder

Jury Indicts Post-Dispatch Crime Writer

$25,000 Bond Set; Reporter Held at Union

Theodore C. Link Sr., Post-Dispatch crime reporter, was indicted Wednesday on a first-degree murder charge in the shotgun and revolver slaying of a farm hand July 11.

A Franklin County grand jury

THEODORE LINK IS RELEASED ON $25,000 BOND

Ted Link's Arrest Ordered in Slaying

Fails to Surrender on Warrant Charging Him With Homicide

Link murder trial before jury today; Death penalty asked in July shooting

Link Is Acquitted of Murder Charge by Gasconade County Jury

The Link story was big news at the time. Clippings are from the St. Louis Post-Dispatch, St. Louis Globe-Democrat, Washington Missourian *and* Meramec Valley Transcript.

sued by Franklin County Magistrate R.H. Schaper, charging him with homicide in the shooting of Clarence Calvin. Bond was set at $10,000.[12]

Franklin County Prosecutor Charles Hansen said that he was dissatisfied with the discrepancy between accounts of father and son. The case would go before a grand jury where Link could be indicted for murder.

On Wednesday, July 27, the Franklin County grand jury at Union, returned the indictment. Circuit Judge Joseph T. Tate set bond at $25,000 and Link was held in the County Jail at Union. Link was released July 28, on the $25,000 bond signed by 17 land owners from the St. Albans area, 15 of whom had signed the previous $10,000 bond. Arraignment was set for September 6, when the bond would be returnable. The case was taken to Hermann on a change of venue before Judge Tate.

The Link murder trial opened January 16, 1961, at Hermann, Mo., before Judge Joseph T. Tate. After selection of jurors, Henry Morris, Link's attorney, on Wednesday morning in his opening statement to the all-male jury, said the Defense would prove that Link shot and killed Clarence Calvin in self-defense last July 11 at the Link's summer home on the Missouri River bluff, east of Labadie. The State was trying Link on a first degree murder charge and asked for the death penalty.[13]

Witnesses for the prosecution were Dr. H.D. Steinbeck, Franklin County Coroner; Sheriff H. Bill Miller, Franklin County; Lt. V.E. Maxey, State Highway Patrol. Several other witnesses were called but all were excused. Charles Hansen, former Prosecuting Attorney of Franklin County, assisted by Charles Moll, newly elected Prosecuting Attorney; Fred L. Howard, assistant Attorney General for Missouri, and Randolph E. Puchta, Gasconade County Prosecuting Attorney, represented the State. The State's testimony consisted almost entirely of the testimony at the coroner's inquest in Union after the shooting.[14]

The Defense was represented by Henry Morris, St. Louis attorney; W.H. Wessel, Hermann attorney; James C. Porter of St. Louis, Frank Jenny of Union and Theodore Link. The Defense called to witness the following neighbors living at St. Albans: Marion "Butch" Thiebes, Albert Schlake, Mr. and Mrs. Clyde Head, Judge Randolph Shaper, James W. Scott, George Gaehle, Alfred Stricker, Mrs. Marion Thiebes, Mrs. Erna Schlake, Alfred Reed and Ulmont Krausch. The Defense based its case on self-defense and justifiable killing, contending Link feared for his own safety and that of his 11-year-old son. The point stressed to the jury in the closing defense argument by William Wessel was that the jurors would have done the same act under the same set of circumstances.[15]

The jury took only one vote.

The verdict: "Not guilty."[16]

FOOTNOTES

1. Baldwin, Carl R., "Underworld, Politics Were This Reporter's Beat," article, *St. Louis Post-Dispatch*, February 28, 1974, p. 4D.
2. Ibid.
3. Ibid.
4. "Theodore Link Shoots, Wounds Man At Home," article, *St. Louis Post-Dispatch*, July 11, 1960, p.1A.
5. "The Constant Companion," article, *Time Magazine*, July 15, 1960, p. 60.
6. "Fatal Shooting by Ted Link Will go to Grand Jury," article, *St. Louis Globe-Democrat*, July 13, 1960, p. 1A.
7. Ibid, p. 6A.
8. "Shooting Victim Had Set Fire to Home, Boy Says," article, *St. Louis Post-Dispatch*, July 12, 1960, p. 3A.
9. Ibid.
10. Ibid.
11. "Theodore Link is Charged with Homicide," article, *St. Louis Post-Dispatch*, July 13, 1960, p. 1A.
12. "Ted Link's Arrest Ordered in Slaying," article, *St. Louis Globe-Democrat*, July 14, 1960, p. 1A.
13. "Defense Begins in Link Murder Trial," article, *Washington Missourian*, Washington, Mo., January 19, 1961, p. 1A-2A.
14. Ibid.
15. "Link is Acquitted of Murder Charge by Gasconade County Jury," article, *Washington Citizen*, Washington, Mo., January 23, 1961, p. 1A.
16. Ibid.

CHAPTER SEVENTEEN

St. Albans Today

"Sale Completed of 5,280 Acres in St. Albans"

The sale of St. Albans Farms to a group of investors marked one of the largest land transactions in Franklin County. The St. Albans Partners was the name of the group of investors involved in the purchase: Dan Devereux, president, Devereux Company; David Kolb, president, Kolb Grading, Inc.; Dennis McDaniel, principal shareholder, Capital Bank Corporation; Michael Ross, CEO Capital Bank Corporation; Joseph Pottebaum, president and CEO, Capital Properties; and Bill Taylor, president, Taylor Excavating.[1] Anthony Novelly of Apex Oil Company was the power behind it all.[2]

The asking price for the property, which comprised the farms of the Oscar and James Lee Johnson estate, was $12 million. Mr. Pottebaum refused to say how much he and his partners paid for the property. Mr. Devereux said the price was higher than the $8 million price tag which appeared in published reports.[3]

> The tract of land is located in Franklin, St. Louis and St. Charles counties. Included in the sale are 22 frame houses, a post office, a stone dairy barn, a hunting lodge, the Wings of St. Albans and many acres of Missouri River bottom land.[4]

The St. Albans Land Development Company was formed for the development of the property. Mr. Tom Patton, vice-president of Bos Group, Destin, Florida, was hired by St. Albans Partners to coordinate creation of the St. Albans community.[5] Plans included fine dining (Malmaison), riding, biking, hiking trails, tennis, swimming, a polo field, a hunt club (Wings), an equestrian center and a shopping center, as well as two 18-hole golf courses and a clubhouse, and homes.

In 1990, St. Albans Partners tried to get exclusive use of the road that loops through the property from Highway T. They wanted to put a guard station at each end of the road to control access of nonresidents. My son, Bernard, his wife and I attended the town meeting that called for discussion of this matter. The town meeting voted against it so the Franklin County Commission rejected it. They also rejected the developers' request to rezone 2466 of the 5000 acres to community development status from agricultural. Residents collected more than 200 signatures in opposition to the rezoning. Instead the developers must get conditional-use permits for each stage of the development that does not adhere to existing zoning.[6]

At the time of purchase, the St. Albans Partners had no immediate plans for development. Mr. Devereux told reporters, "We purchased the property as a long-range investment. We have no immediate plans, other than some improvements, to develop the land. Anything is possible, but to speculate right now on any development opportunities is premature." He said that the group of investors was attracted to the land because of the beautiful landscape and the historical background of the area. He confirmed that the group was looking at a number of recreational development projects, including proposals for small lakes and a golf course.[7]

It so happened that at this time Cherry Hills Country Club, located in Grover, was looking for a new home or to buy land adjacent to theirs. Dr. David Wallington, president of Cherry Hills Country Club, said their golf course was in excellent condition, but their clubhouse was not up to the standards of other country clubs in the St. Louis area. Cherry Hills Country Club and St. Albans Partners merged to form the Country Club of St. Albans in 1989. Cherry Hills Country Club became the

A bird's eye view of St. Albans today, showing part of the golf courses, some homes and the Clubhouse, upper right. Photo courtesy St. Albans Properties, L.L.C.

nucleus of the new 320-acre country club at St. Albans; their members became the charter members of the Country Club of St. Albans.[8] Mr. Paul Kopsky was the first president and Mr. Tom Elliot the first club and food services manager.[9]

Two 18-hole golf courses were planned. The first course was designed by the world renowned golf architectural team of Tom Weiskopf and Jay Morrish. The clubhouse was designed by the Dallas-based clubhouse architect Irv Schwartz; constructed by CMR Construction, Inc. of St. Louis; Timber Craft Custom Builders of St. Louis created the timber framing for Builtbest Enterprises, also of St. Louis, the interior finish contractor.[10]

The Grand Opening of the first course was April 24, 1993. Both Tom Weiskopf and Jay Morrish gave a play-by-play demonstration of how to play each hole and why they built the course the way they did.[11]

The second 18-hole course began construction in 1996. It was designed by another world famous golf course architect, Dr. Michael Hardza. It was officially opened July 2, 1997. The two courses were named "Lewis and Clark" and "Tavern Creek."

Near the stone barn on Tavern Road was *Cedarlane Farm*, known as the Bonner Place. It was originally homesteaded by John William Kierspe (1808–1869) and his wife Henrietta (1809–1861); both emigrated from Germany. Their daughter Henrietta (1838–1912) married Bernard Bick (1841–1902) in 1864.

Bernard Bick was the son of Daniel Bick who left Cologne, Germany, in 1856 with Carl Schatz to visit a cousin living in St. Albans, Missouri. They traveled from Cologne to New York City, to New Orleans, up the Mississippi River to St. Louis, thence to St. Albans. Daniel's two sons, Charles and Bernard, followed in 1857. According to the census of 1880, Henrietta and Bernard had eight children: Henry, Charles, Bertha, George, Lena, Bernard Jr., Emma, Willie and Daniel. Bernard had been trained in Germany to be a cutlery man, so in 1878 he opened a cutlery business in St. Albans.

Bernard Bick received the land from the Kierspe family. This was in turn passed on to the heirs through Lena, second daughter of Bernard and Henrietta. Lena married Henry Bonner. Henry Bonner sold all but ten acres of the Kierspe property to the Johnsons, who were promised the remaining land on the death of Lena Bick Bonner. She died in 1956, but the Johnsons missed her death notice, so the land was put up for auction two years later. Mabel Bick, daughter of Charles Bick (1866–1953) and his wife Nellie Reddein (1887–1952), granddaughter of Bernard and Henrietta Bick, bought the property in 1958. She was able to outbid the Johnsons through an open-end loan given her by her Uncle Rickland, owner and president of the Bank of Cuba, Mo. Mabel was married to Gene Keyes, divorced, and took back her maiden name, Bick.[12]

Mabel Bick died in 1977, leaving the bulk of her estate to William Rosenburg, an old friend from St. Louis. She specified that he could live on the farm for the rest of his life; upon his death the property would go to the Salvation Army for a rest home or children's camp. She also specified that the property was "never to be sold."

In 1992, the Salvation Army decided that a rest home or a children's camp was not feasible and sold its rights to the St. Albans Development company for $10,000. In 1995, Rosenburg and his wife, Jewel, sold their rights for $35,000. Four Bick cousins went to court arguing that the failure of the Salvation Army to carry out Mabel Bick's wishes meant the ten acres reverted to her relatives. The property had been owned by the family for 160 years. The judges finally ruled in favor of the developers because, they said, the cousins were never mentioned in the will.[13] The house was torn down, and the land became part of the second golf course.

Joseph Pottebaum was named in charge of sales. He lived in the "Wings" for six months while the "Village Green," a stone house built in the 1930's for the Farm manager, was being remodeled, In the 1950's the "Village Green" was used as a community library and later rented for private use. It was called "Village Green" because of the ivy covering the house.[14]

A primary concern in planning the roads and placement of the houses was the preservation of the natural beauty of St. Albans. Tim Kloeppell of Volz Engineering and Surveying, the firm that plotted the road network to minimize destruction of trees, stated the goal of the enterprise was "that it all flow together so it looks like a park with houses in it." There are pages of restrictions for building, including 70 percent of the existing trees on a homesite must be preserved; a buffer of existing forest must visibly screen the house from the roadway; and exteriors of the homes must be 60 percent stone or brick on all four sides.[15]

Five residential areas were set out: The Cedar Valley, The Bluffs, The Hunt Club, The Highlands and The Villages of St. Albans. Bay Hill Development Company and Kelly Residential Group were selected to build two display homes. These houses were specially designed to reflect the rural, casual, yet sophisticated atmosphere of St. Albans. The plans call for 1200 luxury homesites. In addition to Bay Hill Development Company and Kelly Residential Group, DeShetler Homes and Rooney Designer Homes are the firms building the homes.[16] Twenty

"The Studio," former home of Mr. and Mrs. Oscar Johnson, Jr. is now used as a conference center. Photo courtesy St. Albans Properties, L.L.C.

European-style cottages will be constructed around the golf course by Timbercrest Corporation. In the Village of St. Albans, 14 Victorian-styled homes are being built by St. Albans Construction Company.[17]

"The Studio," former home of Mr. and Mrs. Oscar Johnson, Jr., was renovated to make a conference center or bed and breakfast. It is used for corporate retreats, rehearsal dinners, weddings and other private parties. There are six double bedrooms. The Studio can accommodate 120 guests inside and at least 200 others in an adjoining tent outside.[18]

The "Wings" was the home of Mr. and Mrs. James Lee Johnson. It is a private hunt club from October to April, but for the rest of the year is available for the same types of events as the Studio. It also has six bedrooms and can accommodate 60 guests inside and as many as 300 outside.[19] It is situated on one of the highest bluffs in Franklin County. Looking down from there you can almost see Lewis and Clark paddling up the river.

FOOTNOTES

1. "Sale Completed of 5,280 Acres in St. Albans Area," by Bill Miller, Jr., *Washington Missourian*, Weekend, April 16, 1988.
2. Jerry Berger, Everyday, *St. Louis Post-Dispatch*, December 5, 1991.
3. "At Home," by Carolyn Olson, *St. Louis Post-Dispatch*, Real Estate, Section E, Friday, February 16, 1990.
4. "Partnership to develop community," Daniel J. Kadlec, editor, *St. Louis Sun*, Money, Monday, October 23, 1989.
5. "St. Albans," by Dan Holman, *St. Louis Post-Dispatch*, West Metro Post, Section W, Thursday, June 21, 1990.
6. Ibid.
7. "Two 18-Hole Golf Courses to be Built at St. Albans," *The Missourian Business News*, Weekend November 18-19, 1989, p. 5A.
8. "Spring Comes to St. Albans," by Ann Sullivan, *Seen*, April 1993, p. 30-36.
9. "St. Albans," by Steve Givens, *St. Louis Business Journal*, October 7-13, 1991, Section D.
10. Ibid.
11. *Seen*, op cit, p. 36.
12. Family history sent to me in 1981 by Bernard M. Brown, a cousin and historian, living in Sullivan, Mo.
13. *St. Louis Post-Dispatch*, April 12, 1997, p. 16.
14. *St. Louis Post-Dispatch*, p cit, February 16, 1990.
15. "St. Albans," insert prepared by St. Albans Land Development, Stories by Roger McGrath, *St. Louis Post-Dispatch.*
16. "St. Albans, A Special Setting," cover story, by Shirley Althoff, *Ladue News*, May 20, 1994, p. 11.
17. Ibid.
18. Ibid.
19. Ibid.

CHAPTER EIGHTEEN

Tavern Cave Today

The St. Albans area's place in history was established in 1804 when the Lewis and Clark Expedition visited the Tavern Cave on their way west.

The cave had been hidden from historians because of the topographical changes. Formerly, the cave was right on the bank of the river, but after the flood of 1903, the U.S. Engineer Corps changed the channel of the Missouri River, and earth filled in on the south bank. Ben Pohlig told me he remembered standing with his father on the cliffs above and seeing the Mordack house falling into the raging river. The cave is now several hundred feet from the water and fills at flood time, leaving more deposit, until today there are large trees and a high mound of earth in front of the opening.

Lucie Huger and Gerald Snyder inside Tavern Cave. Photo by Robert la Rouche.

We heard about Tavern Cave from Ben Pohlig and others down at Head's Store. My family and I walked down to see this cave several times in the 1950's. To get there, we had to walk a mile and three quarters, east, on the railroad tracks. The cave is quite inaccessible, and we had to slide down a steep embankment to find it. It was necessary to tie a rope around a sapling to help you down and up. The cave is located to the right. It has a large opening and at that time, there was a mound of earth in front of it. We measured the opening and examined the walls, finding Indian drawings of birds and beasts and inscriptions left by John Ordway, a member of the Lewis and Clark Expedition and Dr. Peter Kincaid, founder of St. Albans. The words, "ORD, 1804" and "KINCAID 1835" were easily legible. Today the Indian drawings are no longer visible; just daubs of paint. But the names "ORD(way) 1804" and "KINCAID, 1835" can still be seen.

The author in Tavern Cave, pointing to the inscription "ORD 1804." Sgt. John Ordway, member of the Lewis and Clark Expedition, undoubtedly left his mark here May 23, 1804. Photo collection.

In 1968, Professor Ralph P. Bieber of Washington University, St. Louis, visited the cave and found names on the wall. He, too, had been told of the existence of the cave by Ben Pohlig. He claimed to have discovered Tavern Cave. I assume the existence of the Cave was only locally known. Professor Bieber came to St. Albans with a *Post-Dispatch* photographer and reporter who featured it in an article entitled, "Where Meriwether Lewis Slipped."[1]

On the tracks from Tavern Cave. Gerald Snyder of National Geographic, *son Danny on his shoulders, Lucie Huger Reis beside them, Carl Reis and Mary Huger behind. Photo by Robert la Rouche.*

In 1969, Gerald S. Snyder of the National

Geographic Society, Special Publications Division, was assigned to write a book about the Lewis and Clark Expedition. He and his wife, Arlette, and two young children, Michele and Danny, retraced the route of the Expedition. They visited the sites at the same time of year as the Expedition, experiencing the severe temperature fluctuations. He contacted me to arrange a visit to Tavern Cave. On Easter Sunday, 1969, my husband and I and our daughters Mary, Cindy and Lucie and her husband Carl Reis; Gerry Snyder and family, and *Post-Dispatch* photographer Robert la Rouche and his son, trekked down the railroad track to the cave. Gerry was thrilled to explore the cave and see the cliffs above it and find them relatively untouched since Lewis and Clark's visit.

The account of his visit is included in his book, *In The Footsteps of Lewis and Clark.*[2] I called Professor Bieber on March 29, 1970, to verify his visit for inclusion in Mr. Snyder's book when I received the galley sheets from the National Geographic Society. He asked if this were fiction or history. I stressed that Sgt. Ordway was a well known member of the Expedition and we saw "ORD 1804" on the wall of the cave. Dr. Bieber told me he had added "WAY" in chalk to "ORD," making it "ORDWAY."

I have been fascinated by the presence of such an important historic site existing in relative obscurity in the vicinity of St. Albans. I felt it was important to make this known to the general public as well as to preserve it. As a member of the Cornelia Greene Chapter of the Daughters of the American Revolution, I felt acknowledging the historical significance of Tavern Cave was in line with their objectives.

On October 24, 1971, the Cornelia Greene Chapter erected a bronze marker in St. Albans, commemorating the visit of Lewis and Clark to the Tavern Cave and Cliffs. It was a lovely Fall day, and the whole neighborhood turned out for the ceremony. There were about 150 people. The Moolah Shrine Pipes and Drums furnished both music and color for the dedication.[3] This event was part of the celebration of the 200th anniversary of the United States and the 150th anniversary of the State of Missouri. The plaque reads as follows:

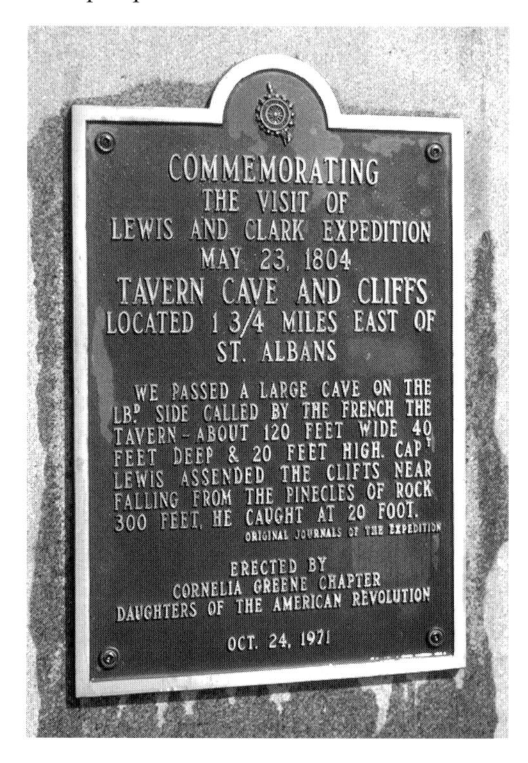

COMMEMORATING
The Visit of
LEWIS AND CLARK EXPEDITION
May 23, 1804
TAVERN CAVE AND CLIFFS
LOCATED 1 ¾ MILES EAST OF
ST. ALBANS

WE PASSED A LARGE CAVE ON THE
LBd SIDE CALLED BY THE FRENCH THE
TAVERN ABOUT 120 FEET WIDE 40
FEET DEEP AND 20 FEET HIGH, CAPt
LEWIS ASSENDED THE CLIFTS NEAR
FALLING FROM THE PINECLES OF ROCK
300 FEET. HE CAUGHT AT 20 FOOT
Original Journals of the Expedition

Erected By
Cornelia Greene Chapter
Daughters of the American Revolution
October 24, 1971

Tavern Cave in a photo taken about 1966 by Jack Zehrt for the National Geographic Society. The mound of dirt in front of the cave was left by the construction of the railroad tracks in the 1880's. The couple's identity is unknown.

Cynthian and Mary Huger unveil the commemorative plaque on October 24, 1971. Photo: Washington Missourian.

The dedication opened with an invocation by Mrs. Wade Smith, Vice Regent, Cornelia Greene Chapter; the National Anthem was led by Miss Helen Earickson, Cornelia Greene Chapter, and the Pledge of Allegiance was led by Mrs. Charles C. Barnett, Jr., State Regent, MSSDAR. Guests were welcomed by Mrs. Robert D. Fitch, Regent, Cornelia Greene Chapter, and, as chairman of the dedication and member of the Chapter, I introduced the special guests.

Gerald Snyder, guest speaker at the dedication. Photo: Washington Missourian.

Mr. Gerald Snyder was the guest speaker at the dedication. Lt. Governor William S. Morris, chairman of the Lewis and Clark Trail Committee of Missouri, presented Mrs. Wade Smith with a replica of the Thomas Jefferson Peace Medal. Lewis and Clark presented this medal to the Indian Chiefs on their journey to the northwest. Mrs. William H. Minderman, State Historian and member of the Chapter, unveiled the marker, assisted by my daughters Mary and Cynthian, both members of the Children of the American Revolution; Rev. Francis J. Yealy, S.J., St. Louis University, gave the benediction.[4]

There was a reception following the ceremonies at the Village Green, where members of the Chapter and Mr. Snyder greeted guests, including William Clark Adreon, great-great grandson of William Clark, and Harvey Colter, great-great-grandson of Pvt. John Colter, also of the Expedition. Mr. Snyder signed copies of his newly published book.

I would like to quote a few passages from Mr. Snyder's speech:

> This mysterious chamber was an important Lewis and Clark landmark. It was not mentioned on any modern-day maps. It had been rediscovered only about 17 years before, and it lay somewhere hundreds of feet from the river, not accessible by boat or road, its secrets still hidden behind a river-built bank of silt.

He quoted from the five journals kept on the expedition, then said:

> One thing we do know for sure, and that is that we have the right place, for the dimensions mentioned by all the journalists are the same and they exactly match those of the cave we know today. — When I left Tavern Cave and traveled West, I came to realize more and more the value of this great rock near St. Albans as one of the few genuine reminders left of the expedition. — In Montana, near the town of Whitehall, I did come across a cavern named Lewis and Clark, but the explorers never visited it. The true Lewis and Clark cavern was right here at St. Albans, Missouri.
>
> What is so sad is that there are so few physical reminders of the expedition left, and that is what makes this recognition of Tavern Cave by the Daughters of the American Revolution so meaningful. — Under the banner of progress,

> we have lost a great part of our heritage to the damming of rivers and the building of factories and huge industrial complexes along the way. — But nevertheless, the cave is a genuine reminder of the Lewis and Clark Expedition, a place, for those who take the time and the effort to visit it, where it still is possible to see the same kind of cliffs that Lewis and Clark saw when they passed by. — we still may not have put Tavern Cave on the map, but at least people passing by will now known something about its history. The Expedition of Lewis and Clark will always come alive here.

First day issue postal commemorative marked the 175th anniversary of the return of the Lewis and Clark Expedition to St. Louis, September 23, 1806.

For many years I have tried to save the Tavern Cave and Cliffs from oblivion. "Save the Cave" has been my motto.

On September 20, 1976, I presented a paper to the Missouri Lewis and Clark Trail State Committee, through the courtesy of a member of the committee, Gus Budde. I presented a paper giving the history of Tavern Cave. I wanted to see if they felt it was important to preserve the site and asked what could be done. They were very much in favor of doing something, and recommended that the owners be approached with the suggestion that it be listed in the Register of National Historic Landmarks. Land, so registered, remains the property of the owner, but with restrictions for its use, and necessary protection of the property.

The following week I drove to Union and met with Charles Hansen, president of the Hansen Franklin County Land, Title and Abstract Company. After studying the railroad right-of-way, Franklin County maps and abstract K-1736, he ascertained that the Tavern Cave and Cliffs were part of the Johnson Estate. The Railroad had only the right-of-way.

I wrote to Oscar Johnson, Jr. on November 5, 1976, to see if this could be done. Unfortunately, Mrs. Eloise Johnson was not well and my letter got misplaced. Several years later, I attempted to contact her again. At that time, Oscar was very sick and died soon after.

The Lewis and Clark Trail was authorized as part of the National Trail System by an Act of Congress in 1978.

On September 23, 1981, the Cornelia Greene Chapter rededicated the historical marker at St. Albans. The program was part of an all-day celebration in conjunction with the Missouri Historical Society. This marked the 175th anniversary of the return of the Lewis and Clark Expedition to St. Louis, September 23, 1806. Stephen O. Spaulding, a descendant of William Clark, placed a wreath at the marker. J. Terrell Vaughn, president of the Missouri Historical Society, presented First Day Issue cachets of a commemorative Lewis and Clark stamp to those taking part in the ceremony.

The First Day of Issue ceremonies were conducted that morning at the Missouri Historical Society by Gordon Morison, senior assistant Postmaster General. Special postal stations were set up in the loggia of the Jefferson Memorial Building for sales of the first day issue postal commemorative. The cachets had the program, post card and the following history:

> The U.S. Postal Service is proud to issue this commemorative postal card, which honors one of the most famous expeditions of exploration

> in U.S. history. The first overland expedition to the Pacific coast and back took place in 1804-06 under the leadership of Meriwether Lewis and William Clark. They followed the Missouri River from its junction with the Mississippi to its source and, crossing the continental divide, explored the Columbia River from its source to the Pacific Ocean.
>
> Preparations for the expedition were initiated by President Thomas Jefferson before the Louisiana Purchase of 1803, and his appointment of Captain Lewis as his private secretary in 1801 was probably with a view to preparing him for leadership of the expedition. Lieutenant Clark came from an old Virginia family. He was the younger brother of George Rogers Clark, who won fame in the American Revolution and who was the subject of an earlier commemorative postal card issued in 1979.
>
> Lewis and Clark, following President Jefferson's instruction, brought back a remarkable set of diaries which stand as some of the most interesting narratives of North American exploration in existence. The records provided a rich mine of information, much of it completely new at the time, and Lewis and Clark thus did much to open the West and to dispel ignorance about the region. The expedition returned to St. Louis on September 23, 1806.

In 1988, when St. Albans Farms was listed for sale, I renewed my quest to "Save the Cave." The property was purchased by a group called the St. Albans Partners. I met with Dan Devereux, one of the partners, in his office. We talked about the certification of Tavern Cave as part of the National Historic Trails. I left a file with him so that he could discuss it with the other partners. I never got my file back, and nothing came of the meeting at that time.

At the 1989 annual meeting of Lewis and Clark Trail Heritage Foundation in Bozeman, Montana, I met Rick Clark, president of the National Historic Trails. He said that they would like to certify the DAR marker at St. Albans rather than Tavern Cave itself, as the cave is practically inaccessible. He told me to work with Tom Gilbert, the Lewis and Clark Trail coordinator. I met with him and asked him to send information to Joe Pottebaum, partner in charge of development at St. Albans. Gilbert wrote to Pottebaum February 4, 1991, sending information, including the following:

> The purpose of a National Historic Trust is to identify and protect the historic route and its historic remnants for public use and enjoyment. There are few historic remnants of the Lewis and Clark Trail to protect; most of our activities are focused on sites where the story of the Lewis and Clark Expedition is told or can be told to the public.

I wrote to Anthony Novelly, senior partner, in October, 1991, requesting a meeting to discuss the certification. No response. Later in June 1994, Peter Bickford told me Mr. Novelly was not against the idea of a National Trail marker, but wanted to wait until the village was finished.

In 1993, when the Country Club of St. Albans was preparing for the Grand Opening of the first of two golf courses, Joe Pottebaum contacted me regarding naming the courses after Lewis and Clark. At that time he showed some interest in the marker dedication.

In early May 1995, I sent the history of Tavern Cave to Dr. Douglas K. Aiken, director of the Missouri Department of Natural Resources. I stressed the cave's importance to the history of Missouri and to the Lewis and Clark Expedition Bicentennial Celebration of 2004. Dr. Aiken and I had met in Ste. Genevieve at the ceremony for the transfer of title of the Amoureaux House. He wrote to me three weeks later, giving the following response:

> Thank you for your letter regarding Tavern Cave near St. Albans. In order to assess the potential for the cave as a possible state historic

site, two members of the staff of the Historic Sites Program visited the cave. At the time of their visit, the cave was filled with approximately four feet of water, and it was not possible for them to make a detailed examination of the walls of the cave.

Two main problems emerge as hurdles to such a proposition as you proposed [I asked them to clean up and preserve the site.] First, the cave clearly falls within the right-of-way of the Rock Island Railroad. As the grade passes over the cave, there is no way that the railroad would wish to dispose of this property as long as they retain ownership of the line. Second, the property is in a very remote setting. Even if the property were acquired, making the site accessible for public visitation would involve a huge capital outlay. We simply are not in any position to obligate ourselves to such an undertaking at this time.

In addition, the historic sites which we operate are acquired on the basis of the need to infill basic interpretive themes which are not currently represented in the state park system. The Lewis and Clark expedition is already interpreted at several parks and historic sites, and I do not believe it would be desirable to acquire an additional site when there are so many other needs.

I do not wish to convey the impression that we think that Tavern Cave is not an important site. Clearly, it is. However, not only are our finances limited in regard to such an undertaking, but the fact that the site is on railroad property makes it seem an unlikely candidate for inclusion in the system at this time.

I was very disappointed in not getting assistance from the State of Missouri. Yet, the Tavern Cave is listed as an historic site with the National Park Service.[5] Here is their description of Tavern Cave:

Tavern Cave, Missouri

Location: Franklin County, along the track of the Chicago, Rock Island, and Pacific Railroad about a mile from the nearest secondary road, some 2 miles northeast of St. Albans.

On May 23, 1804, or 2 days after leaving St. Charles on their westward trek, Clark and probably some other members of the expedition visited this large cave, located on the south bank of the Missouri at the base of a huge sandstone bluff called Tavern Rock. On the homeward trip, the explorers passed it on September 21, 1806.

Although they were the first men known to describe it, since long before their time, perhaps as early as the late 1770's, it had been a well-known landmark and had been utilized by French and Spanish trappers and traders as a shelter. Because they called it the "Taverne" (café or restaurant), some form of a rest stop or inn may have existed there to provide for the comforts of river travelers.

American fur traders visited the cave until the 1840's, as did also such notable Missouri River voyagers as John Bradbury (1809), Henry M. Brackenridge (1811), Surgeon John Gale (1818), and Prince Maxmillian of Wied (1832). From the earliest times, many visitors etched into the sandstone walls their names, dates, and other still-visible inscriptions. None of them, however, can be associated with any member of the Lewis and Clark Expedition.

The cave is now located about 250 feet from the Missouri, whereas at the beginning of the 19th century it was right at its edge. Today it is also about 20 feet less wide than in the early days because of the accumulation of land fill at the north and south ends. This fill apparently consists of debris from the present railroad bed, which is located about 60 feet above the level of the cave. An intermittent stream flows from its east wall. At the mouth of the cave is a huge mound. This likely resulted from repeated floodings of the Missouri and then dumping of refuse from the railroad bed.

The area directly surrounding the cave's entrance is covered with brush and trees. Beyond the river is swampland, apparently created by periodic river floodings and poor drainage. Tavern Rock once rose to a height of 300 feet, but blasting in modern times to form the railroad bed has transformed the bluff's configuration. The Chicago, Rock Island, and Pacific Railroad owns the cave site.

On October 1, 1997, the DAR marker was made part of the Lewis and Clark National Historic Trail. Mr. Ronald G. Laycock was the keynote speaker. Photo by Ken Gilberg.

I do not agree some of the statements in the listing. "Clark and probably some other members of the expedition visited this large cave." The wording "probably" is misleading. The cave is specifically mentioned in *all* the journals of the Expedition. Maybe not everyone on the Expedition visited the cave.

And the statement: "From the earliest times, many visitors etched into the sandstone walls their names, dates, and other still-visible inscriptions. None of them, however, can be associated with any member of the Lewis and Clark Expedition." The etched markings "ORD 1804," strongly suggest, if not prove, that Sgt. Ordway left his mark on the walls of Tavern Cave.

In October 1995, I met with Peter Young, manager of the country club, Dick Williams, director of the National Parks Service, and Darold Jackson of the Lewis and Clark Trail Heritage Foundation. We discussed just what was involved in getting the DAR marker as part of the National Historic Trails. Peter saw no problem and indicated that he would take it up with the board of the St. Albans Partners.

Originally, there was to be a joint celebration of the opening of the second golf course and the dedication. When the second course was ready, however, the St. Albans Partners went ahead with a separate event. The course was opened July 2, 1997. By vote of the club membership, the first course was named "Meriwether Lewis and William Clark" and the second course, "Tavern Creek." The marker dedication was scheduled for the fall.

The DAR marker can be seen as you drive to the center of the village. It is directly under the hill where the Kincaid Cemetery is located and next to the new Chesterfield Day School/St. Albans. On October 1, 1997, it was made part of the Lewis and Clark National Historic Trail.

It was another beautiful fall day, and there were about 200 people attending the ceremony. This program was sponsored by the Cornelia Greene Chapter DAR, the Metro-St. Louis Chapter, Lewis and Clark Trail Heritage Foundation, the National Parks Service, National Historic Trails, the St. Albans Land Development Company and the Chesterfield Day School/St. Albans.

I was pleased to open the ceremony with greetings and introductions to the program. Mrs. John Farmer, Chaplain, MSSDAR, gave the invocation; Mr. and Mrs. George Lanz, Recording Secretary, MSSDAR, led the singing of the National Anthem; the Pledge of Allegiance was led by Ms. Patti Malverne, President, Metro-St. Louis Chapter, Lewis and Clark Trail Heritage Foundation. The flag of the United States and the DAR banner were carried by Cub Scouts Michael Tiller, Russel Leonard, Leah Dicker, Allison Thatcher, Mora Krueger and Jessica Tiller. Mrs. Francis Northrop, Regent, Cornelia Greene Chapter, gave the welcome. Dr. Barbara Fulton, head of the Chesterfield Day School/St. Albans, spoke about the school and introduced Matt Shubert, a fifth grader, who won the essay prize. Matt read his paper. Matt Olson was runner-up. I presented them with a copy of Ann Roger's book *Lewis and Clark in Missouri*, which she later autographed for the school library. Mr. Richard Williams, Director, Lewis and Clark Trail, National Park Service, spoke about the significance of being part of the National Historic Trail. The signs were unveiled by the sixth graders. Mr. Williams presented a plaque to Mr. Joseph Pottebaum, St. Albans Realty, and Mr. Peter Young, St. Albans Country Club. Mr. Ronald G. Laycock of Benson, Minnesota, a member of the board of the Lewis and Clark Trail Heritage Foundation, was the keynote speaker. He told of the preparations and many hardships the Corps of Discovery had in undertaking their hazardous journey. I presented him with an unopened copy, first edition, of *In the Footsteps of Lewis and Clark* by Gerald Snyder. The benediction was given by Rev. Edmund Griesedieck, Pastor, St. Alban Roe Catholic Church. Refreshments were served by the second and third grade classes.

Beau Millman as "Chief Big White." Photo by Mrs. Kathy Millman.

The flag of the United States was carried by Leah Dicker, Allison Thatcher, Mora Krueger and Jessica Tiller. Photo by Mrs. Kathy Millman.

Chesterfield Day School/St. Albans students took part in the dedication. The fifth and sixth graders were dressed in appropriate costumes representing members of the Corps of Discovery: Meriwether Lewis, Matt Olson; William Clark, Landon Schierholz; Toussaint Charboneau, Rachel Dede; Pvt. Moses Reed, Tim Belcher; Pvt. Alexander Willard, Drew Snyder; Pvt. John Shields, Guy Leonard; Pvt. George Drouillard, Raleigh Moore; Pvt. George Shannon, Andrew Crecelius; Sgt. Charles Floyd, Matt Shubert; Sgt. Nathaniel Pryor,

Michael Sheehan; Sgt. John Ordway, Andrew Goldstein; Chief Big White, Beau Millman; Chief Cameahwait, Abby Holekamp; Native American, Amy Goldstein; Pvt. Alexander Carson (father of Kit Carson), Adam Moisson; Sacajawea, Kim Williamson; Caspar Wistar, Holley Tiller; Pvt. John Colter, Van Krueger; Naya Nuki, Katharine Bayer; Pvt. Reuben Field, Taylor Millman; York, Ethan Bradshow; Pvt. Pierre Cruzette, Dillon Sharlet; Pvt. Patrick Gass, Chris Olson.

The fourth grade Girl Scouts were the honor guard carrying the flag of the United States and the banner of the Cornelia Greene Chapter, DAR. The third graders distributed the programs and, with the second graders, passed the refreshments. The first graders and kindergarten children folded the programs.

The Chesterfield Day School/St. Albans was awarded the Lewis and Clark Trail Heritage Foundation 1998 Youth Achievement Award at the Foundation's thirtieth annual meeting in Great Falls, Montana, July 2, 1998. This award was given for their part in the dedication.

FOOTNOTES

1. "Where Meriwether Lewis Slipped," article, *St. Louis Post-Dispatch*, April 17, 1968, p. N4.
2. Snyder, Gerald S., *In the Footsteps of Lewis and Clark*, published by National Geographic Society, 1970, p. 37-39.
3. "Dedicate Memorial to Lewis and Clark," article, *Washington Missourian*, October 28, 1971.
4. Almighty God our provident Father and Lord, we are able to gather here in the peace and security of civilized life because courageous men have, under your guidance and protection, braved terrifying dangers of a vast and savage wilderness to prepare it for the benefits of worthy human life. For this care we thank you. If in the course of our effort to carry further this work, we have done things amiss we ask your forgiveness and we beg your assistance to make this immense and opulent region a haven of justice and benignity for all men.
5. *The National Survey of Historic Sites and Buildings*, Vol. XII, United States Department of the Interior, National Park Service. "Historic Sites" as listed in *Lewis and Clark*, prepared by Roy E. Applemann, Part Two, pp. 298-299.

The Lewis and Clark National Historic Trail wayside exhibit. Decendents of members of the Expedition with the author. Left to right: Charles Coulter, Ruth Colter Frick, Clinton Coulter, Lucie Huger, Katherine Hereford, Bob Backowski, Horatio Potter, Barbara Backowiski, Joe Desloge (not a descendant), Charles Clark, Mrs. and Pierre Chouteau. Photo: Washington Missourian.

CHAPTER NINETEEN

Legend and Lore from St. Albans, Missouri

The "Legend and Lore From St. Albans, Missouri" was written by my daughter Lucie when she was a senior at Maryville College in 1964. The following collection of remedies, signs and superstitions is a snapshot of life in St. Albans as seen through the eyes and memories of the descendants of the original settlers. I have chosen to include this material because it enhances the history of the region and highlights the many colorful characters who made St. Albans the interesting place that it was. I added the little drawings for amusement.—Lucie F. Huger.

For this paper, I have gathered the information from my family, neighbors, and friends. The things that I have recorded here are not relics from an old book in someone's attic, but are part of everyday life in St. Albans. These stories were collected in farm kitchens, in barnyards, in the general store, or any place people gather to talk things over.

The original settlers of this area were for the most part German, with a few English and Scots here and there. They hacked their homes and farmlands from the woods, and, since it is not easy to make a living farming these rocky hills, they had to make use of everything they could. These people turned to the woods for their timber for the houses, their medicines, and much of their food. Today, the area looks much the same as it did then. The wooded hills have been untouched by man, and at night the valleys echo with the cries of the coyote and the bobcat. The people, too, are little changed. They rely on the various signs from nature for the weather forecast. Many of the remedies for man and his animals come from the barks of trees and roots of plants growing on the hillsides. To the city dweller, many of these remedies and superstitions may sound ridiculous, and I suppose some of them are, but I will vouch for quite a few of them. I have tried them, and they work.

Lucie Clara Huger
St. Albans, Missouri, 1964

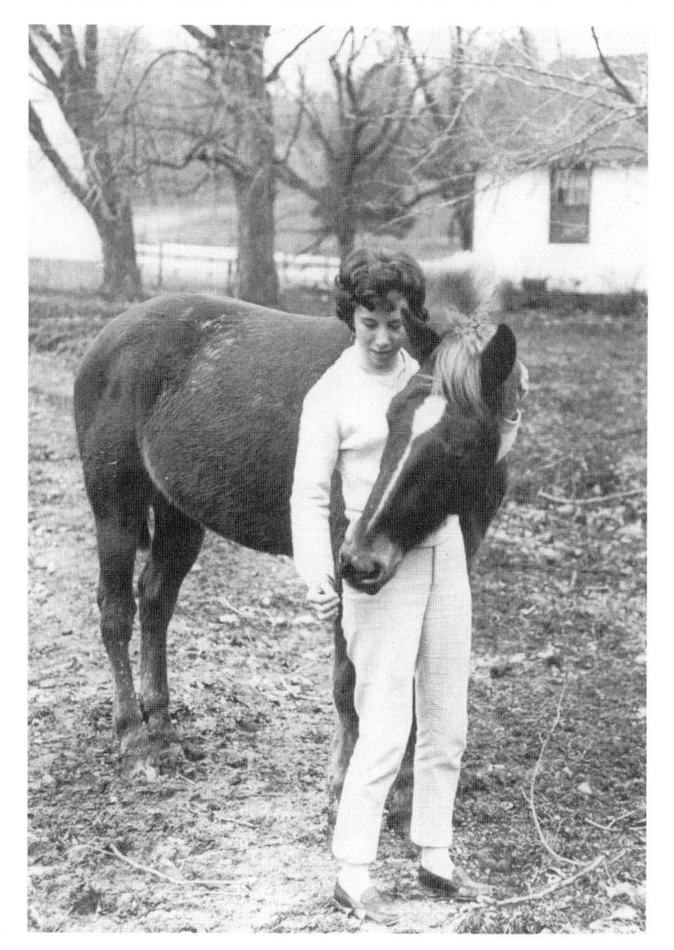

Lucie Clara Huger in 1964 with Wood's Snipperchip, her horse. An unpublished Post-Dispatch *photograph.*

PLACE NAMES AROUND ST. ALBANS

Bassett Road

The Bassett Road got its name from a Dr. Bassett that owned, or bought, the farm at the south end of Bassett Rd. And he just put up signs, 'Bassett Road', and that's how it got its name. That was done about, oh in the nineteen thirties. Somewhere in the nineteen thirties. Before that, some people called it the Hardt Road, and some people called it the Stettes Road, so it really had no name. I never did know anything about it until they put up the signs. See, that was Dr. Bassett, he was quite a famed doctor in St. Louis.

Camp Hollow

Yeah, Camp Holler is on the Wild Horse Creek Road, on the Ossenfort Road and the Wild Horse Creek Road. The beginning of it is at what used to be the old Seiffer farm which is now, Mr. Hoffman owns it I think. And there's also an entrance in it from the upper, the Wild Horse, road. And everybody during the Civil War in that neighborhood took their horses and cattle down in that Camp Holler. And they just camped down there with their livestock. At that time they had a rumor that Price, General Price, was coming through. And they was takin' all the horses and butcherin' the cattle, and so they hid everything in that valley. No, Price didn't come through, he went through farther south. I think he came through Pacific.

Brueckner Hollow

Then there's another valley that people from right this neighborhood went, and that's up here in the Brueckner Holler. That's just back of Fisher's place. You go in there at where Fisher lives, and go back up the valley. And they hid a lot of stuff up there like, oh things that soldiers would take. Charlie Bruechner owned that. I guess they probably bought that from the government. I wouldn't know. Just as long as I knowed, they had it. And the old lady Brueckner, she was an old lady when I was just a youngster. And I always heard the old folks talk about the Brueckners lived there.

Charles Brueckner, Hermit

"There was a hermit named Charles Brueckner who lived up the valley from the Fishers. He lived with a dog in a little log cabin on small piece of land. He originally came from Aachen, Germany. When the road was built to Lee Johnson's house, Brueckner would not take any money for a part of his land. He was afraid of being robbed. Instead, he accepted a Victrola and a stack of records. I remember hearing his music every summer night.

He raised his own vegetables, chickens, flowers, fruit trees and tobacco. I recall seeing the tobacco hanging up to dry. He had a buggy in a shed—but no horse. He walked everywhere. He walked to our place (the Fisher's) and brought us vegetables. He walked to Head's store where he bought bacon.

He lived to be fairly old; died of pneumonia. His things were sold at auction. We bought a dresser and a chest, five foot by two foot, with 'Aachen' painted on the side. We still have the chest.

His log cabin burned down after he died. He is buried in a lone grave nearby."

—As told to Lucie F. Huger by Jean Fisher Gibbs.

Bouquet Road

And the Bouquet Road was named after the family

Tavern Rock is the largest bluff in the group of outcroppings in the distance. Honeybee Point is the large outcropping closer to the town of St. Albans. Charles Becker's home is in the foreground. Photo is from Theodore Link's scrapbook from c. 1910. Courtesy: Ted Link, Jr.

named Bouquet. He was a veterinary. And it was named after that family. That's spelt 'Bouquet', it's a French name. Actually, 'boket' would be, but they call it 'bokay'. But the family went by the name Bucket. Yeah, Bucket Road. Everybody said Bucket instead of 'bokay'. But actually, the Bucket was spelt 'Bouquet'. No, they called 'em Bucket fer short.

Honeybee Point

When they built that road up on that point, there was a small, not too large a tree, just a medium sized tree. And it was full of honey from one end to the other, and there were bees in it, of course. And Mrs. Johnson said we'll call that Honeybee Point. That was Mrs. Irene Johnson. That was about nineteen-twenty-seven, I'd say. {Mr. Krausch was one of the men who built the road.}

Port Royal

Below Tavern Rock there was a little town there named Port Royal, which was a lime kiln down there. It seemed to be quite a flourishing little town until they run out of limestone. And then when the railroad moved their equipment shed away from there, the town just disappeared. That was down below the Tavern Rock about several, couple, miles. The other side, on down the railroad track between here and Centaur. And that was quite a flourishing town at that time. Oh, not....well, it was a railroad station. Called Port Royal.

Ossenfort Road

Well, the Ossenfort Road was named after the Ossenfort family. Yeah, they lived where, next to Truebloods, DeHarts live. That's the old Ossenfort place. It was quite a large farm.

Little Tavern Valley

Well, that's Little Tavern Valley. You see, Little Tavern Creek runs through that valley. It runs all the way up, well, past what is now Jones's. It drains their water from all the way up, well where Scheuddigs used to live. It runs all through your place.

Tavern Rock Cave

These creeks are called Tavern on account of the Tavern Rock Cave down there. That was open to the river. And all the transportation on the river, such as, well Lewis and Clark for instance, they camped there. They wintered in that cave one winter. And people going up and down the river, they camped there of a night. If they'd get there they'd camp in that shelter of a night.

(Big) Tavern Creek

And then the first creek they came to was Tavern Creek. They called that Tavern Creek and that was a big creek.

Little Tavern Creek

And then the next one was Little Tavern. And that's how they got that name. That's the way I was told that they got it.

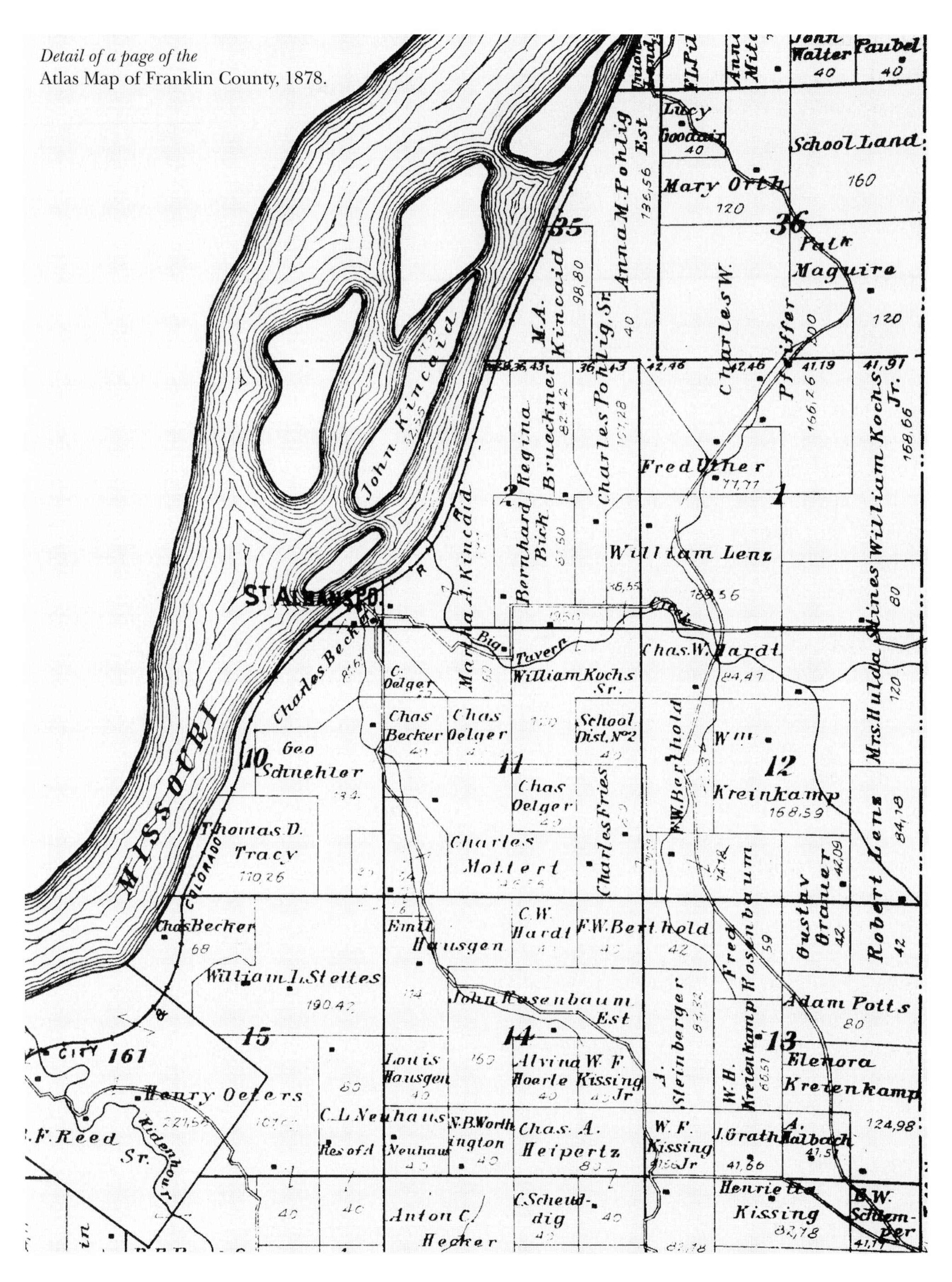

Detail of a page of the
Atlas Map of Franklin County, 1878.

Lick Hollow

Well, the hollow at the old pump station, that valley goes up there, that's Lick Holler. That's the one where Callie Steffens lives, in that holler. That's Lick Holler. Well, 'cause there was a deer lick down there. They salted, put salt out and the deer came there to lick that salt. And they called that Lick Holler.

Freeman Hollow

And the next one down the track from that is Freeman Holler, known as Freeman Holler. That's the holler that comes out right at Butch Thiebes' road there. That holler goes all the way to the river. And that's Freeman Holler. A man by the name of Freeman lived in that. It's been Freeman Holler as long as I knew it, and I think that a man by the name of Freeman lived down there. Once in a while it went by the name of Club Holler 'cause there was a club house there. But actually, it's the Freeman Holler.

Eddy Hollow

And the next holler down towards St. Albans from that is Eddy Holler. There was a huge eddy in the river right at the entrance of that holler. Well, they said the water there was, they thought, over a hundred feet deep. They never could touch bottom there. Well, the river went around there. See, the river used to run right past St. Albans. And that Eddy Holler, they call that the Big Eddy. And its branches; one branch of it is the Big Eddy, and the other branch is the Little Eddy. Well, if you go over that little field right at Butch Thiebes' road, and bear to the right, that little road takes you into Eddy Holler. It's a terrific big valley. Yeah, that's Eddy Holler. And one branch of it goes out towards the studio at St. Albans. It's up on the hill you know.

Link's Bluff

We always called that bluff up there where the Links have their house Link's Bluff.

Informant: Ulmont Krausch

The Grand Army Road

You know when that war was fought between the North and South? What was that called, the Civil War? Well, that's where the Grand Army men it was there; and the Rebels, I don't know, was them the Southerners? Anyway, that Grand Army Road was where the Grand Army men marched over from Pacific. My grandpa was in that. And he got sick and died afterwards.

Informant: Mrs. Minnie Stricker

The naming of Owensville, Missouri

My grandfather, Lester, and a feller named Owens, pitched horseshoes. And the man who won got to name the town. And my grandfather won. And my grandfather said it would sound better to call it Owensville than Lesterville.

Informant: Clark Lacy

How Wild Horse Creek Road was named

I'll tell you the legend of Johann Kuschwanz. Now in the early, early days of Wild Horse Creek, here before it was called Wild Horse Creek, there were some settlers living around the town of Centaur. And Johann Kuschwanz was a sort of eccentric old bachelor who lived there. And people were always having trouble with a white horse that he had, a great big white horse. He'd roam around and get in the gardens and paw up their vegetables and so forth. And they were always after him to keep the horse bottled up, and he never would do it. He was a kind of eccentric. Well, one night there was a terrible storm. And the lightning crashed, and the winds blew, and the rain came down, and there was a clattering of hoofs. And those who were up that late looked up in the flash of the lightning and they saw Johann Kuschwanz seated backwards on his horse, facing the rear, clattering off down the creek. And that is the last that they ever saw of him. The horse and he all disappeared, and that's why they call it Wild Horse Creek.

Informant: Dr. William Small

WEATHER SIGNS

Rainbow as a sign of rain

If a rainbow appears in the morning, it's a sure sign of rain that day. But if it appears in the afternoon, no rain in sight. Any time a heavy cloud goes over in the afternoon and you see a rainbow, you won't see any more rain that day. Now I know that. I've watched that a-many and a-many a-time and I know it's true.

Wet and dry moons

When the moon's laying on its back it'll rain in a few days. That's a wet moon. It's catchin' rain. If it's standin' upon a point it won't rain 'cause it's poured out. That's what you call a dry moon. I've always watched this, and almost every time it works. I've heard older people say this ever since I was a kid.

Now you watch this this summer whenever it's real dry. If the moon's standin' on a point, it won't rain.

BELIEFS ABOUT THE WEATHER

You've heard that if your bones ache, it's going to rain. Grandma used to say, 'Oh, it must be fixin' to rain, my bones is sure achin'.'

When we was kids, every time we killed a snake, we'd turn it so its stomach was up to be sure it rained. Then we were happy, 'cause we knew we could quit choppin' cotton. I can't remember if it worked or not.

Any time you see storm clouds moving against the wind, it will rain because there is something stronger in the cloud. If it doesn't change soon, it will go the other way 'cause the wind is stronger.

Well, we always said when your corns were hurting, it's a sign of bad weather.

They say when a dog eats grass it's goin' to rain. We always went by that too, but that ain't true.

'Thunder before seven, rain before eleven.' Now I want you to watch that, 'cause it's always true. Now, I don't know about night, but of a mornin'.

The first twelve days of the year predict the twelve months of the year. Like if it rains on the first day, the first month will be wet. That's what they always say, but I don't know.

'Rainbow at night, sailor's delight—rainbow in the morning, sailors warning.' That'll work too.

They say, if there's dust whirlwinds, it's gonna be dry. We've always went by that.

When you hear the locusts singing, it's a sign of dry weather.

If the shucks on the corn are heavy, it's supposed to be a hard winter. That don't work either. Several years ago, I never seen such heavy shucks as there were. Arb said we were going to have a bad winter 'cause there were such heavy shucks. But we didn't have a real hard winter at all.

Well, when the water pipes sweat, there's going to be a change in the weather. Yeah, that works.

If the smoke lies close to the ground, and doesn't blow away, it's going to rain. [This was also told to me by Michael Cremins, 21, University City, Mo., a student at St. Louis University.]

Before a cold spell, the hogs always make themselves nests. You can see 'em carrying their sticks and straw and everything they can find, makin' a bed.

They always say, bad thunder will kill goslings in the shell.

There's an old saying, 'A sunshine shower won't last half an hour.' That's true. It won't rain while the sun is shining.

If the sun shines while it's rainin', it will rain the same time the next day. To me, it don't stand true like some of them other things.

Lightning in the east is a sign of dry weather. Lightening in the north is a sign of wet weather. Now I've watched that one too. That one will work just about every time.

When the mules start runnin' and rippin' around near the house, you can just bet that it'll be cold in just a few hours. This is true too.

When there's a red sunset in the summer, the next day'll be a windy day. If it's a real dark fiery red sunset, you just try that this summer and see if it don't work.

Informant: Mrs. Cordie Lee Bolin

THE BIRDS AS WEATHER SIGNS

If people'd just look at the birds, they'd know what the weather was goin' to do.

Well, you take if you seen one of these redbirds get in the tip-top of a tree and whistle of a mornin', it will rain before sundown. That's a fact too. I've seen that happen in dry weather of a summer. It will be just the prettiest day, when a redbird will whistle. And, sure thing, it will rain before long.

Sunset on the Missouri River. This view from the St. Albans bluffs is much the same as when Oscar Johnson, Jr. took this photo in the 1930's. Ken Gilberg collection.

I've been down here, and it will be just lookin' like a storm, and a whippoorwill will holler, and it won't rain. If a whippoorwill hollers in the first part of the night, it won't rain before midnight.

You take if you see snakes a-crawlin', or a lot of terrapins, that's a sign of rain. That'll work now.

Well, if you see hogs a-carrying sticks that's a sign its gonna turn cold.

They claim if you have a red sunset of an evening on Friday, it'll be windy the next day.

Well, whichever way the milky way points in the sky, the wind will be out of that direction the next day.

Whatever way the wind is on January First, the wind will go back to that direction once every twenty-four hours in January. It may not stay there long, but it'll be there.

Informant: Clark Lacy

The rain crow

If ever you hear a yellow-billed cuckoo call, you can be sure that it will rain soon. I've been told this by my mother and many other people. It's generally true. The yellow-billed cuckoo is known as the rain crow.

Blackberry winter

Every May, when the blackberries bloom, we have what is known as blackberry winter. It always gets cold, and you have to turn the furnace on. We always wait until after blackberry winter to turn on the air-conditioning. This is the opposite of Indian summer, I guess.

Evening red, morning gray,
Sends the traveler on his way.
Evening gray, morning red,
Brings the rain upon his head.
This is almost always true.

If there's a ring around the moon, it will rain in a few days.

If the leaves on the trees curl so the bottom side is up, it will rain.

If the chickens and wild birds stay out in the rain or snow, it won't stop for awhile.

If the flies are sticky in the summer and gather around the kitchen door, it will rain. This is true.

You can always tell if there's going to be a storm 'cause the stock get restless.

If the animals get winter coats that are thick early, it will be a long, hard winter.

Informant: Lucie C. Huger

ANIMAL TREATMENT

Dog distemper

It's supposedly an old Southern cure for distemper. You just take a bucketful of chicken feathers they can be from a chicken or out of a pillow, and you burn them. And then you have the dog inhale the fumes, after they've burned, they're not burning anymore.

Informant: Terry Goggio

Cow's hollow horn

Another thing I saw my grandfather do, when a cow got what they call a hollow horn he'd split their tail open and fill it with salt. Well, about that far, (about two feet) quite a little stretch, down through the switch anyway. About half way up on the tail he'd just take a pocket knife and split that skin, and fill that full of salt. It seemed like it cured it. Some time, he'd drill a hole in the horn and put turpentine in it too. I think that sounds more like it than splitting the tail for hollow horn. 'Course you know when they'd get down with that hollow horn, they'd call that, well, let's see, they'd call that wolf in the tail, yeah, *'wolf im schwanz'*, but actually, that was no more than the same as a rabbit or cat gets a worm in their neck.

They call that a wolf in the neck, but actually what it is, is a grub worm.

[We were talking about wolves on the backs of cattle, and Mr. Krausch said, "Usually cattle that are wintered pretty rough get that pretty bad."]

Caked bag

Take mullein tea, the leaves from mullein and boil 'em and make a pretty thick tea out of it. And apply that to a cow's bag if they get a caked bag. And bathe it good in that several times a day, will most of the times cure a caked bag on a cow. Do it two or three times a day, I imagine. Sometimes, a couple of applications will take it down. Yeah, that works. We've did that lots.

Informant: Ulmont Krausch

Caked bag

When William Bolin was taking care of our milk cows, one of them had a badly caked bag. He asked me to get some linseed oil, and, after applying this about three times to the bag, the cow was all right. William told me that he always used this on his own milk cows with excellent results.

Informant: William Bolin

Horse cure for a sweeny

Yeah, that's an old German remedy. When a horse got fallen muscles in the shoulder which is called sweeny, soak a thick cloth in vinegar, and take a hot flatiron and iron over that so that shoulder gets good and hot. I guess a 'lectric pad would do the same nowadays, but them days they used a hot flatiron. I have seen that done already.

Grease to make a horse's hair come back

If you have an animal, a horse or a mule, that gets stung by a bee, or a bumblebee, you put lard or any grease on. It will keep the hair from coming out white from the sting. Otherwise, the hair'll come out white. My father used to put, if he was mowin' in the field and they got a bee sting from usually bumblebees, he'd just put regular lubricating oil on because he had the oil can there on the mower. And he'd just drive off the end of the field away from the bees and put regular machine oil on. That way the hair wouldn't come out white, see the bee sting'll make the hair come out white. When they come back in they'll be white if you don't put some sort of grease on. What that does to 'em, I don't know, but it makes 'em come out like they were.

[Whenever our horses get cut up or bitten, I put bacon grease on the sore place. This is to make the hair come back the right color. It really works, and it seems to make the hair come in faster too. L.C.H.]

Distemper in a horse

They used to take wasps nests, old wasp nests. And burn 'em and hold 'em under a horse's nose for to cure distemper. I guess it'd cure most anything 'cause you really had to tie 'em down good to make 'em breathe that smoke. But I've seen that done. Whether it cured 'em or not, I don't know. I guess it's like a cold, it got better, run it's course, 'cause distemper I don't think is anything but a cold, really.

Informant: Ulmont Krausch

Cure for a sore horse

Mr. Daily said that years ago before there were veterinaries around, one of his horses got hurt on the railroad track. When he got the animal home, it was in such bad shape that it could not get up. It could raise itself up in front, but not in the back. A neighbor came over to doctor the horse. He took a knife and made two cuts on the animal's back, just in front of the rump. Then he cut some hair out of the horse's tail and put salt on them, and pulled them through the two cuts. Mr. Daily says that this was to draw all the soreness up to one place. He says that it worked too. The next morning the horse was able to stand up, and it soon recovered.

Cure for distemper in a horse

Mr. Daily said that a lot of the old-timers use this when a horse gets distemper. You heat tar and let the animal breathe this smoke. He claims that it cures them.

Cure for a sweeny horse

Mr. Daily told me that when he was young there were no vets and so they used nothing but home remedies when their animals were sick. When a horse is sweeny, there is an indentation in the shoulder muscle. These old horse doctors used to lance the place and insert a quarter in the hole. A lump would form under the skin around this foreign object, and this would fill the place and make the horse look perfectly all right.

Informant: Bill Daily

Cure for the poll evil

Horses, for the poll evil, it's generally caused by a bruise. They jus' keep gettin' worse and you have to treat it yourself, 'cause I don't know of any medicine that'll cure it. Now you take an axe, you doctor this horse at sunup, of a mornin', just as the sun's a comin' up and now you have the blade of this axe in the ground, and you take this axe out of the ground, just as the sun's comin' up. And you rub it in the horse's head and it will cure it. The metal that's in the axe, that will cure it. You use the sharp part of the blade.

*Poll evil is a bump that a horse gets behind his ear and it keeps gettin' bigger until you do somethin' about it.

Informant: Clark Lacy

Old blue, cure for an injured animal

When we were very small, my dad used to go out and buy these young mules, and bring 'em in for the boys to break to work. He liked them with a lot of life in 'em. One time he brought a little old mule in, we always called him Old Blue, 'cause he was a real blue in color. And we farmed some land over by the railroad track. And the men, the engineer men, would always blow their whistles and holler when they came by. And Dad would always wave back at them. So they blew their whistles this particular time, and this little mule called Blue got so scared, it jumped into a fence, and almost cut its foot plumb off. And my Dad used healing oil and stove soot mixed together. He made a plaster, and kept it on this mule's foot as much as he possibly could. And we always thought that's what healed it up. I'm sure it was. Yep. It healed up perfectly.

Informant: Mrs. Cordie Lee Bolin

CURES AND REMEDIES FOR HUMANS

For coughs and colds

For a cough, they used to take a big hunk of rock candy and honey and boil it in milk.

[They would use this as a cough syrup. L.C.H.]
For a cold, they used to put garlic, you know, the buds, on a string around their throat. It's supposed to work.

Informant: Mrs. Ida Spiegleglass

This is an old German custom. This is for chest ailments. You take potato peelings and you put them on a person's chest. You know the old coffee grounds that are still wet? Pack it on the chest. It's supposed to draw the soreness out of the chest. They tried this on my uncle. It didn't work. He got tuberculosis.

Informant: Terry Goggio

File to cure fever

Put a eight inch file, that's what Grandma always used, between the springs and the mattress. Supposed to keep the fever down. The electricity from the fever is supposed to go to the file. I can remember Grandma keepin' that file between her mattress. Sleep on that file. Never, never take it out from under the bed. Leave it there forever.

Pipe smoke to cure an earache

Anyone that smokes a pipe can cure an earache. When we'd have the earache, Dad'd just light up his old pipe and blow smoke in our ears. This works. I guess it's the warmth of it that does it. Every time we had the earache he'd blow smoke from his pipe in our ears.

Cure for colitis

You take the inside out of the chicken gizzard. It's called the 'striffins,' that's what the old people used to call it. I can remember them savin' striffins many a time when I was a kid. Boil it in a cup of water to cure colitis. Well, I've seen it done at home but, like I said, I never did do it. I got it from my grandmother.

Arthritis preventative

There's an old woman that we went to church with all the time down at Poplar Bluff that wore a copper bracelet. It was real copper too, to keep away arthritis.

Informant: Mrs. Cordie Lee Bolin

Mullein leaf tea for soreness

Another thing fer takin' swelling out. You know, if you have a swollen leg? Or an ankle or something like that? You take this mullein leaf, and cook that, you know, in vinegar. And use that fer to rub on. You cook it in vinegar and that's awful good. You take the leaf and kinda squash it on the leg or whatever you use it on.

Onion tea for cough

Onion tea, that's good fer a cough, isn't it? I think so. Yeah, that's good. You take so many teaspoons and swaller it, and it's good fer a cough. You just take that there onion and squeeze it. You do it, it works.

Red pepper tea for sore throat

I used red pepper tea for sore throat. It really took the lining out of my throat, but it cured it. It sure did. And that was in the summertime when I had it. It was in June. And I'll tell ya. In those days, I used to help my husband feed yet, of course. And I went to the barn, and my throat was so sore that I had a handkerchief tied around my neck, because my throat was sore. And when I got out there to the barn, I tell you, it just looked like the whole lining came out of my throat. And after that it got well. But I drank that red pepper tea, you know, for it. And after that my throat was a whole lot better, and it got better. But that really took it.

[Mrs. Stricker also advocated tying an old sock around your neck at night for a sore throat. I always do this myself.]

Several teas

Yeah, they used to make peppermint tea to drink. I don't know what that was for though, anymore.

And there was another tea, it grows down there on the old Hurley place. [This is now part of our farm. L.C.H.] There used to be a big bush we'd pass every time we'd go to school. You know, walk to school. And you could make tea out of that to drink.

Cure for the seven year itch—Indian herbs

Well, I don't know, I tried everything. I had it myself one time. And what I used was some herbs from an Indian doctor. I cooked them and made 'em into a medicine-like, and then took so much, I ferget what I had to take of it, I believe it was a tablespoon, three times a day. Well, that man come around and sold those herbs, and I got eighteen dollars worth. And that cured me though I tried everythin' and that cured me. He looked like an Indian, anyway. He was dark and everything. But it was Indian herbs that I used. I had that seven years on my shin. It was just this long a place (about seven inches) and it itched so! Oh, that was something!

And then that man came around, and he said if that didn't cure me. He'd give me my money back. And it cured me! I ferget where he was from. It seems like he was from Washington, Mo.

Remedy for bee stings

You know the best thing fer that? The wax outa your ear. It is, it's the best thing you can do. I tell you, you see over there on that hillside there? It was up here, my grandson was with me, up here in the pasture. And I got stung seventeen times. And I just happened to have a bobbie pin in my hair, and I took that and got the ear wax outa my ear, and put that on. And that relieved it right away, otherwise, I don't know what would have happened to me.

Slippery elm bark

Slippery elm bark, you boil that down. Let's see, ain't that good for rheumatism and stomach ache? I know we used to do that years ago, you know, when we was little kids. You know that my Mother and Dad used those things. But I don't know if you rubbed that in, or just took it without.

Informant: Mrs. Cordie Lee Bolin

Ice water to cure a fever

When you have high fever, I know they'd take a real cold cloth. You know, they'd wet it in cold water. Them days, they didn't even have ice, you know, refrigerators. They'd take real cold water, and dip the rag in that, and wring it out, and put it on your forehead, and then when the coolness was off, you'd put it in cold water and put it back again. You know, as a poultice like.

Warmooth' for upset stomach

Let's see, there was a kind of a root that you'd dig and use that for stomach cure, Warmooth, or somethin' like that. You can put that in whisky you know, and drink a little of it. Anyway, where Herman, my brother, lived, that lady used to raise that stuff. Well of course, once you plant it, it comes back every year, you know. We always used to have some of that there.

Uses for turpentine

Yes, I took turpentine a lot of times for worms. Just take a teaspoon, or not quite a teaspoon, of sugar and put so many drops, I believe it was according to your age. If you was five years old, you'd take five drops, and if you was older, you'd take more, and if you was younger, you'd take less. That was all we'd use them days fer worms.

Oh, that was one of the best remedies. You know, if you had a cut or anything like that. That would really help. If you'd step on a rusty nail, you'd kinda soak it in good hot water, and then put turpentine on it, and that would really help. Was very seldom that people had blood poisoning like they have nowadays.

Cure for fits—molasses

Well, we had a girl you know, 'course maybe I shouldn't tell this, anyway, the one daughter had like a spasm. It was nervous convulsions, that's what it was. And it was because she didn't have enough sugar in her system. And you know what they did fer that? We doctored with quite a few doctors, and then we was told to go to Dr. Zahorsky. Oh, we spent a lot of money on that girl, and she'd always get 'em back, get 'em in the middle of the night. She'd start out and it was just like she had fits. And you know what he give her? Three tablespoons of sorghum molasses. Well, you know, people used to eat more sorghum molasses and they were healthier than what they are now eatin' too much sugar. I know that black strap, that was just fer cattle anyway, and that was dark.

[My mother's father is a firm believer in the powers of black strap. Whenever anything is wrong with any of us, he says a little molasses will cure it. We've had enough of it too, thanks to Grandpa. When we ran out of hay one winter we put it on straw for the cattle. I've never seen anything that will fatten up an animal like black strap. L.C.H.]

Horehound

Yes, we used horehound for coughs, made it into a syrup-like with honey. You dissolve it just like a cough medicine. That was very good. Yeah, you can put it in if you have got the whisky on hand. You know, lot of times we didn't have it to put in it. Whenever we had it, we'd put it with it, you know, like the horehound and that together.

Cure for snake bites

Well, vinegar and those mullein leaves is good fer snake bite too. You cook those mullein leaves, and put vinegar on them, and bathe it in that. You can fix it in a hurry. There was a cow that had snake bite down there on the farm, you know. We had a nice cow, her name was Lady. She was a Jersey. And if there was anything ailing her, we always felt so bad about it. And my Dad found out that she had gotten snake bite. And of course he picked mullein leaves right away and brought them to the house, and we fixed that in vinegar. He just bathed the cow's leg in it. Well I'll tell you, he just took a bucket and set her foot into that fer a while, and just squashed the water over it. It dasn't be hot, but not too cold either, but as hot as she can stand it. You couldn't put a cow's leg in anything too hot, or she'd kick ya. But she was a cow that wouldn't hardly ever kick.

Well, turpentine's good too. If you should suck this juice out, spit it out, of course, I mean the poison. That's good to do that right away because it won't go through your system if you do that way. I guess there's lots of things that people can use fer that. Nowadays, of course, they have to go to the doctor right away to get treated..

Remedy for stomach ache and poisoning

Well, they used to take milk and a little nutmeg is good fer that. Kind of lukewarm sweet milk with a little nutmeg in it.

For poisoning, whip the white of a raw egg and make them eat that. The two Steinberg boys had it. Well anyway, when my sister was first married, she lived up at the old Steinberg place. And the grandpa, he was dustin' potatoes with that arsenic of lead. And he left that arsenic of lead set out in the shed, and those two boys got hold of it and ate some of it. And they made them eat the whites of eggs, and they vomited. Of course, they called the doctor, but I think it was the egg whites that did it, 'cause it took the doctor a long time to get there them days.

Cure for poison ivy

Well, if you take Epsom salts and dilute that well with warm water, just make a little paste, like to put on you, it's not irritating.

Sweet cream is good too. You just pat it on. Try that once. Of course, don't let it go too long. I think it's harder to cure when you leave it go.

Goose grease to cure a fever

I tell you what, if they'd have high fever, I'd take like goose grease and some quinine and make a salve out of that, and rub 'em with that. And that'd take the fever down. There was just a little turpentine put in that. That's right. You know how they used to have those capsules? They were in cellophane, you know. You'd take the quinine, it would come in a bottle, and you'd fill them yourself, say about three tablespoons of goose grease, and then this capsule of that quinine, and a few drops of turpentine. And that was good for colds and things like that.

Cure for dysentery

I was going to tell you about this remedy. You know, for dysentery? It's the narrow dock tea. You know, when it's good and ripe. Yeah, dock. It's called narrow dock tea. One is a wide leaf, and one is a narrow leaf. It's good for dysentery; you make a tea out of it. Then cool it and take so much at a time. I believe it's a tablespoon fer a dose. And that's good fer that. Very good.

Informant: Mrs. Minnie Stricker

Folk remedy to stop bleeding

You take cobwebs'll stop anything from bleedin'. You take in an old building, the dust that's in them cob webs, that's what stops bleeding.

You take the soot that's in the compartment of wood stoves, that'll stop bleedin'.

Well sugar, you can take sugar and put it on a cut place. And that will stop it from bleedin', you know.

Folk remedy for mumps

For mumps, you tie a black yarn string around your waist. And it will keep the mumps from going down.

Informant: Someone sitting around at Head's Store, St. Albans, Mo.

Rattlesnake grease for rheumatism

Did you ever hear that rattlesnake oil was very good for rheumatism? You just rub it on. I never did try to render the fat out of a rattlesnake, but I've been told that years ago you could buy it. I don't know whether you still can or not. I imagine you can. Oh, I've heard the different people that used it, and the way they rendered it, they skinned a rattlesnake, and hung her up in the sun, and let the sun. Put a little cup underneath so that grease would drip in that cup. It's not too plentiful, but then there is some grease that comes out of 'em if you get a fat one. It don't take very much.

Skunk grease for colds

Years ago we'd always use skunk grease for, well, chest colds, aches and pains. And it doesn't at all resemble a skunk. It's pure, it's just like any other grease. But it really penetrates. If you're careful and remove that scent bag, a skunk is no different than any other animal. And you fry out that grease and render it. I know that during World War II, a boy was in Germany or France, and he wrote home and he said, for heaven's sakes, send him some skunk grease, that he just couldn't get along without it, that he had a chest cold and he needed some skunk grease. And they sent him some skunk grease, all the way over to Germany.

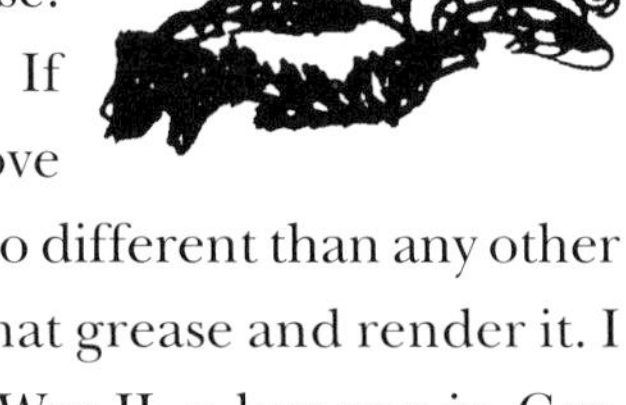

Blackberry root tea for diarrhea

Another old remedy is blackberry roots, a tea out

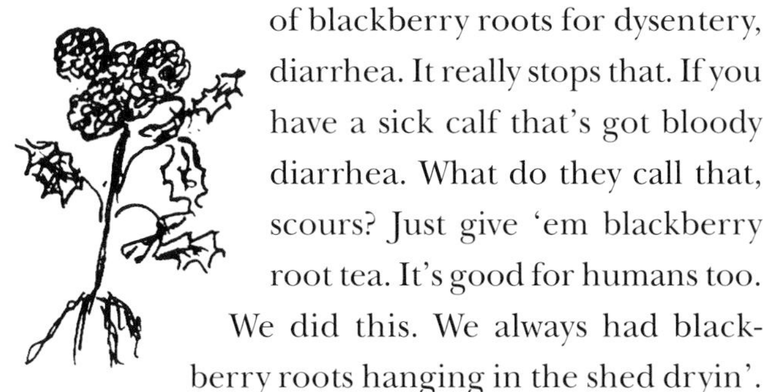

of blackberry roots for dysentery, diarrhea. It really stops that. If you have a sick calf that's got bloody diarrhea. What do they call that, scours? Just give 'em blackberry root tea. It's good for humans too. We did this. We always had blackberry roots hanging in the shed dryin'.

Cure for diarrhea

You use the mule tail weed. Oh, it grows up something like a lead pencil and leaves all, you know what I mean, yeah, that's supposed to be a cure for diarrhea. No, they don't make a tea out of it. I used to work with a man that'd chew it. Whenever you'd see him runnin' around with a piece of that mule tail in his mouth, why you knew that he had the bellyache.

Bring out the measles

Oh, when I had measles, they didn't want to come out. I had a fever and just a few measles. So I was given a tea that really brought 'em out. It didn't taste too bad, but it tasted rather green. It was a dark greenish-brown liquid. And I thought it was real good stuff. And as I was about half grown, why then they took courage enough to tell me what it was. It was a tea made out of sheep droppings. So I guess it did the job, and I didn't die over it. So try it sometime.

Ice water for nosebleed

If anybody's nose is bleedin' when they're not expecting it dash ice water on the back of their neck, and that stops their nose from bleedin' Yeah, it works sometimes. When we were first married we'd do that to each other, she'd do it to me when I had a nosebleed, and I'd do it to her when she had one. She'd be down at the spring bathin' her nose and I'd take a cup of that cold water and pour it over the back of her neck, and then run. Then I'd better run 'cause she'd be after me.

Cures for ringworm

Take a penny and rub it over it, a copper penny and rub it over the ringworm.

A silver thimble, if it fits around the outside, you press that on, and actually I guess what that does is stop the circulation. It's supposed to be a silver thimble. Yeah, it works.

I ferget what they did up at the barn for ringworm. Calves get it a lot, you know. And I don't really know what they did do for it. But they had something. I think they put on cracked bluestone and lard. Bluestone is what? What do they call it? London purple? I think they just call it bluestone. It's a blue stonelike that you crush up. A blue... blue vitriol is what it is, I think. And they use that on ringworm quite a bit. Otherwise, I wouldn't know what they would use.

Mullein leaf for sore throat

You take a mullein leaf and soak it in hot water and wrap that around your neck and put a cloth over that for sore throat. It takes the soreness out of your throat. As soon as it cools you change it. It'd even be good to take the soreness out of your tonsils. Try it some time.

Hot vinegar and salt for sprains

Oh, I thought of another one. Well, you treat sprains with hot vinegar and salt. Soak a rag in that and put it on the sprain, a sprained ankle. Use it like a poultice, and just keep on till your ankle gets well.

Carrying elder leaves in the summer

Well, the saying is that if you carry elder leaves in your pocket, you'll never get chafed or 'galded'. I have did that lots of times in the summer when I worked in the hay and dirty jobs. And I guess it worked. Well, you get sore under your arms from the perspiration and your skin rubbing together. The skin comes off and gets very red and awful sore. That's about it.

Spicewood tea

You take the spicewood twigs, break 'em up in about two, three inch pieces, and boil 'em, not too long. Makes a very good tea fer a beverage, makes a beverage tea. Taste one and smell it. Course that's from last year. It should be gotten now before the sap. [Mrs. Krausch added] See, that's so hard and dry, you just have to put five, six of these on for two cups. And I would say to boil it till you get the strength out of it, and then you just pour it in a cup and drink it.

[They said that spicewood was hard to find and that they knew of one place in their valley where you could get it. It's a small tree, growing in dark places along a creek bed. They gave me some to take home so I could make some tea. Apparently they drink it all summer as iced tea. The next day, my father found a grove of these trees on our property. L.C.H.]

Sassafras tea

Well, you get the sassafras root, you dig 'em, 'course I pull 'em out with a tractor, I'm too lazy to dig 'em. And there's two kinds, the white sassafras and the red. The red is the best tasting, the white is a little more bitter. And it don't take a big section of root. You just cut 'em in pieces and boil 'em, just make a tea out of 'em, very good. No, we usually do it just the spring. Supposed to thin your blood a little bit. And then last year somebody came out and said it caused cancer. 'Course we did it anyway. See you can peel the bark off the roots like that. [Mrs. Krausch added] Yeah, I do that, 'cause if you keep the big roots, you have to have a bigger jar to put it all away, where I just shave that soft bark of the roots. I'll tell you what that tastes like, sassaferilly. You know what that taste like? I haven't tasted that for a long time. Years ago, you know, we had sassaferilla [sarsaparilla].

[You boil these roots to make a tea. Mrs. Krausch made a cup for me and it was quite good. She also gave me some bark to take home so I could make my own tea. They said that their whole family likes this tea, especially the children. L.C.H.]

Informant: Ulmont Krausch

Blood purifier

For blood purifier is burdock root. You jes dig the roots, and wash 'em, and chop 'em, and let 'em set in somethin'. They'll ferment, like grapes would if you was a makin' wine, you know.

Cure for a corn

The way to cure a corn is to take a grain of corn and rub it on the corn and throw it to a chicken and not see which chicken eats it. You throw the grain over your head.

Folk remedy for the croup

For the croup, well, we always give 'em skunk grease. You give 'em a little and then you rub their chest with it. That's the finest thing for little kids. I take skunk grease myself. You jus take about a tablespoon of grease. It goes easy down the throat. I'd rather take skunk grease than most anything.

Cure for a cold

You can get relief for a cold by makin' tea from mullein. You just take the leaves. You can get 'em in the winter.

Cure for rabies

There is only one deer tha's got the madstone. And that's what you call a white buck deer, and tha's the one that's got the madstone. That'll work 'cause I knowed a feller that had the madstone, John Lickleiter of Red Bud. Well, they put this madstone on wherever the dog has bit him, or whatever bit, you know. And when it comes off, you put this madstone in sweet milk. And you keep a' repeatin' this as long as this madstone will stick to that place.

And it turns the milk real green. And I guess whenever the stone gets real full of poison you have to draw the poison out of the stone before you can put it back on, you know.

Cure for seven year itch

Here's an old time remedy for the seven year itch. That was the worst thing that anybody ever could have. Well, you take poke roots an' you boil 'em, and then you take and wash with it, and that'll cure it.

Goldenseal

And you take goldenseal is good to wash any kind of a sore with. It'll cure anything.

Cure for poisonous snake bites

Now you take a live chicken and just pull it apart and put it to the bite. The heat from the chicken is what draws that there poison out of the bite. I ain't never been bit by no poisonous snake, but if I was, I'd sure try it.

Informant: Clark Lacy

Buying warts

This old woman, she had a little restaurant across the street from school. And the children'd come over there and they'd say, 'Mrs. Rosenbaum, how 'bout buyin' my warts?' And she'd say, 'OK'. And she'd give 'em a penny for their warts, and they'd go away. Few days they's come back and they'd say, 'Well, my warts are gone.' And they were. That's it. But she wouldn't tell us what she did.

Cure for warts

When you're out in the woods walkin' and you come across some animal bones and you have some warts, pick up the bone. Watch, pay attention to how you pick it up. Rub it over each wart. Lay it back down just in the same spot that you picked it up. Don't ever go back and try to find it, and your warts will go away, I've seen the kids at home try that. Never seen if they come off or not. Don't look back toward it, they'd say.

Informant: Cordie Lee Bolin

Cure for warts

They claim that you can wash your hands in stump water and that will take warts off. You know, the water that's settin' in the top of a stump.

You want to steal dish rags. Just so you steal 'em so nobody knows you steal them. You can steal them from your mother, but it's better to steal from someone else. You just take it and rub the wart with the dishcloth in the first place, or else it won't work. When it decays, the wart'll leave. An' you won't know when it leaves. That's the funny thing about a wart, you never know when it leaves.

Informant: Clark Lacy

Cure for warts

Well, let's see. For every wart you have tie a knot, I always thought they said in an old greasy string. Walk to a crossroads, take the string off and bury it. Turn your back on it, and don't look back, and your warts is supposed to go away. I just always heard that'd work; like I said, I never had no warts so I couldn't swear to it.

Castor oil is good for warts. Just put it on. Rub it on several times a day., and that way as often as you think of it, you know.

Oh yeah, they used to give us pennies, you know. And we'd give pennies to a certain party, they'd buy 'em from you and you'd give 'em the pennies, you see, to pay for it. Yes, they went away. Mrs. Freis' sister-in-law, she bought 'em from me one time. I had this whole finger covered with warts, and she bought 'em from me, and they went away.

Or even a meat rind. You take a meat rind, and rub it on, and go and bury it. You bury it anywhere. How deep it is, that's when it rots. In my later years, I never had no warts, but when I was a kid I really had a lot of 'em. Yes, when it rots, the warts go away.

Mrs. Stricker also knew about the dish rag cure.

Informant: Mrs. Minnie Stricker

LUCK SIGNS

Birds in the house

They claim if a bird gets in the house and you kill him, you won't have bad luck. But if you let him go, you'll have bad luck. A lot of people believe that. I never did think too much of it though.

Making a wish

If you want anything to come true, make a wish an' when you hear the first whippoorwill holler, it will come true.

Black cats

I am superstitious about black cats 'cause they bring me bad luck. Whenever I start fishin', when a black cat crosses my path, I might as well turn home 'cause I won't catch no fish. I'm afraid of black cats.

I wouldn't kill a cat at all because they claim it's seven years bad luck, you know, and I wouldn't want that.

If a black cat crosses your path when you're in a car, you can drive back three times and it crosses it's path out. And then they claim you won't have bad luck. You know, if you cross his path out.

Informant: Clark Lacy

Bad luck to pick flowers on graves

My aunt used to tell us when any time we walked through a cemetery, not to never pick the flowers from bokays, because, if we did, we'd have something, some bad luck, come to us, before we got home.

Luck signs

We always made a wish when we seen a redbird. They always say that any wish you make when you see a redbird will come true.

They always said if you came across a pin and the point was towards you, it'll bring you sharp luck all day. You have to pick the pin up.

They say to put a penny on your right shoe for good luck.

Oh yes, we've always heard it's bad luck to kill cats.

It's bad luck for a cat to cross your path, or a bird to fly into the house.

I never heard that it was bad luck for an engaged girl to cut the ribbons on her gifts, I always thought they was just being polite, but at every shower I've ever been at, somebody else has cut the ribbons. I guess that's why.

I've always heard that a two-dollar bill is bad luck. [Quite the opposite, I've always carried one for good luck. L.C.H.]

They say it's bad luck to put your hat on in the house. You're supposed to have bad luck too if you open an umbrella in the house.

If you've forgotten something, never return to the house to get it, 'cause you'll have bad luck.

It's supposed to be bad luck to find a five-leaf clover. [A four-leaf clover brings good luck L.C.H.]

They say it's bad luck to put your dress on backwards. My brother's mother-in-law in Michigan got hers on backwards one morning, and she wouldn't change it fer nothin' 'til after twelve o'clock. We all laughed at her, but she wouldn't take it off 'til after twelve.

When you make a wish on a falling star, turn your back on it, if you look back at it, your wish won't come true.

I've always heard it was bad luck to pay back salt if you borrowed it. Now my parents never would do that. They never would take back salt or pay it back. Way out in the country, when you ran out of salt, you had to borrow it. I don't think they ever did replace it with anything.

Grandma'd say if a hen crows, it'll put some kind of a jinx on us, bring some kind of bad luck to us, and we'd have to kill it right away. I've seen her get the boys out and make them run a hen down the moment it crowed so as it wouldn't have the chance to crow another time.

Informant: Mrs. Cordie Lee Bolin

Wishes and luck

When you drive under a bridge, honk your horn three times and make a wish. I always do this.

You should always put a penny in a purse that you give to someone.

Never give anyone a knife. It will cut your friendship. [Mrs. Cordie Bolin knew this too.]

Ruthie Bennett, a cousin, used to say that she'd hold her thumbs for good luck. 'I'll hold my thumbs for you,' she was always saying.

You make a wish on the first star you see at night.

"Star light, star bright,
First star I see tonight.
I wish I may, I wish I might,
Have this wish I wish tonight."

[Cordie and I knew this too. I always say it in the evening when I see the first star. L.C.H.]

Informant: Mrs. Lucie F. Huger

Signs of death

Well, the sayin' is that if a redbird comes and flies agin' the window, and continually keeps on, it will be a sign of a death in the family. But I don't think that's true 'cause it happened here and none of us died, yet.

Informant: Ulmont Krausch

You know, they claim that whenever you go to a funeral, the one that's the first one to leave the cemetery will be the first one to die. That's an old superstition. I don't know if it may be the fact or not.

Now this here, I actually believe that. This is not a superstition. This is something that really happened. We all heard that. That ain't superstition when you hear that and somebody else hears it. You know, you've heard of death angels a-knockin'. This was a Campbell boy. Lester Campbell was his name, and he had sugar diabetes. And he was in the house, he was settin' close to the door. And we heard a loud knock on the door, and opened it, and looked for whoever it was, and there was no one in sight. And that boy took sick that next evenin', and he died the next day. It was two days 'til he died. It really happened. It was actually. The wife and all the boys can tell you.

My wife's grandmother, she had a boy that died of diphtheria, and the dog howled then. And then one of the other boys took sick and the dog howled. And then she took and killed the dog 'cause she thought the dog caused him to die. And then he got all right.

I drempt that I was a-walkin' through the woods and I walked into an undertaker's parlor. You know, where there's caskets a-settin'. And I drempt there was birds a-flutterin' inside the buildin'. And I then I drempt whenever I left out of there, there was two big dogs. And they walked along with me. And they was a-tryin' to bite my hands. I'll tell you about them dogs later. And that's all I drempt, 'cause then I woke up. I didn't say anything. I didn't want to tell my dream before breakfast 'cause they claim that if you dream a dream and you tell it before breakfast, it will come true. And I didn't tell it.

[Lacy later told me that he had quite a bit of trouble with his brothers over his mother's estate. They apparently broke a contract that they all had signed. He firmly believes that the two dogs in his dream were his brothers and that this was a sign of how they would treat him. L.C.H.]

Informant: Clark Lacy

Signs of death in the family

If a rooster comes to the door and crows outward, not into the house, it's a sign that somebody will die and be taken out that door in a short time.

If a bird flies in the house, it's a sign that someone in the house will die soon.

When a baby's cradle suddenly starts rockin' without any reason, the baby's not likely to live to outgrow the cradle.

If a dog hangs around the house and howls, and howls, and just keeps it up, there'll be someone die in the family.

I've always heard it said never let a child see itself in the mirror before it's a year old because it's not likely to live to see its second birthday.

My brother's father-in-law was real bad sick, and he kept pickin' at his covers. And his daughter said, 'Oh dear, I guess Dad doesn't have long to live. He keeps pickin' at his covers.' But he lived. This happened at Kennett in December this year.

There's lots of whippoorwills down there. If a whippoorwill lit on the top of your house and hollered as much as three times, there'd be someone die in your family. I heard that at Poplar Bluff from some of the neighbors. Of course, that's just hearsay.

At home, they'd always stop the clock just as soon as someone passed away. And they'd always put a sheet over the mirrors. I can remember when anyone died in the house. I think the reason they stopped the clock was to have accurate time of death. I always wondered why they covered the mirrors though. Two, three years ago, I read in the papers that that was an old Jewish custom, 'cause if you looked in the mirror, you'd see the corpse and be the next to die.

They used to say that the dying person, if they asked for someone in particular just before they die, that person will be the next one to die. That's just an old sayin'. I know for a fact that ain't true.

At home, just the minute that anybody died, all the bedding went outside on the clothes line. It would hang there until after the funeral. And then it was all picked up and burned, pillows, mattresses, and all.

Informant: Mrs. Cordie Lee Bolin

Premature funeral

And then about that lady that was dead and didn't know it. And the funeral, the preacher was there an' all the neighbors, that time they didn't embalm 'em you know. Buried 'em on their own ground, you know. An' somebody seen her raise up her hand. An' oh, she had the store here for about ten years. Minnie Bartolds was her name the time she was supposed to be dead. Mrs. Curley was her name down here. She got alive again and she had the store in here for ten years., and she just died here about two years ago. Really died then. That's about sixty years ago when she was supposed to be dead.

Informant: Ben Pohlig

Signs of visitors

They claim that if you see a redbird, you'll see a man; and if it's a mother redbird, you'll see a woman.

And they claim that if you drop a fork, there'll be a man a-comin'; and if it's a spoon, there'll be a woman.

Informant: Clark Lacy

When a rooster jumps up on your front porch and crows in your front door, it's a sign that you'll have company in a short time.

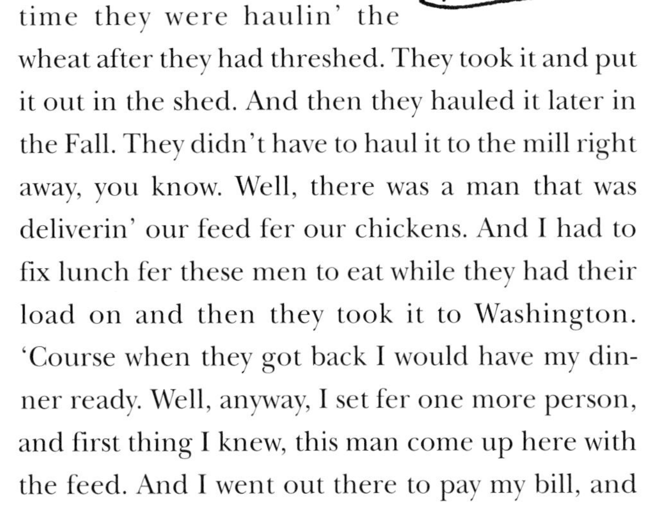

If you drop a dirty dishrag on the floor, it's a sign that someone will visit you dirtier than you are. I've heard that one but I never did go by it.

If you drop a fork, it's a sign that a man's a-comin' to visit. If you drop a knife, it be a woman.

If you take out the same thing on your plate twice, someone's comin' hungry.

If two roosters fight, it's a sign there'll be two menfolks come. If it's hens, there'll be two women.

If your nose itches constantly, it's a sure sign you're having company.

Informant: Mrs. Cordie Lee Bolin

Well, when your nose itches, or the cat washes her face with a paw. Used to, when a cat would wash herself with a paw, why, somebody would come.

Yeah, I heard that if you dropped a dirty dishrag, somebody dirty would come. I remember one time I dropped a dirty dishrag, and there was a peddler came. And he was real, you know how they are. He was from a different country, I believe he was Japanese. And he was dark complected, anyway, and he looked darker than he was. He looked more dirty in fact.

If you set fer more than your family, you make a mistake, sometimes somebody else is a comin' too. Did you know that? Anyway, one time they were haulin' the wheat after they had threshed. They took it and put it out in the shed. And then they hauled it later in the Fall. They didn't have to haul it to the mill right away, you know. Well, there was a man that was deliverin' our feed fer our chickens. And I had to fix lunch fer these men to eat while they had their load on and then they took it to Washington. 'Course when they got back I would have my dinner ready. Well, anyway, I set fer one more person, and first thing I knew, this man come up here with the feed. And I went out there to pay my bill, and he asked what my husband was doin' and I said, 'He's eatin' lunch.' And I asked him, 'Don't you want to come along and eat with us?' And he said yes, he'd come along in. So he came along in and ate with us.

Informant: Mrs. Minnie Stricker

Courtship and marriage

Did you know that red is a sign of true love? That's why they give red roses so often.

Well, they say that if you peel an apple, and whirl the long piece of peel around three times and then drop it on the ground, it will fall like the initial of the boy you will marry. That's what they used to tell us. I don't know if I tried it or not. I guess I did.

We used to break the petals off a rose and throw them over our shoulder and say, 'He loves me, he loves me not.' Whichever way it ended up, that's how you stood with the boy. [We always used a daisy. L.C.H.]

We always used to repeat this old saying:

'Married in blue, always true;
Married in green, ashamed to be seen;
Married in red, wish you were dead;
Married in yellow, ashamed of the fellow.'

You can know what your future husband's going to do by counting your buttons: 'Rich man, poor man, beggar man, thief, doctor, lawyer, merchant, chief.' [My mother also knew this one. L.C.H.]

There was another old sayin' that we used to repeat: 'Married in black, wish yourself back.'

It's supposed to be bad luck for the bride to see the groom on their wedding day before the wedding. [My mother and I both know this too. L.C.H.]

Sleep on a piece of wedding cake to dream of the one you will marry.

Never get married when it's raining, 'cause you'll shed as many tears in your married life as fall that day.

Here is another one that everybody knows. The bride should wear something old, something new, something borrowed, something blue.

First time a girl sleeps in a strange room that she's never slept in before, she names each corner a boy. And the first corner she looks at when she wakes up will be the boy she'll marry.

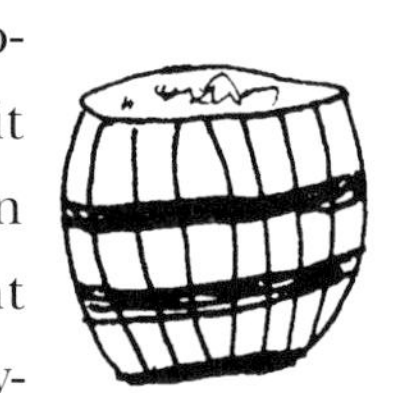

Grandma used to tell us girls to go out and look in the rain barrel on May Day mornin' and we'd see our true lover, the man we're supposed to marry. She said she tried it and her husband's face appeared in it. A bunch of us girls spent the night with me and we got up before anybody dared open their eyes and went down and peered in that rain barrel and nothing appeared.

Take a white sheet and spread it over a clover patch the first morning of May. And a snail will crawl up on it and write the name of the boy you're supposed to marry. Grandma said she tried it and it worked.

Informant: Mrs. Cordie Lee Bolin

Wishbones and picking a mate

If you take a pully bone of a chicken and two people break it, one who gets the big end will get his wish, you know. And you put it up over the door. And the first person who comes in will be the person you'll marry.

Informant: Clark Lacy

Beliefs about birth and infancy

They say a pregnant woman can mark her baby by looking at things when she is under strain. The baby will have a mark that looks like the thing she saw.

A baby born with a caul is supposed to be a genius or have strange powers. That's what they always said.

Bald-headed babies are supposed to have curly hair. That's true. Ever'one I ever seen, when it comes in, it comes in curly.

I've always heard tell that you have to watch a baby around cats. Cats will suck the baby's breath away they say. [Countless visitors have been horrified that the little children in our house sleep with cats. They all tell my mother that the cats will suck the baby's breath. L.C.H.]

Children have worms if they pick their noses. That's a pretty good sign, no kidding.

If a child has it's baby tooth pulled and never touches the hole with its tongue, a gold tooth will come in the place. Yes, we've always heard that, but that ain't true. They couldn't keep from touching the place with their tongue.

They used to tell us when we was pregnant, to not ever really crave for anything. Be sure to have your husband to go and get it because the child would come into the world cravin' for the same food or the same drink, or whatever it was you needed. And it wouldn't get off real well, you know what I mean, until it got old enough to partake of whatever this was you wanted. If I ever did want for anything in my life when I was pregnant with one of my children, it was Coke one night. I couldn't sleep that night for thinking of that Coke. That's why when Jane was born, I let her drink a whole Coke soon as she was able to, 'bout four months. I didn't want her to always have that cravin' for Coke.

When I was pregnant with Jane, I went to my grandmother's and she said, 'Cordie, I'm gonna have fried chicken for lunch today.' I said, 'Oh good, it sounds so good.' So we set down at the table, she said, 'I want ever'body to leave that bowl of chicken alone, and I want Cordie to have all she can eat.' I don't know if I really enjoyed it any more than eatin' it before, but she thought I was really cravin' that fried chicken. She sure wanted me to have all that I could eat. But I said that never did stick with me at all. Nothin' ever stuck with me but that Coke business.

I had a friend one time that never did dip snuff, only when she was pregnant. But when she was pregnant, she had a cravin' for snuff, that she said she couldn't even think about doing anything till she got her dip of snuff of a mornin'.

Grandma used to say that if a woman walked under a mare's neck during pregnancy, she would go eleven months like the mare. I heard a lot of old people say this. Even my real grandmother would caution us girls not to do such things.

Never scare a woman that's pregnant 'cause whatever you scared her with, like if you would pick up somethin' and throw it at her, you know, why wherever this touched her, her baby would have that kind of splotch on it. It would be like, one time this happened. This happened one time when I was carryin' Jane, when I was pregnant with Jane. We was movin', and Arb found some mice. And I was scared to death of 'em, just scared to death of 'em. So he pitched one at me, (it was dead). And it hit me. And my grandmother says 'Oh, you shouldn't of done that. That baby'll probably have a mouse on it somewhere.' You know, the shape of a mouse, a birthmark on it somewheres. She didn't. No, but that was the old sayin'. Just never scare a pregnant woman because you're liable to mark the baby.

Back years ago they gave black pepper tea. They'd put a teaspoon of black pepper in about a half a cup of water, and heat it real hot, when you was goin' into labor, you know, to have the baby, and make you drink that, which would make the labor pains closer together. I know, they gave me that for Jane. They gave me everything for Jane though.

They gave me shots and everything for Jane. I don't know what finally did it, but anyhow, they did give me that pepper tea. Sure did.

Care of a baby

They claim that whenever you go to dress a little, bitty baby, whichever hand you take 'em by that's the way they'll be. You know, left handed or right handed.

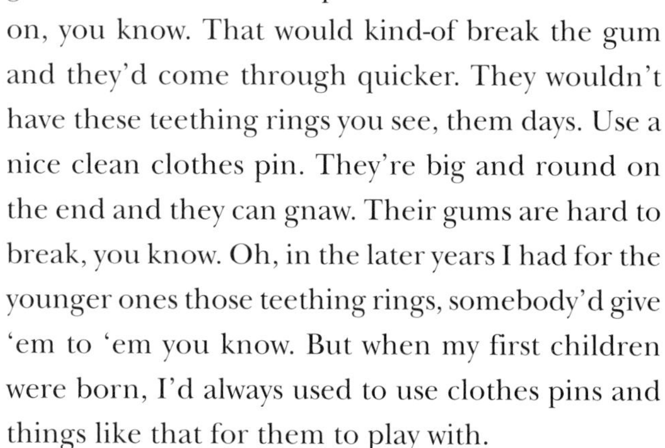

Well, I'll tell you what they used to give the babies a clothes pin to chew on, you know. That would kind-of break the gum and they'd come through quicker. They wouldn't have these teething rings you see, them days. Use a nice clean clothes pin. They're big and round on the end and they can gnaw. Their gums are hard to break, you know. Oh, in the later years I had for the younger ones those teething rings, somebody'd give 'em to 'em you know. But when my first children were born, I'd always used to use clothes pins and things like that for them to play with.

[My mother always let us teethe on clothes pins. She says they are better than anything you can buy. L.C.H.]

Things to make a baby stop crying

Well, we used to take some whisky you know. A few drops of whisky and warm water and a little sugar. And if they had any colic, that would kinda take that away. There was a kimmel whisky, that's good. My mother always kept that when she had little babies. Yeah, she used fennel too, made fennel tea. Well, I did too for my first ones, but after that I couldn't buy it at the drug store, and then I didn't use it anymore.

Well, we used to have something called asafidity. Do you know what that is? That's made outa onions and it's just like milk. You know, kinda chalky-like. You get so many drops of that, and that helps. Some people wouldn't even give it to their children, but it's a doctor's 'scription, so it should be good. And I don't think it would hurt 'em, so I give it to 'em because you had to do something sometimes because my, if they'd have colic all the time, why, that was awful too.

Baby fingernails

They alus told us that if a baby bit his nails, he wouldn't go very far in life. If a baby boy bit his nails off, he wouldn't go very far in life. You know, his life would be short. Yeah, I've heard that one.

I've always heard it said don't never trim your baby's fingernails with a pair of scissors before it's a year old. When it grows up, it will become a thief.

Teething

Take a mole's skin if a child's had trouble a-cuttin' his teeth. And kill the mole, and tie a piece around the child's neck on an old string. And let him wear it till it wears out, and the tooth will come through the gums better. Just for molar, that's all I ever heard it used for. Make the string black, though.

Nursing women

A nursing mother, a mother that's got a right young baby, eats a lot of onions, they say it's good for the nerves, for the baby you know. Quiet the baby, and make its nerves be still, and let it sleep well and not have a tummy ache, and anything else. That'd be the onion tea bit as far as that goes.

Eat lots of peanut butter and make good milk, make healthy milk for a baby. It does too, yeah. It sure does. I'll tell you what, you can feed an old cow peanut hay, maybe you all never did have no peanut hay, but we did, and the milk, just so rich that you can't hardly use it. From peanut hay. Yes, that's right. 'Course they eat the peanuts and all. They don't just eat the hay.

Sign of a new baby in the house

Used to, when there was a new baby born in the community, they'd say, 'We'll take this new baby to so-and-so's house.' Because wherever you take the last new baby to visit, that's where the next new baby will come. They'd take the baby there and they thought that would bring 'em good luck and they'd have a new baby. I'd tell my friends, right after I was married, when I was havin' my children, I had three just as fast as I could, yeah. And I'd say, 'Don't bring that new baby to my house because I don't want nary another baby right now.'

Informant: Mrs. Cordie Lee Bolin

Lots of old timers used to make watermelon seed tea. That's a remedy for babies whenever they get water bound. That's the old time remedy. I've seen it give, and I know it's good.

Informant: Clark Lacy

Children's rhymes and games

Johnny's mad, and I'm glad,
And I know what will please him.
A bottle of wine to make him shine,
And a pretty little girl to squeeze him.

Cry baby cry,
Stick your finger in your eye
Tell your mother it wasn't I..

Informant: Mrs. Cordie Lee Bolin

One misty, moisty morning, when cloudy was the weather,
I chanced to meet an old man all clad in leather
He began to compliment, and I began to grin.
"How do you do?" and "How do you do?" and "How do you do?" again.

Looking through the knot-hole in Grandpa's wooden leg.
Who'll wind the clock when I am gone?
"Run get the axe. There's a fly on baby's head."
A man's best friend is his mother. No other.

O-U-T spells out, and out you go,
Right in the middle of the deep blue sea
With a dirty, dirty dishrag tied around your knee.

[These are rhymes that my mother taught us when we were small. She learned them from her grandfather and other members of the family. Some I learned at school. L.C.H.]

"Step on a crack, break your mother's back.
Step in a hole, break your mother's sugar bowl."

[This is a game we used to play when we were walking down the sidewalk. Sometimes we almost fell on our heads trying not to step on a crack or hole. L.C.H.]

Riddles

What has eyes but can't see? Answer: A potato.

What walks on four legs in the morning, two at noontime, and three at night? Answer: A man, that's pertaining to years, you know.

What runs all over the sink but doesn't have any legs? Answer: Water.

What runs all over the country without moving? Answer: Roads.

What runs all over the country of a daytime, but sets under the bed with his tongue stuck out at night? Answer: A wagon.

What is that runs but can't walk, hollers and can't talk? Answer: A train.

As I was going through the garden gap
Who should I meet but Dick Red Cap;
A stick in his hand and a stone in his throat;
If you answer my riddle, I'll give you a groat.
Answer: A peach.

A man went away on Sunday, stayed a week, and came back on Sunday. How was that?

Answer: His horse's named was Sunday.

Old Mother Twichit has but one eye
And a long tail which she lets fly;
Every time she goes through a gap
A bit of her tail she leaves in a trap.
Answer: Needle and thread

Deep as the ocean, full as a cup;
All the king's horses can't pull it up.
Answer: A well.

Round as a biscuit, busy as a bee;
Guess, oh guess what this can be.
Answer: A watch.

What's round at both ends and high in the middle?
Answer: Ohio.

"Wellerisms"

"Well, tha's as easy as fallin' off a log backwards," they always used to say.

"I won't have the guts to do that again," said the bug as he hit the window.

"I'm de-lighted," said the firefly as he backed into the fan.

"I spec so," said the fly.

"Well, it won't be long now," said the monkey when he got his tail caught in the lawn mower." [Fan, also dog instead of monkey. L.C.H.]

"I'll meet you at the corner," said the ceiling to the wall.

"So long," said the chimp as he slid off the giraffe's neck.

"I see," said the blind man as he picked up his hammer and saw.

"Every little bit helps," said the monkey as he spit in the ocean.

Informant: Mrs. Cordie Lee Bolin

Special powers

Water witching. You ask if I know any water witches, well sister, you're a-lookin' at one. You want to know how come I came to know I was a water witch ? Back in Kentucky, there was an old man witchin' a well fer a feller, and I was a kid. I says to myself, 'I cun do that m'self.' I was just a-jokin'. I was just a kid then. I didn't know I could do it. It worked for me just like it worked for him. And that's how I came to know I was a water witch. Oh, I witched several wells. I never did fail to get water either. I can witch all right. If there's any water there, I can find it. . I found water where there never was water found before. Why down in Oklyhomy, there was this farm. And everybody round there had to haul water. They had a hundred and four head of Black Angus cattle. I found water. And they never did have water on that farm before. I can take you there and show you the pump today. That was that big farm there. All that pasture land there, and not a bit of water on it.

Well, you cut you a forked limb, and you just reach and grab it, and hold it just like this. [The arms are held straight. The single prong extended first and the double prongs grasped firmly, one in each hand, with the thumbs out.]

And if that durn thing'll work, it'll come back 'n twist itself in two. It'll come plumb over and twist itself in two. It shore will 'cause I've seen it happen. You just start walkin' and when you can begin to feel the stick movin', you start countin'. Every step you take you count your steps and figure so many feet. And that's how far down you have to dig. I betcha I can tell pretty close how far it was. That stick'll twist in two in your hand. I always use a peach tree limb. It has to be green. They claim there's one out of every family that can do it. One witch out of every family. That's what they claim.

Informant: Pearl Webb

Water witching and following bees

There was a neighbor of ours down there by the name of Calvin, Perry Calvin. He used to could go and find water, water veins. There was none in our family unless it was my Dad. He did locate that well. Do you know where that well is on the place? Well, he located that. He sure did. Well, he just dug there and got the water. I think it was only sixteen feet. That's what they say. He used a peach twig. And this Calvin, he'd come up to our place there, we had a spring. And he'd come there and watch the bees when they were drinkin' water. And he could locate where the bee trees were in the woods. He'd watch which way they would fly, you know. He was Bill Calvin's grandfather.

Informant: Mrs. Minnie Stricker

Breaking up a storm

My grandmother, she used to would go outside when there would be a storm a-comin' up. She'd say to us, she'd say, 'Now children, don't be scared. I'm gonna split this cloud wide open.' She'd take the old double bit axe and come down with a hard stroke on an old stump in the yard. She'd always stick it in the way the cloud was comin'. She'd always say to us, 'Never fear children, this ole axe will split the cloud in two.' To us the cloud always went away. It really did. Yes sir, after a while it would break up and one part would go one way, and one the other. Us kids were always happy then.

Informant: Mrs. Cordie Lee Bolin

Animal legends

We used to sit up till midnight on Christmas, 'cause Momma said the animals would kneel and pray. But I never did stick with that, 'cause I never did hear them pray. Oh, every now and then a cow would moo or a horse whinny, I guess that was supposed to be it. If we didn't hear them, Momma would say they were praying to themselves. She'd say, 'If you kids go out to the barn, you'll see the cows kneel.' You know what I think that was. Whenever you'd go to the barn they'd get up, and you know how they get up on their hunkers first, so it looks like they're kneeling. I don't know if they really believed it, or if it was excuse to let us up until midnight on that night. Come to think of it, I always thought it was the old year out and the new year in when the cows would pray.

Informant: Mrs. Cordie Lee Bolin

Snakes

Did you know how poison snakes protects their little ones? You know poison snakes stay with their little ones the first year. And the way they defend the little snakes, whenever anything comes around, the little snakes goes down their throat. I never seen 'em, but I had fellers, and I know they was true, tell me that they seen 'em. My mother said, when she was a girl, she seen an old copperhead make a noise and all the little snakes popped in its throat.

Informant: Clark Lacy

Several years ago we had some people from northern Missouri, near Chillicothe, working on our farm. They had a great fear of what they called hoop snakes. Whenever we would see a large grey snake, they would yell, 'Look out! That's a hoop snake.' These people thought that the snake would roll up and clasp the tip of its tail in its mouth. They then said that it would stand itself up and come rolling at you, like a bicycle tire. The snake would come rolling head-over-tail at its victim so fast that it was impossible to get away. They had many tales of people who had been attacked and bitten by hoop snakes.

Informant: Lucie C. Huger

Beauty treatment with a cucumber

Well, just slice a large yellow cucumber open and massage your face real good with it. And don't wash your face until morning; leave it on overnight. Just wash it off with soap and water then. It was used for bleaching purposes. It'll sure draw your skin 'til it's so tight. I remember using it once., but I never used it again 'cause I couldn't stand it. It draws your face up 'til the pressure is terrible. Mom used to tell us to do it. Grandma knew it too.

Itching hands

If a woman's right hand itches, she's gonna shake hands with some unexpected guest. And if it's her left hand that itches, she's gonna handle money.

Informant: Mrs. Cordie Lee Bolin

A good hog raiser

They say a man with hair on his back is a good hog raiser. I don't know if that means that they had to look like a hog to raise hogs.

Informant: Ulmont Krausch

Burning ears

Well, anyway, my sister had a habit that if her ears would burn, they'd just, you know, like if somebody was talkin' about her, she'd say somebody was talkin' about her. They'd just get so hot, and she'd feel on her ear.

Informant: Mrs. Minnie Stricker

The wonder driver

Well, one day we were driving through the field with a full load of hay on the wagon, about forty bales. And Arthur Johnson leaned down off the wagon and said, 'Well, we've got a wonder driver, boys.' 'What's a wonder driver, Arthur?' 'Well, he's a feller who's a drivin' and wonderin' where he's goin'. Greg was the wonder driver.

Heart dropsy

The first time we met old Arb we were picking up loose hay in the field. We didn't even know his name yet. So he leans down on his fork and says, 'Boys, I feel a fit of heart dropsy comin' on.' Ray says, 'Hey, what's a fit of heart dropsy?' Arb says, 'Well boys, it's when you drop down and don't have the heart to get up again.'

Informant: Bernard, Gregory and Raymond Huger

Planting and harvesting

You take a cucumber, here's the time to plant the cucumber. You want to plant that when the sign's in the Twins for a good yield.

Corn should be planted when the sign's in the Crab. It will stand dry weather, 'n it makes a better yield 'n it will root deeper in the ground.

You don't want to cut hay when the sign's in the Scorpion 'cause it's bitter.

The hills of St. Albans through the summer haze, 1993. Photo: Ken Gilberg

Well, a p'tater. Now you first break your ground (that'd be plow the ground). Then you work the ground and make a seed bed, that's pulverizin' the soil. 'N then you lay this off in rows three foot apart and you plant these p'taters about five inches under. It should be done when the moon's on the wane, that's in the last quarter. Now you plant these p'taters, one p'tater in a hill sixteen inches apart. You know, distance from one another. Whenever you plant p'taters, they want to be cut in quarters. Most generally you cut them that way. That'll be two or three eyes on each quarter. And the p'tater should be placed in the ground with the eye side down, that gives you more p'tater per hill. The dirt should be brought to the p'tater. As long as you cultivate the p'tater the dirt should be brought to the p'tater. That keeps the sun from gettin' to the p'tater.

Any crop, anything that makes its yield above the ground, that's planted by the light of the moon or before the moon fulls. Anything that you want to grow bigger you plant in the light of the moon...beans, flowers and the like.

Whenever watermelons start to makin' runners, you cut the runners off. And then they'll make big watermelons. You get less vines and they make big melons.

Informant: Clark Lacy

OLD BELIEFS AND SAYINGS

You'll never see it on a galloping horse.

A wise man changes his mind, a fool never does.

This is a saying I always used to hear:

> Beauty is only skin deep,
> Ugly is to the bone;
> Beauty lasts only a day,
> Ugly holds it's own.

They say you can never tell by the looks of a frog how far he can jump.

Grandma used to say that to us when she'd give us a job to do, one that we didn't like and we'd say, 'Aw, he didn't do it, why should I?' She'd say, 'Is the pot calling the kettle black?'

Take care of the pennies, and the dollars will take care of themselves.

It's easier to pull down than to build up.

The old woman's pluckin' her geese. (It's snowing)

Somebody's as big a fool as Thompson's colt. (They don't have any sense.)

Beat the devil around the stump. (To accomplish what you set out to do, and soothe your conscience at the same time by calling it by another name.) That means that you're doin' somethin' when you're not.

They always say, you can build a house, but you have to make it a home. (We always said, "It takes a heap of living in a house to make it home." L.C.H.)

Another thing that I always heard is that gasoline and whiskey don't mix.

There's an old saying: "Sing before breakfast, cry before supper."

Don't take cats with you when you move, 'cause somethin' bad will happen to you. Never bring a broom with you when you move either. It's supposed to be bad luck. Leave it standin' where it is. I never did that though. I always moved my broom with me.

After a big heavy thunderstorm, they say milk will sour real easy. But I guess that's just fer when they didn't have iceboxes.

We always heard that if a butterfly lit on you, you'd get a dress the same color. 'Light on me, light on me,' we always used to say, 'cause then we'd get a dress the same color.

This is an old saying that we used to repeat:

> Cold hands, a warm heart;
> Dirty feet, and no sweetheart.

They say that a preacher's children are always onery. It's true too. I'll tell you why, they're always movin' from place to place, and having to meet all sorts of people, everyone's always lookin' at them and talkin' to them. I remember once , when we were in church, a young preacher was giving the sermon. And his kids were in the back of church, makin' all kinds of noise and carryin' on. He stopped his sermon and said, "You've always heard that old saying, 'Preachers' children are always onery,' and I've got some back there to prove it."

You've heard the old sayin', If company comes on Monday, you will have company all week.

If you hand salt to someone at the table, you're gonna have a fight with them. You have to put the salt down first.

You know that if you cross your fingers when you tell a lie, the lie doesn't count. (We always called this "kings". L.C.H.)

Informant: Cordie Lee Bolin

FOLKLORE INFORMANTS

Mrs. Cordie Lee Bolin, 50, St. Albans, Mo. She grew up in the Boot Heel Of Missouri, near Kennett.
Fairfield, St. Albans, Mo.

William Bolin, 59?, California, Mo. A farmer from the Missouri Boot Heel.
Fairfield, St. Albans, Mo.

Bill Daily, St. Louis, Mo. He has had horses all his life.
Fairfield, St. Albans, Mo.

Terry Goggio, 24, University City, Mo. Learned from an "old Southern mammy".
Carl's Westlane Beauty Salon, Clayton, Mo.

Bernard, Gregory and Raymond Huger, my brothers
Fairfield, St. Albans, Mo.

Lucie C. Huger
Fairfield, St. Albans, Mo.

Mrs. Lucie F. Huger, 47, my mother.
Fairfield, St. Albans, Mo.

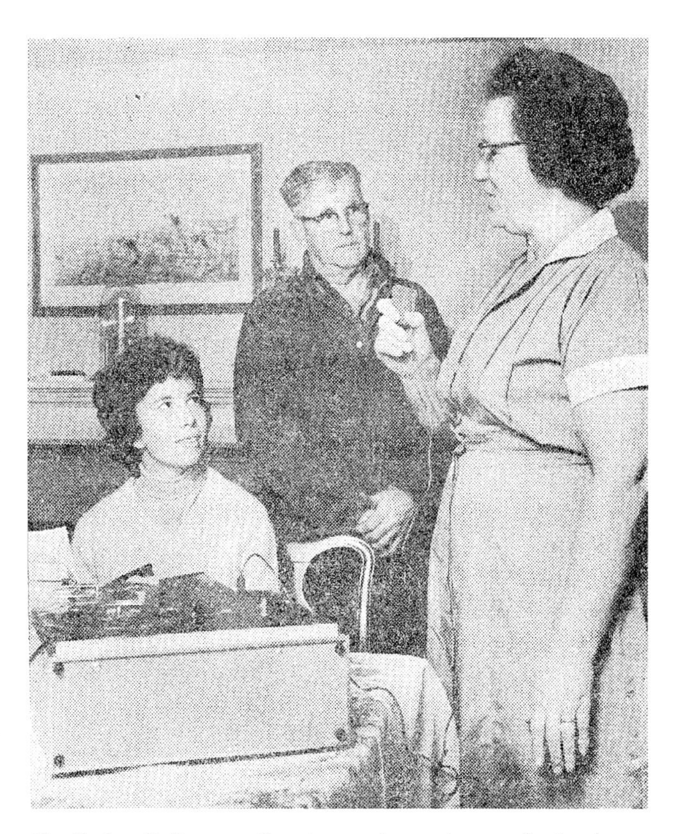

Cordie Lee Bolin recording her stories and songs for Lucie Clara Huger. Looking on is Calvin Steffens, a local handyman and neighbor at St. Albans. Photo from the St. Louis Post-Dispatch, *March 18, 1965.*

Ulmont Krausch, 67, St. Albans, Mo., a descendant of the original German settlers in this area, he farms the old family place on Bassett Road.
Tavern Creek Farm, St. Albans, Mo.

Clark Lacy, 59, Owensville, Mo., night-watchman, Rock Island Railroad, St. Albans, Mo. Lacy has spent most of his life in or near Owensville.
Head's Store, St. Albans, Mo.

Ben Pohlig, 78, St. Albans, Mo., employee, St. Albans Farms Inc. St. Albans, Mo. Ben, a descendant of the original settlers of this area, was born in St. Albans and has always lived here.
Head's Store, St. Albans, Mo.

Dr. William Small, St. Louis, Mo. Dr. Small has a place out here and has been coming to St. Albans for many years.
Head's Store, St. Albans, Mo.

Mrs. Ida Spiegleglass, Clayton, Mo.
Carl's Westlane Beauty Salon, Clayton, Mo.

Mrs. Minnie Stricker, 75, Labadie, Mo. a descendent of the original German settlers in this area.
Labadie, Mo.

Pearl Webb, 55, Labadie, Mo. He grew up in Auxier, Kentucky, the same town in which the notorious Hatfields lived.
Fairfield, St. Albans, Mo.

"The Bluffs of St. Albans." Painting by Ralph Broughton, 1966.

APPENDIXES

APPENDIX A—KINCAID

1. KINCAID HISTORY

I had several visits with Lelia Hardt Godair, granddaughter of Peter Kincaid, at her home in Pacific. She told me stories about the family. Robert Kincaid served in the Civil War; went by wagon train to Helena, Montana, met his wife out there, went back many times to visit. His wife had a farm in Shelby, Ohio – lived and died in Ohio. John Kincaid worked the family farm; he had an island with cattle on it. Alex also worked the farm. He was handsome, liked to dance, skate and swim, never married. John was taller, big, heavy and never danced. Julia talked so much about Edinburgh. John, Alex and Julia lived at the house when it burned down; chest full of Dr. Kincaid's carvings burned up. Mrs. Johnson built them another house. Lelia said her grandfather could carve anything. She remembered a bust of his sister Eliza; one of the King of Scotland; her grandmother and grandmother's sister. He was well-educated and spoke seven languages.

In her letter to me dated September 20, 1965, Evelyn Gilsinn described the children of Peter and Martha Kincaid as follows:

> As to the family, the older boys, Robert and Charles, were the bookish ones. Their father had taught them some Latin, French and German. (German was also taught in the school which the Steines family and other Germans taught.) My great-grandmother was German, but Mother said she never spoke German. She had probably come over as a child. She had lived in Manchester, where she met her future husband while he was treating her father for dropsy. According to her, he cured him. John was the farmer, a big handsome man that made me think of Santa Claus. He had a kind of floating moustache and filled the door as he stood in it. He was quite jovial. Apparently he managed the farm for the mother and the younger children until it was too late for him to consider marriage. In the time I remember, he and Alex and Julia lived there. Alex was a quiet man who liked to fish and thought socialism was just fine. Julia was the artistic one who puttered around the house and garden, played the mandolin and designed odds and ends for around the house. She read some theosophy and gave up meat in her later years. She would rant at John when he came home occasionally in high spirits after a trip to Union. She thought as little of liquor as she did of meat.
>
> The oldest son of Peter by his first wife must have been twelve years old when Peter married Martha. Jane, the daughter, was ten. These children were either born in Scotland or had been taken back to Scotland—possibly after the mother died, because my grandmother told of how the little girl —I'd think the boy—had climbed up the rigging of the sailship and had to be coaxed down. He left home as a young man to go to California and supposedly was drowned. Jane married someone named Burns and lived up around what is now the Lake of the Ozarks. Charles lived in that area too. He was postmaster of some little town. Robert had a ranch in Montana and later settled on a farm in Ohio. He kept the farm until his death, though he lived in town. The girls, Martha, Liza and Caroline, married farmers. James came to St. Louis. George had one child that died at an earlier age.

The (Eliza Kincaid) Ossenfort-Lenz Family Tree gives the following account:

> Peter Kincaid MD 1786 (Father of Elizabeth)—the colorful one on our family tree—was doctor in Wellington's Army at Waterloo. Graduate of Edinburgh Univ. Berlin School of Surgery. Owned property in downtown St. Louis before 1830. Bought 100 arpents of land on

Creve Coeur Creek 1830. Moved his family from St. Louis to St. Albans, Mo. 1837. Year of cholera epidemic in St. Louis. The story handed down—he traded the 40 acres downtown for a barrel of whiskey (the cure for cholera) and a white mule. He rode horseback from St. Albans to Ballwin (20 miles) and started the Masonic Lodge there.

Information from Dorothy Lenz Ossenfort, Curtis' wife adds to the Kincaid family history.

Dr. Kincaid later acquired more land as patients often paid their medical bills with land. The river originally came up to where the railroad tracks are. There was an island just beyond, where Kincaid's son lived. It is told that he had statues carved by his father and a trunk which he inherited but never opened. —— Dr. Kincaid is said to have been knighted for his service to Wellington in the battle of Waterloo and was known as Dr. Sir Peter.

20 acres inventoried in the John Kincaid Est.

Robert Kincaid	(brother)	Shelby, Ohio
Alex Kincaid	(brother)	Pacific, Mo.
Julia Kincaid	(sister)	Pacific, Mo.
Caroline Niesen	(sister)	St. Louis, Mo.
Martha Howard	(sister)	————
George Kincaid	(brother)	

Peter Kincaid)
Charles Kincaid) nephews, children of a brother
Howard Kincaid) Charles Kincaid
Delah Fisher)
Clara Meyer)
Nettie Bruner) nieces, children of James Kincaid
Florence Kemper) a dead brother
Grace Sabor)

Affidavit of Heirship

State of Missouri) ss
County of Franklin)

Now comes John Kincaid, who being duly sworn, says that he is the son of Peter Kincaid; that said Peter Kincaid died intestate in the year 1861, leaving heirs named as follows: Martha Kincaid, widow, and the following named children: Peter A. Kincaid, Jane Burns, Chas. A. Kincaid, Robert Kincaid, John Kincaid, James Kincaid, Alexander Kincaid, Julia Kincaid, Caroline Kincaid (Now Niesen), Martha Kincaid (now Hardt), Geo. L. Kincaid, and Eliza Kincaid, now deceased, but leaving as her children and heirs Fred. W. Ossenfort, Charles H. Ossenfort, John P. Ossenfort, Hattie Berthold, August L. Ossenfort and Edward W. Ossenfort; That Martha Kincaid, the widow, purchased Jane Burns' interest which is 1/12 interest; that the said Martha Kincaid died intestate in the year 1897, leaving heirs named as follows: Chas. A. Kincaid, Robert Kincaid, John Kincaid, James Kincaid, Alexander Kincaid, Julia Kincaid, Caroline Niesen, Martha Hardt. Geo. L. Kincaid and the children of Eliza Ossenfort, the husband of said Eliza Ossenfort also being dead, named as follows: Fred. W. Ossenfort, Charles H. Ossenfort, John P. Ossenfort, Hattie Berthold, August L. Ossenfort and Edward W. Ossenfort; that the Peter A. Kincaid and Jane Burns were step children of said Martha Kincaid.

That the option given December 2nd, 1903, of record is vol. 58 at page 582, executed by Martha Hardt and husband, Caroline Niesen, and Julia A. Kincaid, and the option given November 14th, 1903, of record vol. 58 at page 583, executed by James Kincaid and wife, both in favor of Newell C. Knight and Joseph O. Morris are long ago run out, and that said Newell C. Knight and Joseph O. Morris do not claim any more right under said option, as far as I know

Signed John Kincaid

Subscribed and sworn to before me, this 20th day of September 1912.

Emil O. Griese
Notary Public
My com. Exp. Mch. 6th 1913

Charles Ossenford) [*sic*]
John ")
Eddie ") nephews & niece, children
August ") of decd. Sister Eliza
Ossenford
Hattie Berthold)

Hilda Ossenford (now married) Grandniece a daughter of Fred Ossenford, decd. who was a son of Eliza Ossenford, decd.
Mamie Graham, GrandNiece, daughter of Ellen Spellman, Decd. who was a daughter of Charles Kincaid, decd.

RR P O Box 220 Indianapolis, Ind.

2. KINCAID GENEALOGY

Peter Kincaid, b. Nov. 15, 1785, Scotland; d. Oct. 12, 1861, St. Albans, Mo.
Dr. Peter Kincaid was married to Ann McKinnon. Ann deserted him June 10, 1836. It is not known whether or not she was the mother of his two children

1. Peter, b. 1828 in Missouri; died in California.
2. Mary Jane, b. 1831 in Missouri; d. 10/21/1914
   m. Thomas Burns, some time after 1851
   Issue: Burns
   1. Mary
   2. Charles
   3. Thomas
   4. David
   5. James
   6. John
   7. Malissa
   8. Sarah Elizabeth, b. 9/6/1868; d. 2/12/1937
      m. 1881 Joseph Martilus Phelan, b. 6/19/1858; d. 11/12/1937
      Issue: Phelan
      1 Toy Jesse, b. 1/29/1894; d. 1/18/1955
        m.10/28/1916 Anna Mildren Cowden, b. 6/12/1902; d. 1/22/1965
        Issue: Phelan
        1 Cornelia Myrtle Elizabeth, b. 2/2/1922; d. 12/12/1965
          m. 12/3/1942 Preston Reece Morrison, b. 5/14/1921
          Issue: Morrison
          1 Naomi Rita Mae, b. 8/22/1943
            m. (1) Henry Lee Schulle
            m. (2) Elwood H. Carpenter
            m. (3) Hoyt Ray Jones
            Issue: Jones
            1. Rheetah

Dr. Peter Kincaid married Martha Mueller 1841.
Martha Mueller, b. 8/22/1819; d. 9/14/1897
Issue: Kincaid

I Charles A., b. 9/20/1842
  m. Martha Wright

Issue: Kincaid
1. Peter
2. Charles
3. Howard
4. Ella
5. Noni
6. (girl)

II Robert, b. 1/28/1843
He moved to Montana and had a ranch; married widow with one son in Montana. Moved to Ohio where he and his wife settled on a farm; died in Ohio. No issue.

III John, b. 9/14/1846; d. 1927
Never married; lived at St. Albans; buried in Kincaid Cemetery, St. Albans, Mo.

IV James, b. 1848; d. 1916
m. (1) Louise Ronsick
Issue: Kincaid
1. Delah, m. Fisher
2. Clara, m. Dr. Chris Meier
Issue: Meier
1 Hazel, m. Kenneth W. Bower
2 Esther, m. Ducey
3 Nettie, m. Bruner
Issue: Bruner
1 David Kincaid
4 Florence, m. Kemper
5 Grace, m. (1) Sabor
m. (2)2/13/1922, Isobel Daly Schepp

V Alexander, b. 8/5/1849; d. 1/28/1937
Never married; lived at St. Albans; buried in Kincaid Cemetery, St. Albans, Mo.

VI Elizabeth (Eliza), b. 5/21/1852; d. 7/21/1885
m. William Frederick Ossenfort, b. 10/27/1847; d. 3/5/1897
Issue: Ossenfort
1. Frederick William (twin of Charles), b. 8/26/1873; d. 1/15/1945
m. Pauline Zellharben(r)
Issue: Ossenfort
1 Hilda, m. Steines
2. Charles H., (twin of Frederick), b. 8/26/1873; d. 8/3/1952
m. Caroline Lenz
Issue: Ossenfort
1 William Frederick, d. 6/5/1985
m. Viola
Issue: Ossenfort
1 William Frederick

2 Dovie
m. William Simmons
Issue: Simmons
1 William
m. Diane Boullicouit

3. John Peter, b. 6/18/1875; d. 6/12/1940
m. 9/9/1909, Clara Zeta Reckart, b. 12/17/1877; d. 5/10/1951
Issue: Ossenfort
1 John Peter II, b. 3/22/1913; d. 6/5/1985
m. 8/12/1939, Barbara Kathryn Jean Kleefisch, b. 5/20/1914
Issue: Ossenfort
1 John Peter III, b. 12/15/1940
m. 6/19/76, Cheryl Gaye Kliefoth, b. 5/15/1946
Issue: Ossenfort
1 John Peter IV, b. 4/8/1978
2 Caroline Lee, b. 5/23/1980
2 William James, b. 3/24/1942
m. 2/23/1964, Marcia Juanita Lee, b. 5/17/1946
Issue: Ossenfort
1 Cynthia Lee, b. 3/17/1966
2 William James, b. 10/17/1970
3 John Peter, b. 2/7/1977
4 Christopher Henry, b. 6/4/1980
3 Barbara Judith, b. 5/19/1946
m. 8/1/68, Jerome John Murphy, b. 3/28/1942
Issue: Murphy
1 Scott Michael, b 2/20/1970
2 Molly Ann, b. 1/18/1972
3 Andrew Christopher, b. 7/11/1974
4 Jerome John, b. 8/12/1975
5 Timothy Patrick, b. 8/11/1976
4 Jean Lee, b. 10/26/1954
m. 5/31/1981, Richard B. Specter, b. 9/6/1951
Issue: Specter
1 Lauren Elizabeth, b. 3/16/1982
2 Lindsey Ann
3 Allison

4. Henriette, b. 6/7/1878; d. 1/30/1966
m. 5/9/1899, John Christian Berthold, b. 4/10/1870; d. 11/30/1938
Issue: Berthold
1 Harold John, b. 7/31/1900; d. 8/1/1977
m. 10/15/1921, Grace Ann Glaessman
2 John Christian, b. 2/20/1902; d. 4/18/1903
3 Mildred Leona, b. 12/14/1905; d. 2/13/1979
m. 11/24/1949, Frederick Mintz
4 Marjorie Marie, b. 2/5/1914
m. 2/3/1940, August Daniel Beyer, b. 11/1/1912

Issue: Beyer
1 Elizabeth Kincaid, b. 12/22/1940
m. 2/8/1964, Samuel Morey
2 Hilary Claire, b. 9/21/1943
3 Charles Alexis, b. 1/18/1947
m. 5/16/1970, Janyce Wasling
4 Gregory Berthold, b. 12/15/1948; d. 7/1/1949

5. August L.Dudley (twin of Edward), b. 12/24/1879; d. 5/20/1942
m. (1)Lenore Rittenhaus
Issue: Ossenfort
1.August Dudley, b. 2/19/1910; d. 12/17/1984
m. 9/29/1934, Mildred O'Connor, b. 9/8/1910
Issue: Ossenfort
1 John Dudley, b. 7/17/1941
m. 7/20/1963, Roberta Byington, b. 4/25/1942
Issue: Ossenfort
1 Carol Jean, b. 8/31/1964
2 John Dudley, b. 8/3/1965
3 Paul
4 Clifford

6. Edward W.(twin of August), b. 12/24/1879; d. 11/7/1937
m. Rosa Lenz
Issue: Ossenfort
1.Curtis
m. Dorothy Riddle
Issue: Ossenfort
1 Dorothy Lenz
2 Clifford
3 Charles
4 Edward

VII Julia, b. 7/29 1854; d. 12/1/1939
Never married; lived at St. Albans, buried in Kincaid Cemetery, St. Albans, Mo.

VIII Caroline, b. 4/21/1855; d. 6/8/1930
m. 12/17/1877, August Niesen, b. 12/2/1854; d. 3/17/1897
Issue: Niesen
1. Victor, d. 7/12/1883
2. Amanda, b. 10/23/1878; d. 10/30/1926
m. 12/8/1898, Frederick A Schroeder
3. William J., b. 7/26/1880; d. 11/16/1925
m. Florence Addie Bever
4. Edna J., b. 7/22/1884; d. 11/7/1971
m. Francis Xavier Gilsinn
Issue: Gilsinn
1 Evelyn, b. 6/19/1904

2 Francis Andrew, b. 1/21/1906; d. 12/22/1968
m. 5/25/1932, Ida Danner, b. 8/24/1910
Issue: Gilsinn
1 Joan, b. 9/20/1934
m. 10/14/1958, Lawrence Baricevic, b. 3/20/1933
Issue: Baricevic
1 John Alan, b. 10/21/1959
2 Mary Elizabeth, b. 10/17/1963
3 Mark Lawrence, b. 10/18/1965
2 Susan, b. 11/7/1943
m. 5/27/1967, Bruce Howard Guignard, b. 4/19/1934
Issue: Guignard
1 Bruce Howard Jr., b. 1/12/1972
2 Amy Suzanne, b. 1/14/1975
3 Robert Anthony, b. 6/13/1911; d. 10/3/1973
m. 1/12/1935, Margaret Benecke, b. 3/19/1915
Issue: Gilsinn
1 Jeanne, b. 3/21/1936
m. 11/10/1956, Floyd Edward Seipp Jr., b. 7/18/1932; d. 5/3/1993
Issue: Seipp
1 Daniel Craig, b. 4/30/1961
2 Barbara Jeanne, b. 11/2/1968
m. 10/12/1996, Ali Gildor, b. 1/18/1969
4 Rosemary Gilsinn
m. (1) Lowell Meyer
Divorced
m. (2) Edward O'Brien

5. Howard C., b. 10/31/1889; d. 3/31/1971
m. Eleanora Wilson

6. Pearl M., b. 1894

IX Martha Jane, b. 4/21/1857; d. 6/18/1927
m. 10/10/1878, Charles Arthur Hardt, b. 4/9/1854; d. 2/2/1937
Issue: Hardt
1. Clara, b. 12/24/1879; d. 7/20/1965
m. Charles Wiedner
Issue: Wiedner
1 Earl
m. (1)Sullivan
m. (2) ________
Issue:
1 Marie
2 Chris
3 _____
2 Marie
m. Harry Ottman
Issue: Ottman
1 Jane
2 Harry

2. Nellie E., b. 8/13/1881; d. 8/17/1974
m. Alex Halbach
Issue: Halbach
1 Gerald
2 Iola
3. Alex, d. 2/16/1968
m. Alice Paffrath, d. 2/14/1963
Issue: Hardt
1 Elmer
2 Bernard
3 Irvin
4 _____
5 _____
6 _____
4. Alice,
m. Joseph Baier, d. 6/18/1967
Issue: Baier
1 Isabelle,
m. Clifford Poertner
2 Lester
3 Marvin,
m. Loraine K.
4 died in infancy
5 died in infancy
6 died in infancy
5. Lelia, b. 1/15/1892
m. 1/17/1914, Milton Godair, b. 8/5/1887; d. 5/2/1974
Issue: Godair
1 John Arthur, b. 11/20/1914; d. 10/15/1993
m. 6/30/1944, Jean Young, b. 8/18/1922 married in Melbourne, Australia
Issue: Godair
1 David Scott, b. 4/6/1945
m. (1) 10/26/1974, Sandra Marie Withoelder
No issue. Divorced
2 Ann Elizabeth, b. 8/11/1952
m. (1)7/15/1972, Gordon Coleman
Issue: Coleman
1 Scott Adrian, b. 12/15/1975
Divorced
m. (2) David Duckworth
Issue: Duckworth
1 Waylon David, b. 8/6/1979
2 Irma Lavinia, b. 11/16/1916; d. 5/20/1993
m. 1/21/1939, Francis Paul Binfield, b. 12/19/1913
Issue Binfield
1 Paul Alan, b. 4/14/1940
m. 3/18/1961, Shirley Ann Mason, b. 3/28/1942

Issue: Binfield
1 Ronald Alan, b. 12/14/1961
m. (1) 6/6/1981, Cindy Eldred, b. 5/10/1962
Issue: Binfield
1 Sarah Rene, b. 9/1/1983
Divorced
m. (2)8/19/1986, Michele LaVonne Johnson, b. 9/12/1963
Issue:Binfield
1 Erica Stella, b. 11/7/1987
Divorced

2 Vicki Jo, b. 2/17/1966
m. 2/10/1984, Stephen Mark Anderson
Issue: Anderson
1 Brooke Elicia, b. 10/2/1988
2 Brittany Nicole, b. 10/19/1989
3 Holly Marie, b. 10/26/1991

3 Kari Lynn, b. 9/6/1968

3 Roy Donald, b. 9/12/1923
m. 11/27/1947, Lorene Wilma Hardt, b. 1/20/1925 (3rd cousin)
Issue: Godair
1 Margaret Ann, b. 3/8/1950
m. 2/14/1976, John Robert Preiss, b. 5/22/1941
Issue: Preiss
1 Kathryn Louise, b. 1/8/1980
2 Elizabeth Johanna, b. 10/26/1986
2 Carolyn Louise, b. 11/3/1951
m. 12/28/74, Gerard William Warmann, b. 2/15/1951
Issue: Warmann
1 Emily Kathryn, b. 1/9/1979

4 David Harris, b. 9/14/1925
m. 11/25/1950, Joan Schuler
Issue: Harris
1 Betty Jean, b. 12/10/1954
m. 11/16/1974, Michael Lange, b. 12/26/1950
Issue: Lange
1 Christopher David, b. 8/26/1979
2 Jared Michael, b. 2/7/1983

5 Verna Jean, b. 7/24/1927
m. 11/16/45, Chester Preston Stoval, b. 7/28/1921
Issue: Stovall
1 Susan Marie, b. 4/25/1949
m. 9/14/1968, Glenn Harold Koch, b. 1/26/1942
No issue

X George L. Kincaid, b. 1859
m. Annie Bouquet
Issue: Kincaid
1 Caroline Ann, died young

APPENDIX B—LINK

1. "HOTEL REGISTER"

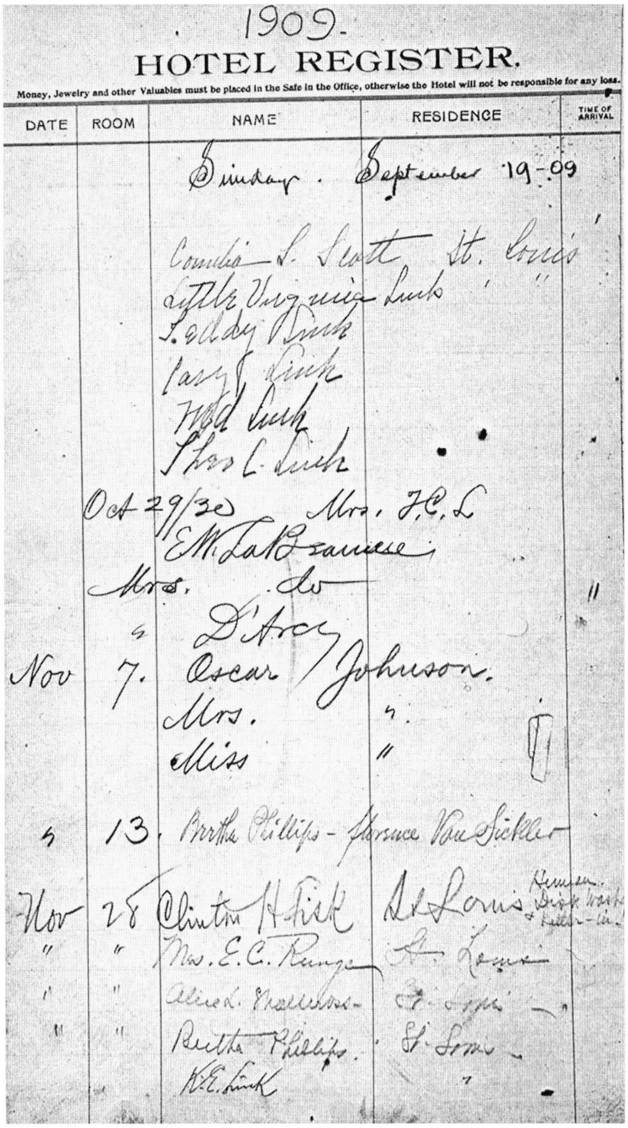
1909.

HOTEL REGISTER.

Money, Jewelry and other Valuables must be placed in the Safe in the Office, otherwise the Hotel will not be responsible for any loss.

DATE	ROOM	NAME	RESIDENCE	TIME OF ARRIVAL
		Sunday. September 19-09		
		Cornelia S. Scott	St. Louis	
		Little Virginia Link	"	
		Link		
		Link		
		Link		
		Thos C. Link		
Oct 29/30		Mrs. T.C.L.		
		E.M. LaBeaume		
		Mrs. do		"
		D'Arcy		
Nov	7.	Oscar Johnson		
		Mrs.	"	
		Miss	"	
"	13	Bertha Phillips - Florence Van Sickler		
Nov	28	Clinton H. Fisk	St. Louis	
"	"	Mrs. E.C. Runge	St. Louis	
"	"		St. Louis	
"	"	Bertha Phillips	St. Louis	
		K.E. Link		

A sample page from Link's "Hotel Register" from 1909 with signatures of the Link and Johnson Families.

The guest book of Annie and Theodore Link, the "Hotel Register," dates from 1903. In it are signatures, greetings, sketches and photographs. The original book is now in the possession of Theodore C. Link, Jr.

Tribute to Theodore C. Link Sr.

There was a man in our town
And he was wondrous wise,
For on a cliff his home he built
And dwelt there near the skies.

And when he found that friends of his,
With all their might and main
Did love the place – he asked them there
Again and yet again.

And oh! The jolly times they had
In doors and out doors too,
With "jack pots" and with "roodles"
With chips red, white and blue.

And now that Christmas time is here
These friends have tried to think
If they could give something nice
To their dear friend Mr. Link.

But pictures, rugs and ornaments
And furniture galore
He had in such profusion that
They could not give him more.

And so, although they thought and thought
They were quite in despair,
For everything that they could name
He had already there.

At last a memory came to them
Of how they scrubbed with might
Upon the so-called "silver" spoons
But could not make them bright.

Then to the store with well-filled purse
They hastened with elation,
And bought these nice new spoons without
A moment's hesitation.

Now Mr. Link, they're sent to you
With hearty Christmas wishes
By Bertha, Ned and Alice,
The ones who washed the dishes,

And struggled with the old spoons
In such a cheerful way.
They hope you'll let them try to wash
The new ones, too, some day.

Christmas 1909

(Author unknown)

Tribute to Oscar Johnson

Gentle he was and free from boast or passion
Gracious in bearing, with a manner kind.
Made in a mold for strength, and not for fashion
Liberal of deeds and generous of mind.

Honest in purpose with a humble learning;
Rich in experience of men & things;
He kept the lamps of early dreams still burning –
E'en while his hopes of victory took wings.

Here in the hills, he was a prince in seeming
Simple in manner – by success unspoiled;
No man might know of what his soul was dreaming –
But all might share the things for which he toiled.

Bright be the land where now his soul rejoices
Templed and crowned with vales and hills so fair
Sweet with the happy sound of woodland voices
Unknown to sorrow & devoid of care.

W. M. C. 1917

Ode to ST. ALBANS

When the sun shines brightly o'er St. Albans,
Bees and birds a merry chorus sing
There the river murmurs to the hill tops,
The forests in glad echoes ring.
In bygone days I spent sweet childhood hours
On sunny ways a plucking wildwood flowers.
Where nature's kiss so fair
Gives to the balmy air
A perfume, rich and rare.
O beautiful St. Albans.

When the moon beams gently o'er St. Albans,
Bees and birds asleep in dewy beds,
There the river whispers to the hill tops,
Where twilight's hour the shadow weds.
Oft in my dreams I wander back again,
To ripling streams, my old home down the lane,
I love thy rocks and rills,
Thy fields and vine clad hills,
My heart with longing fills
For beautiful St. Albans.

Mrs. Walter L. Smith,
Centaur 11-14-19

APPENDIX C—BECKER

1. *CORDWOOD—1856-1863*

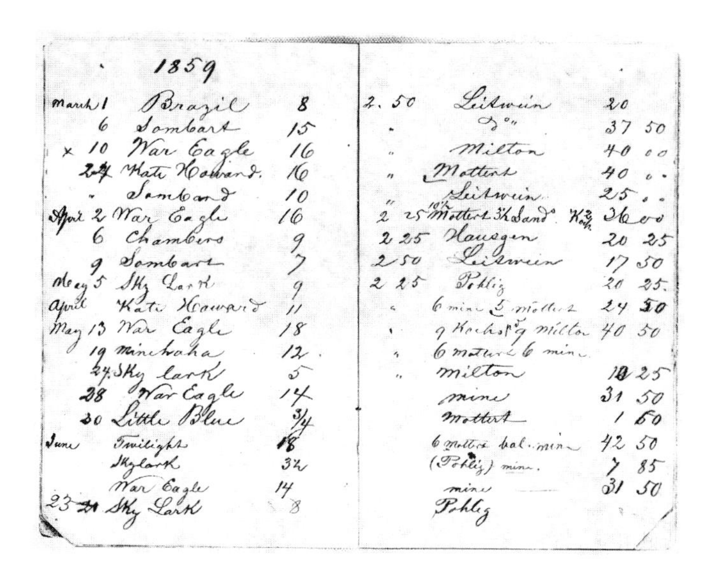

1859

March 1	Brazil	8	2.50	Leitwein	20
6	Sombart	15	"	Do"	37 50
x 10	War Eagle	16	"	Milton	40 00
24	Kate Howard.	16	"	Mottert	40 ..
"	Sombard	10		Leitwein	25 ..
April 2	War Eagle	16	2 25	Mottert [illegible]	36 00
6	Chambers	9	2 25	Hausgen	20 25
9	Sombart	7	2 50	Leitwein	17 50
May 5	Sky Lark	9	2 25	Pohlig	20 25
April	Kate Howard	11	"	6 mine 5 mottert	24 50
May 13	War Eagle	18	"	9 [illegible] 9 Milton	40 50
19	Minehaha	12	"	6 mottert 6 mine	
24	Sky lark	5	"	Milton	12 25
28	War Eagle	14		mine	31 50
30	Little Blue	3/4		Mottert	1 60
June	Twilight	18		6 mottert bal. mine	42 50
	Skylark	32		(Pohlig) mine	7 85
	War Eagle	14		mine	31 50
23	Sky Lark	8		Pohlig	

The Becker "Cordwood 1856-1863."

The descendants of Francis Becker have his small record book *Cordwood—1856-1863* giving the date, steamboat, number of cords taken up, price, whose wood, amount. For example: "April 6 Chambers 9 2.25 Hausgen 20.25" meant that on April 6, the steamboat *Chambers* took on 9 cords of wood at $2.25 per cord, supplied by Hausgen for which Hausgen was paid $20.25.

Here are the names of some of the steamboats listed: *Herald, Dan Tatum, Key-Stone, Admiral, Polar Star, Martha Jewett, Ogden, Morning Star, Bend Bold, Emma, St. Mary, Edinburgh, Violet, Kate Howard, Asa Wilgus, White Cloud, Watoso, New Lucy, Delaware, South Wester, Minehaha, T. L. McGill, Wm. Kampbell, Platt Valley, Star of the West, War Eagle, Peerless, Perry, Brazil, Sombart, Sky Lark, Little Blue, Florinz, Sioux City, Aubray, Estella, Isabella, Robt. Campbell, Omaha City, Shreveport, Spread Eagle, Clarabell, Glascow, Mattie Stevens, Calypsa, Wenona.*

Becker also listed the price he received for the wood:

Price of cordwood		
March	1856	$2.75
June	56	$2.50
August	57	$2.75
April	58	$3.00
May		$2.75
July		$2.50
April	59	$2.25
July	59	$2.00
June	60	$1.50
July		$1.75
Aug	61	$1.00–$1.75
April	62	$2.50–$1.25
Mar	63	$2.50

APPENDIX D—HORN

1. LETTER FROM WILBERT HORN

Labadie, Mo.
January 31, 1986

Dear Friend Mrs. Huger,

I am giving you a copy of Our Dear Gertie and Memories, I suppose you will wonder why. Since Gertie passed away I have lived my life over in thoughts. Your Christmas card brought back many memories of the Hugers. When we first met you and your family that very cold snowy cold winter day you were on the way to church at St. John's and you stoped at our home because your car was frozen up and your family were very cold. We were glad to share our fire with you while Mr. Huger and I thawed out the radiator.

Who would have every guessed at that time what the future held for our family. We were so different and yet so much the same. You were Catholic we prositent. We were farmer you were city folks in a way as Mr. Huger was a profesinal person. But there were some likeness we worshiped the same God we both loved our familys and had high goals. Our contacts were seldom but there was quite some likeness and some differences. It reminds me of the lines on the globe that go from pole to pole they can be half a world apart and yet arrive at the same place. It was so nice to see you at our 50th wedding aniversity. How nice Mr. Huger looked in his white summer suit. I am sorry I do not rember how nice you looked but your presents was not overlooked.

Your party when you moved to the city we appreciated the invitation very much and enjoyed meeting your family.

The loss of your daughter in the bloom of life and our son must have given some likeness in our lives.

I think the Book we wrote shows in principle that (you may not agree) we have straind to live life to it best potencials and have achieved to a certain point. Gertie was very intristed in the Church Universal and devoted very much of her energy to achieve her goal and apairently that is your goal.

The reason I send you this book is because I feel you and Mr. Huger have shown your purposes in life were for the better thing achieved by following the Precepts of Our Lord and Savior Jesus Christ.

Your friend,
Wilbert A. Horn

P.S. May be some of the pictures of St. Albans will intrest you as I know you have a great love for St. Albans.

P.S. again
If I am out of order please forgive me. I am 87 I enjoyed writing this it is such pleasant memories. Thanks.

APPENDIX E —MOTTERT

1. EARLY RECOLLECTIONS

The Mottert house, now lost to fire. Sketch by Herman.

The Republican Tribune
Union, Mo., 1935

Mrs. Emma Mottert celebrated her 90th birthday January 20, 1935.

All brought well filled baskets and at one o'clock a delicious dinner was served. The afternoon was spent in playing cards and relating stories of Grandma Mottert's early days in Franklin County.

Mrs. Mottert was born in Germany January 19, 1845. She came to this country at the age of 20 years. Of the 70 years that she spent in this country, 65 were spent in the neighborhood of St. Albans and nearly 63 years of this time on the same place where she now resides.

She loves to tell how they hauled cordwood to the boat landing at St. Albans, then quite a river port. How well she remembers the old ox teams and the wood wheeled wagons, wheels that were cut out of huge sycamore logs and made without spokes, then came the days of horse and buggy, the R.F.D. , the telephone, the radio, the airplane, and it happened that on Saturday January 19th, the Government began to operate the Beacon Light that the planes may operate by night as well as by day.

In her early days here in the county the traffic along Little Tavern Road was scarcely more than one oxteam per day. Now she can sit on her front porch and count an endless caravan of cars on the farm to market road that passes her home.

HOMESTEAD.

Receiver's Office, Boonville Mo Dec. 3rd, 1870.

RECEIVER'S RECEIPT, No. 8160. APPLICATION, No. 8160.

RECEIVED of Charlie Mottert Jr. the sum of Fourteen dollars — cents; being the amount of fee and compensation of Register and Receiver for the entry of E ½ of N E ¼ of Section 15 in Township 44 of Range 2 East under the acts of Congress approved May 20, 1862, and March 21, 1864, entitled "An act to secure homesteads to actual settlers on the public domain." Containing 80 acres

$14 — Jno. N. Gott Receiver.

A copy of the certificate whereby Charles Mottert purchased 80 acres for $14, dated December 3, 1870.

BIBLIOGRAPHY

Books

Atlas Map of Franklin County, Missouri, St. Louis Atlas Publishing Company, St. Louis, Mo., 1878.

The Catholic Encyclopedia, Encyclopedia Press, Inc., New York, 1913.

History of Franklin, Jefferson, Washington, Crawford & Gasconade Counties, Missouri, Goodspeed Publishing Company, Chicago, 1888, Reprinted by Ramfre Press, Cape Girardeau, Missouri, 1958.

The History of Missouri, Family and Personal History, Vol. IV, Lewis Historical Publishing Co., Inc., New York and West Palm Beach, 1967.

History of Southeast Missouri, with Biographical Appendix, Goodspeed Publishing Company, 1888.

Missouri, American Guide Series, sponsored by The Missouri State Highway Department; Duell, Sloan and Pearce, New York, 1941.

National Encyclopedia of American Biography, Vol. 24.

Standard Atlas, Franklin County, Missouri, 1919.

Appleman, Roy E., prepared Second Printing, *Lewis and Clark Historic Places Associated with Their Transcontinental Exploration (1804-06),* Robert G. Ferris, Series Editor: The Lewis and Clark Trail Heritage Foundation and The Jefferson National Expansion Historical Association, St. Louis, Missouri, 1993.

Applebaum, Roy E., prepared Part Two, "Historic Sites" as listed in "Lewis and Clark"; The National Survey of Historic Sites and Buildings, Vol. XII, United States Department of the Interior, National Park Service.

Bond, Christy Hawes, *Gateway Families,* Ancestors and Descendants of Richard Simrall Hawes III and Marie Christy Johnson; The New England Historical Genealogical Society, Boston, Mass., 1994.

Carleton, Will, *Farm Ballads,* Harper & Brothers, Franklin Square, New York, 1882.

Chittenden, Hiram Martin, *History of Early Steamboat Navigation on the Missouri River,* in 2 vols., P. Harper, New York, 1962, Vol. 1, p. 81.

Duden, Gottfried, *Report on a Journey to the Western States of North America and a Stay of Several Years Along the Missouri (During the Years 1824, '25, '26 and 1827).* An English Translation; General Editor, James W. Goodrich; The State Historical Society of Missouri and University of Missouri Press; Columbia & London, 1980. Introduction.

Drummond, Malcolm, *Historical Sites in Franklin County, Missouri,* Harlan Bartholomew & Associates, 1978.

Edwards, Richard, and Hopewell, M., Edward's *Great West and Her Commercial Metropolis, Embracing a General View of the West, and a Complete history of St. Louis, From the Landing of Liguest in 1764, to the Present Times, with Portraits and Biographies of Some of the Old Settlers, and Many Prominent Business Men,* St. Louis; Published at the Office of *Edwards Monthly, a Journal of Progress,* 1860.

Handlin, Oscar, *The Uprooted—The Epic Story of the Great Migrations That Made the American People,* Boston; Little Brown and Company, 1951.

Houck, Louis, *The Spanish Regime in Missouri,* in 2 volumes, Chicago, Illinois, R.R. Donnelley & Sons Company, 1909.

Kiel, Herman Gottlieb, *The Centennial Biographical Directory of Franklin County, Missouri,* compiled and published by Kiel, 1925.

Lavender, David, *The Way to the Western Sea,* Anchor Book, published by Doubleday by arrangement with Harper & Row, Publishers, March 1990.

Leonard, John W., ed. , *The Book of St. Louisians,* St. Louis, The St. Louis Republic, 1906.

MacGregor, Carol Lynn, edited and annotated *The Journals of Patrick Gass, A Member of the Lewis and Clark Expedition,* Mountain Press Publishing Compnay, Missoula, Montana, 1997.

Nasatir, A.P., ed. , Before Lewis and Clark, *Documents Illustrating the History of the Missouri, 1785–1804,* in 2 vols., St. Louis Historical Documents Foundation, St. Louis, Missouri, 1952.

Rombauer, Robert Julius, *The Union Cause in St. Louis in 1861—An Historical Sketch,* St. Louis; Press of Bixon, Jones Printing Co., 1909.

Scharf, John Thomas, *History of St. Louis, City and County, from the Earliest Periods to the Present Day; Including Biographical Sketches of Representative Men*, in 2 vols., Philadelphia; Louis H. Everts and Co., 1883.

Snyder, Gerald S., *In the Footsteps of Lewis and Clark*, National Geographical Society, Washington, D. C., 1970.

Stevens, Walter B. , *Centennial History of Missouri 1820–1921*, University of Missouri Library, Columbia, Mo.

Stoddard, Amos, *Sketches, Historical and Descriptive, of Louisiana*, Philadelphia, Published by Mathew Carey, 1812.

Thurston, Herbert, S.J., and Attwater, Donald, *The Lives of the Saints*, J.P. Kenedy & Sons, New York, 1956.

Thwaites, Reuben Gold, *Early Western Travels, the Journal of the Lewis and Clark Expedition: August 30, 1803–August 24, 1806*, compiled by the Center for Great Plains Studies at the University of Nebraska, Lincoln; published in 8 volumes as *The Journals of the Lewis and Clark Expedition.*

Weaver, H. Dwight, *Missouri, The Cave State*, Discovery Enterprises, 2006 Daisy Lane, Jefferson City, Missouri, 65101, Dark Pathways Series, Book Four, 1979.

Woestemeyer, Ina Faye, *The Western Movement*, N.Y., Appleton-Century Co. Inc., 1939.

Manuscripts and Periodicals

Anderson, Hattie M., "Missouri, 1804–1826: Peopling a Frontier State," *Missouri Historical Review*, XXXI, Missouri Historical Society, St. Louis, Mo., 1936.

Balesi, Charles J., "The Time of the French in the Heart of North America, 1673–1818," Alliance Française Chicago, with the support of Mr. Barry MacLean, 1992.

Bek, William S., "The Followers of Duden," translation of "Gottfried Duden's Report, 1824–1827," seven articles, *Missouri Historical Review*, 1919-1921, Missouri Historical Society, St. Louis, Mo.

Becker, Charles, "Day Book," 1903–1907.

Becker, Francis, "Day Book," 1868.

Becker, Francis, *Cordwood—1856-1863.*

Billion, Frederick Louis, *Annals of St. Louis in its Territorial Days, from 1804 to 1821*, Printed for the author, St. Louis, 1888.

Blum, Virgil C., S.J., *The German Element in St. Louis 1859–1861*, unpublished Master of Arts Thesis, St. Louis University, 1945.

Bogler, Jim, "How Big Are the Trees of Engelmann Woods?", letter to the Missouri Department of Conservation, 1992.

Bower, Hazel Meier, "A Family History," November 1975.

Brackenridge, Henry M., *Recollections of Persons and Places in the West*, Philadelphia; J.B. Lippincott and Company, 1868.

Cochran, Alice Lida, *The Saga of An Irish Immigrant Family: The Descendants of John Mullanphy*. Unpublished Dissertation for Degree of Doctor of Philosophy, St. Louis University, 1958.

Darby, John F., *Personal Recollections of Many Prominent People Whom I Have Known, and of Events—Especially of Those Relating to the History of St. Louis—During the First Half of the Present Century*, St. Louis, G. I. Jones and Company, 1880.

Food Service News, "Barn Inn," Electrical Information Publication, Inc., Madison, Wisconsin, November 1950, Vol. 12, No. 1.

Franklin County Records, Courthouse, Union, Missouri.

Goodwin, Cardinal L., "Settlements of Missouri and Arkansas 1803–1822," *The Missouri Historical Review*, Vol. XIV, Missouri Historical Society, St. Louis, Mo.

Gray Summit, Missouri, "Telephone Directory," October, 1954, Southwestern Bell Telephone Company.

Gregory, Ralph, *Price's Raid in Franklin County, Missouri*, Missourian Publishing Co., Washington, Mo., February 1990.

Horn, Wilbert A., *Our Dear Gertie and Memories*, Wilbert A. Horn, Labadie, Missouri, 1986. Revised 1987.

Horn, Wilbert A., A manuscript on the life of Charles and Louisa Becker.

Ladue News, St. Louis, Mo., "St. Albans a Special Setting," May 20, 1984.

Madden, Fred W., "The 'Beauty Spot' Family at St. Albans Farms, Inc." *Guernsey Breeder's Journal*, February 21, 1951.

McDermont, John Francis, *The Early Histories of St. Louis*, St. Louis Historical Documents Foundation, St. Louis, Mo., 1952.

Mercantile Library, Barringer Collection, "Rock Island Lines."

Missouri Historical Bulletin, St. Louis, Mo.

Missouri Historical Review, St. Louis, Mo.

Ramsey, Robert L., *The Name Places of Franklin County, Missouri*, University of Missouri Studies, Columbia, Missouri, 1954.

Saddle & Bridle, "Fleetmount Farm," Mid-West Publishers, Inc., St. Louis, Mo., Vol. 3, 1929, Vol. 4, 1930, Vol. 4, 1931, Vol. 5, 1932.

Newspapers

Franklin County Tribune

March 12, 1909, Charles Becker moved to Labadie

Guernsey Breeders Journal

February 21, 1951, "The 'Beauty Spot' Family at St. Albans Farms, Inc."

Meramec Valley Guide, Pacific, Mo.

July 14, 1971, "Old Bethel Church Filled with Years of History"

Meramec Valley Transcript, Pacific, Mo.

January 19, 1961, "Link murder trial before jury today; Death penalty asked in July shooting."

October 7, 1964, "Rebel Raid Here 100 Years Ago"

Missouri Business News

November 18–19, 1989, "Two 18-Hole Golf Courses To Be Built at St. Albans"

Republican Tribune, Union, Mo.

August 15, 1919, "Origin of Franklin County Names"

St. Charles Post, St. Charles, Mo.

June 21, 1990, "Road to Yesterday"

St. Louis Business Journal, St. Louis, Mo.

October 7–13, 1991 "St. Albans"

St. Louis Globe-Democrat, St. Louis, Mo.

September 8, 1933, Brown Settlement

June 10, 1951, "Mystery Cave"

April 8, 1952, "Guernsey Herd Sale"

July 12, 1960, "Farm Hand Dies in 2-Gun Blast by Ted Link"

July 13, 1960, "Fatal Shooting by Ted Link Will Go to Grand Jury"

July 14, 1960, "Ted Link's Arrest Ordered in Slaying"

July 28, 1960, "Ted Link Charged with First-Degree Murder"

July 29, 1960, "Ted Link Free on $25,000 Bond"

August 8, 1971, 1821 Gateway to the West

August 21–22, 1971, 1971 Missouri 150 Years Statehood

June 14-15, 1981, "New Catholic Parish Formed"

September 24, 1981, "Ceremonies rededicate marker for Lewis and Clark expedition"

August 30, 1983, "Oscar Johnson Jr. Guernsey Herd"

The St. Louis Home, St. Louis, Mo.

June, 1993, "The Perfect Country Home"

March, 1994, "Buying New"

St. Louis Post-Dispatch, St. Louis, Mo.

c. 1931, "St. Albans"

April 7, 1935, The Browns

April 2, 1952, Guernsey Sale

April 9, 1952, Guernsey Sale

July 11, 1960, "Theodore Link Shoots, Wounds Man at Home"

July 12, 1960, "Shooting Victim Had Set Fire to Home, Boy Says"

July 13, 1960, "Theodore Link is Charged with Homicide"

July 28, 1960, "Theodore Link is Released on $25,000 Bond"

April 11, 1968, "Old Barn Inn closed, Once Top Restaurant"

April 17, 1968, "Where Meriwether Lewis Slipped"

August 8, 1971, "Settlers Ended Missouri's Long Indian Era"

August 8, 1971, "Fur Was the West's Lure"

October 17, 1971, "St. Albans Event To Mark Visit by Lewis and Clark"

February 28, 1974, "Underworld Politics Were This Reporter's Beat"

April 28, 1986, "Country Store"

October 26, 1988, "Cherry Hills Club May Be On Move"

September 14, 1989, "Malmaison: A Touch of France in the Country"

February 16, 1990, "At Home"

June 21, 1990, "St. Albans"

December 5, 1991, Jerry Berger

June 24, 1993, "Labadie"

July 25, 1993, "The Flood of 1951"

October 6, 1996, "Heirs, Developer Fight Over Estate in St. Albans"

April 12, 1997, Bick Property "St. Albans" insert prepared by Roger McGrath

St. Louis Review

June 13, 1980, Parish of St. Alban Roe

St. Louis Star

August 6, 1931, "Brown Island"

St. Louis Sun

October 23, 1989, "Partnership to Develop Community"

Seen

April, 1993, "Spring Comes to St. Albans"

Time Magazine

July 15, 1960, "The Constant Companion"

Tri-County Journal

July 16, 1971, "In Retrospect—Bethel Church-Labadie"

Washington Citizen

January 16, 1961, "Begin to Qualify Jurors Monday in Link Murder Case"

January 23, 1961, "Link is Acquitted of Murder Charge by Gasconade County Jury"

Washington Missourian

January 19, 1961, "Defense Begins in Link Murder Trial"

August 5, 1971, "Mother Church of Methodism in County"

October 28, 1971, "Dedicate Memorial to Lewis and Clark"

February 21, 1972, "Old-Timers at Labadie Have Their Night"

November 16, 1988, "Malmaison Recalls Beauty of Former Times"

INDEX

Numerals in bold indicate a caption, photograph or illustration of the subject mentioned.

A

B

C

I

J

M

P

Q

R

S

T

LIFE AT FAIRFIELD

ABOUT THE AUTHOR

Lucie Furstenberg Huger has always been interested in history, particularly the American West. She was born in 1916 at St. Louis, Missouri, lived there until 1927, when, with her family, she moved to Liberal, Kansas. There, she experienced the "Great Dust Bowl" of the 30's. Returning to St. Louis in 1934, she received her B.A. in American History from Maryville College, writing her thesis on Wild Bill Hickock.

In 1942, Lucie married St. Louis attorney Bernard J. Huger. In 1950, seeking a more idyllic place to raise their growing family, the Hugers moved to St. Albans. They bought the Funsten place, some 400 acres of gorgeous woodlands, and named it *Fairfield.* The Hugers lived at *Fairfield* until Mr. Huger died in 1977. It was at St. Albans she first learned about Lewis and Clark's visit to Tavern Cave in 1804.

In addition to her family of seven children, Lucie's focus is on charitable and historical projects. She was active in the children's schools, her parish of St. Anselm, and the St. Louis Abbey.

For five years, Lucie and Delphine McClellan organized "The Master Calendar of St. Louis" for the benefit of Desloge/St. Louis University Hospital. This was a full page calendar in the *St. Louis Globe-Democrat* listing local events.

As a member of the Daughters of the American Revolution she succeeded, in 1971, in having a DAR marker placed in St. Albans commemorating the Lewis and Clark visit. In 1997, this marker was made part of the National Lewis and Clark Trail by the National Park Service. For her DAR work with the American Indian Cultural Center of St. Louis, she was made an honorable member of the Hopi Indian Tribe with the name "Ama Da Wi" (Bright Light). Also as a DAR, she stood atop (outside!) the St. Louis Gateway Arch to dedicate a 4000 watt beacon to "The Brave Pioneer Women Who Went West."

In addition to DAR, Lucie was one of the organizers of the Friends of McDonnell Planetarium, and its first full-time president; past president of the Fleur-de-Lis; member of "Les Amis"; the Foundation for the restoration of Ste. Genevieve, and many other cultural and historical societies.

Lucie has written one other book, *The Desloge Family in America,* a genealogy, published in 1959.

Lucie now lives in Kirkwood, Missouri, and plays bridge, goes on St. Ansleme Guild trips (which she herself organized for ten years), attends DAR Chapter activities, travels to visit her children both here and abroad, paints in watercolor, writes her family history and genealogy, and attends Lewis and Clark meetings and events.

For three years, Lucie has endeavored to find a statue and suitable location for it to commemorate the Bicentennial of the Lewis and Clark Expedition. Her answer to this quest came from R. H. Dick, a local artist, who has designed such a statue, and Chancellor Blanche Touhill of University of Missouri–St. Louis, who has offered a site on the campus and to share in the funding of the project.

Lucie is still seeking a way to "Save the Cave."

Bernard J. Huger at Tavern Cave. Author's photo.

SAVE THE CAVE

Tavern Cave needs to be preserved. Annual flooding and possible disfigurement by visitors can cause this historic, one-of-a-kind, relic of the Lewis and Clark Expedition to be lost forever. It is vital that this singular historic piece of our national history be preserved for future generations.

Now, on the banks of the Missouri River, there is a new St. Albans. A St. Albans that has a recorded history that began long ago with the Indians and German settlers. From 1804, with the visit of the Lewis and Clark Expedition, to 1988, when St. Albans Farms was closed, it was a community almost frozen in history. Now, recent developments have brought monumental changes. A new village has been formed; golf courses and a substantial residential area have been built.

What remains is a sweet memory of a small and unique community. The Indians, Lewis and Clark, Dr. Peter Kincaid, German settlers, St. Albans Farms and the Johnsons have all left an indelible mark on this historic area. For those who visit or make their home here, St. Albans will forever remain a place with a proud history.

Lewis and Clark stopped here...

Photo: Ken Gilberg

ABOUT THE AUTHOR

Lucie Furstenberg Huger has always been interested in history, particularly the American West. Born in 1916 at St. Louis, Missouri, she received her B.A. in American History from Maryville College, writing her thesis on Wild Bill Hickock.

In 1942, Lucie married St. Louis attorney Bernard J. Huger. In 1950, seeking a more idyllic place to raise their growing family, the Hugers moved to St. Albans and lived there twenty-eight years until Mr. Huger died. It was at St. Albans that Lucie first was fascinated by Lewis and Clark's visit to Tavern Cave.

As a member of the Daughters of the American Revolution she succeeded in having, in 1971, a DAR marker placed in St. Albans commemorating the Lewis and Clark visit. In 1997, the marker was made part of the National Lewis and Clark Trail by the National Parks Service. For her DAR work with the American Indian Cultural Center, St. Louis, she was made an honorable member of the Hopi Indian Tribe with the name "Ama Da Wi" (Bright Light). Also as a DAR, she stood atop (outside!) the St. Louis Gateway Arch to dedicate a 4000 watt beacon to "The Brave Pioneer Women Who Went West."

In addition to DAR, Lucie was one of the organizers of the Friends of McDonnell Planetarium; past president of the Fleur-de-Lis; member of "Les Amis"; the Foundation for the Restoration of Ste. Genevieve, and many other cultural and historical societies.

Lucie has written one other book, *The Desloge Family in America*, a genealogy, published in 1959.